THE CATHOLIC RELIGIOUS POETS FROM SOUTHWELL TO CRASHAW

The Catholic Religious Poets from Southwell to Crashaw

A CRITICAL HISTORY

A. D. Cousins

Sheed & Ward
London

ISBN 0 7220 1570 4

First published in 1991 by
Sheed & Ward Ltd
2 Creechurch Lane
London EC3A 5AQ

Book production by Bill Ireson

Filmset by Fakenham Photosetting Ltd,
Fakenham, Norfolk
Printed and bound in Great Britain by
Biddles Ltd, Guildford and King's Lynn

*To my Mother and
in memory of my Father*

Contents

Acknowledgements

This book, as its title suggests, attempts a critical history of Catholic religious poetry's major phase in the English Renaissance. So much has been written about the English Protestant religious poets of the late sixteenth and earlier seventeenth centuries, and so little (relatively speaking) about their Catholic counterparts, that such an attempt needs no apology. Instead of offering one, then, I am happy rather to thank those friends and colleagues who have lightened my task. For their help and encouragement I am grateful to Mauro Di Nicola, H. B. Vickery, Manfred Mackenzie, Erica Veevers, the late H. W. Piper, Ken Pankhurst, Jan Brady, and Harold Love. Conal Condren and Earl Miner found time to read and to comment on parts of my manuscript; my work has been the better for their suggestions (while I alone am responsible for its faults). To the staffs of the Vatican Library, the National Library of St Mark, Venice, the Cambridge University Library, and the Macquarie University Library I am thankful for their efficiency and courtesy. I am grateful to Judy Faulkner for her careful typing. My greatest thanks go to my wife Carolyn for her constant support while I have been writing this book.

Some material in Chapter One was originally published in *Parergon*, N.S.5 (1987), 155–162. A different version of the material in the Appendix appeared in *English Literary Renaissance*, 9 (1979), 86–107 at pp. 91–95.

Preface

In studying the Catholic religious poets from Southwell to Crashaw, this book focuses especially on the interplay in their verse between natively English and Counter-Reformation devotional literary traditions.[1] As it does so, it puts forward particularly two arguments: that (in contradiction to some views) most of the more important Catholic poets write verse which expresses a Christ-centred vision of reality; that the divine *agape* receives almost as much attention in the Catholic poets' verse as does devout *eros*. Finally, though, everything in this book is directed towards the formation of one encompassing argument: that the work of the Catholic religious poets deserves closer examination and higher valuation than it has usually been given.[2]

Before discussion of the poets begins, however, a few things need to be remarked on, including the book's emphasis on the interplay in their verse between native and foreign devotional literary traditions. If Counter-Reformation, and necessarily some more general, elements of what is customarily called the baroque can be discerned as significantly present in the Catholic religious poets' verse, its presence does not imply a writer therefore to be both intellectually and stylistically sophisticated, nor does its absence imply him therefore to be unsophisticated in intellect and style. Southwell's best work, in my view, is just about evenly divided between his more natively English poems and his more continental; much the same could be said of Alabaster. Further, none of Constable's, and virtually none of Habington's religious poems have any direct connection to the baroque – and neither is intellectually or stylistically naive.[3]

Having mentioned the arguments that are especially put forward in this study, I should like now to glance at some that are not presented in it. To begin with, in what follows there is no discussion of Donne or of Jonson as being, in any ways, Catholic religious poets.[4] Recent work on Donne's sacred poetry, most notably that of Barbara K. Lewalski (which is reinforced by John N. King's account of English Reformation Literature) persuasively suggests that both its theology and its literary strategies are Protestant, as of course Donne himself was when he wrote it.[5] The case for omitting consideration of Jonson's religious verse from this study is much the same. Although Jonson was for twelve years a Catholic, there is no reason to believe that he was one when he wrote his devout poems; furthermore, they bear no distinguishing signs of either Catholic belief or Catholic literary practice.[6] On the basis of what is known about the two poets, it seems to me that neither could reasonably be portrayed as a writer of Catholic religious verse.

Another exclusion in the subsequent chapters is that of a general argument about the Catholic poets as being political dissidents insofar as they were members of an oppressed religious minority.[7] That they were religious and, to quite different degrees, literary dissidents within English Renaissance society is clear; the former means that in a broad sense they were necessarily also political dissidents.[8] But the practicability of generalizing about their political dissidences seems, to say the least, doubtful. If they were all religious dissidents, their experiences of being so – and thus the extents to which their Catholicism set them at odds with the governments under which they lived – were diverse. Southwell, for example, publicly declared his loyalty to the Crown (in his *Humble Supplication*) at the same time as he was breaking a number of its laws through the enactment of his religious principles.[9] He was not, yet was, in opposition to Elizabeth's government; his poetry, whilst not treating of Elizabethan politics, was nonetheless politically dissident, since it formed part of his illegal ministry as a priest. On the other hand, Habington was a member of Henrietta Maria's privileged Catholic circle: his religion appears to have given him no personal cause for political dissent, and no dissidence born of his Catholicism seems discernible in any of his verse (a recent analysis of his play *The Queene of Arragon* indicates, however, that he was a shrewd critic of Charles's rule).[10] The heterogeneous political and social environments within which the Catholic religious poets lived, the differences among their relations to and treatments by those environments, the frequent lack of detailed biographical information about them, and the very different revelations in their verse – secular as well as sacred – of hostility to or dissociation from their environments because of their Catholicism, appear to make generalizations about them as political dissidents less feasible than desirable.

All in all, then, it seems reasonable to suggest this: in attempting a critical history of the Catholic religious poets from Southwell to Crashaw, one necessarily emphazises them to have been a various and disparate group of writers; one also acknowledges their verse to be an often innovative, and an often impressive, presence within the poetry of the English Renaissance.

THE CATHOLIC RELIGIOUS POETS FROM
SOUTHWELL TO CRASHAW

CHAPTER ONE

English and Counter-Reformation Traditions

To appreciate the verse of the Catholic religious poets it is essential to know something of the main devotional literary traditions on which they draw, for it is through those traditions that they tend primarily to organize their poems and so to communicate their perceptions of experience.[1] A thorough account of each of those traditions would require a lengthy volume to itself; many thousands of words, then, would need to be written before discussion of the poets themselves could begin. Yet without completeness being essayed, the traditions can still be usefully described in the space of a chapter. They number five: the theory of the plain style as a Christian rhetorical mode in Tudor times; the practice of the plain style in Tudor religious verse; Counter-Reformation poetic theory (chiefly Jesuit); the theory of the emblem; ideas of meditation (again, chiefly Jesuit). The first and second traditions are native to England or, rather, so naturalized as to appear native. Being English and writing for their countrymen, the Catholic poets of course draw on devotional literary traditions well established, popular, and fashionable in their society. The remaining traditions are not only European but, in the forms used by the Catholic poets, usually Jesuit since four of the poets discussed below are Jesuit priests (Southwell, Heywood, Brereley, Hawkins) and three seem to show Jesuit influence (Alabaster, Beaumont, Crashaw). Other traditions are also drawn upon, as would be expected; they will be considered later, however, for the verse of the Catholic poets is – for the most part –

elementally shaped by interaction with the traditions to be examined here.

The theory of the plain style as a Christian rhetorical mode in Tudor times

The traditions now to be examined have received much and varied analysis. For all that, they have never been studied together in relation to the Catholic poets; moreover, as no account of them is (or ever will be) definitive, new information still remains to be put forward and fresh interpretations suggested. The place to start would seem logically to be with those traditions which were well established in Tudor England before Southwell and the other poets began to write, the theory of the plain style and its practice, primacy being given to the theory. That tradition derived ultimately from St Augustine, who had established the plain style as a Christian rhetorical mode in *De Doctrina Christiana*, and whilst it was therefore not natively English it had nonetheless been in England long before the sixteenth century.[2] In Tudor times Augustine was respected by Catholics and non-Catholics alike as a patristic authority; *De Doctrina Christiana* was for both parties a basic text on Christian communication. But Augustine's already influential thinking on the plain style was significantly consolidated in Tudor England by the *Sileni Alcibiadis* (1515) of Erasmus, where the saint's ideas were affirmed and elaborated upon by a modern writer himself widely influential among members of the old faith and to be so among those of the new. He was not of course alone in expounding Augustine's thinking afresh. Other contemporary writers did so, notably Calvin, yet although that broadened the appeal of the plain style as a religious literary mode, still it can be fairly said that the theory of the plain style as a Christian form of discourse was established and essentially perfected in sixteenth-century England through the writings of Augustine and Erasmus.[3] What that theory was and why it should have recommended the plain style to religious authors can readily be seen in *De Doctrina Christiana* and *Sileni Alcibiadis* themselves.

In *De Doctrina Christiana* Augustine revalues and sanctifies ancient rhetorical theory, mainly that of Cicero, by centreing it on Christ.[4] He focuses in particular on Christ's love for mankind as manifested in his humility: "Thus the Wisdom of God, setting out to cure men, applied Himself to cure them, being at once the Physician and the Medicine. Because man fell through pride, He applied humility as a cure" (1,14,13). Augustine argues that through his compassionate humility the Logos, the Divine Wisdom, "accommodated" himself to mankind: first, by his Incarnation; second, by embodying his divine truth in the simplicity of his preaching. Of the Incarnation Augustine says: "[S]o the Medicine of Wisdom by taking on humanity is accommodated to our wounds ..." (1,14,13). A passage in his *Confessions* reveals exactly what he means:

> For thy Word, the eternal Truth, being so highly exalted above the highest of thy creatures, reaches up those that were cast down, unto itself: having here below built for itself a lowly cottage of our clay, by which he intended to abate from the height of their own imaginations, those that were to be cast down: that so he might bring them about unto himself; allaying the swelling of their pride, and cherishing of their love: to the end they might go on no further in the confidence of themselves, but might find their own weakness rather; seeing the divinity itself enfeebled at our feet, by taking our coats of skin upon him: that so being weary at length, they might cast down themselves upon it, and that rising, might raise up them together with it. (7,18)

The second aspect of Christ's accommodation of himself to human frailty, his preaching, is described by Augustine in Pauline terms: "Thus in the Wisdom of God the world could not know God through Wisdom. Why did He come ... unless it pleased God, by the foolishness of preaching, to save them that believe?" (1,12,12). The lowly simplicity of Christ's preaching, its "foolishness," Augustine thinks in fact typical of the Bible as a whole – characteristic, in other words, of the way God communicates with man (2,42,63).[5] In *The Confessions* Augustine remarks of the Bible:

> [Y]ea, and the authority of that Book appeared so much the more venerable, and so much the more worthy of our religious credit, by how much the readier at hand it was for all to read upon, preserving

yet the majesty of the secret under the profoundness of the meaning, offering itself unto all in words most open, and in a style of
speaking most humble, and exercising the attention of such as are
not light of heart; that it might by that means waft over some few
towards thee: yet are these few a good many more than they would
have been, had it not obtained the eminency of such high authority, nor allured on those companies with a bosom of holy
humility. (6,5)[6]

For Augustine, then, the principle of accommodation lies at
the very heart of God's entering history in the person of
Christ: thus his centreing of ancient rhetorical theory on
Christ actually means a centreing of it on Christ's accommodation. On the basis of that principle he shapes rhetorical
theory anew, putting forward the plain style as a distinctively
Christian mode.

Augustine argues in *De Doctrina Christiana* that when a
speaker or orator, motivated by charity, wishes to teach divine
truth he must do so plainly, accommodating it even to the
weakest mind:

But in all [his] utterances [he] should first of all seek to speak so
that [he] may be understood, speaking in so far as [he is] able with
such clarity that either [the listener] who does not understand is
very slow or that the difficulty and subtlety lie not in the manner of
speaking but in the things which [he wishes] to explain and show,
so that this is the reason why [he is] understood less, or more
slowly.   (4,8,22; cf. 1,22,20 and 1,37,41)

He concludes: "The speaker should not consider the eloquence of his teaching but the clarity of it" (4,9,23; cf. 4,10,24).
Thus the plain style, that customarily used for teaching,
becomes defined as the natural and primary Christian rhetorical mode (see 4,12,27). Augustine proposes that the other two
styles of rhetoric should be drawn on when lucid instruction
alone is not enough to impress divine truth upon the listener
(4,12,27–28). In asserting that, Augustine radically alters
Ciceronian theory. He agrees with Cicero that the speaker
must have command of all three styles (the plain to instruct, the
middle to delight, the high to move – see 4,12,27 and *Orator*,
29,100) but he gives primacy to the plain style whereas Cicero,

countering his Atticist detractors, had insisted that in particular the true and complete orator must have mastery of the high style. For Augustine the last is first and the first inferior: the plain style (which Cicero and others had thought relatively unimportant) takes first place because it leads to salvation; the high style (which Cicero and others had thought most important because of its persuasive force) takes a lesser place with the middle style, for it is useful to the Christian speaker, but inessential (4,12,28). The elemental difference between the rhetorical theories of the two thinkers seems to be as follows: Cicero argues that the high style promotes civilized life in the cities of men; for Augustine, as for St Paul, Christ has shown that through the plain style men can be led to eternal life in the City of God.[7] At once adopting what is usable from pagan rhetoric (cf. 2,40,60–61; 4,2–3) and engaging in a dialogue with Ciceronian theory, Augustine models the true and complete Christian speaker on Christ himself, implying that his "foolishness of preaching" revalued and revolutionized the ancient rhetorical tradition (1,12–15; 2,40–42).

Yet Augustine's emphasis on the plain style cannot be seen only in those terms, for though they suggest why a Christian speaker should use the plain style they do not fully explain how its fits into his role as a sharer of divine truth. To understand that one needs to consider the plain style, as Christ's chosen rhetorical mode, in relation to the other aspect of his accommodation – the Incarnation. Augustine urges that the Christian speaker should "so order his life that he not only prepares a reward for himself, but also so that he offers an example to others, and his way of living may be, as it were, an eloquent speech" (4,29,61; cf. 4,27–28 and 1 *Cor.* 9,15–11,1). That is to say, his plain speaking of divine truth should be inseparable from its clear expression, the incarnation of it, in his life. Augustine argues that the Christian speaker should not only talk like Christ but lead a Christlike life; as a sharer of divine truth he should manifest both aspects of Christ's accommodation. Thus Augustine reveals what the Christocentric rhetoric he has been fashioning finally means for the Christian speaker: simultaneously embodying Christ's truth and recreating his communication of it to become an *imitatio Christi*. Displacing man from the centre of the ancient rhetorical tradition and modelling it anew on Christ, Augustine adds a spiritual function – which he puts before all others – to rhetoric's familiar, secular use in political, forensic, or epideictic causes.

In affirming and elaborating upon Augustine's concept of the plain style, Erasmus too focuses on the twin aspects of Christ's accommodation. But he perceives accommodation as a principle for reinterpreting history, not only rhetorical tradition, as a principle which generates a new understanding of learning, of spirituality, and of language in the service of both. He unfolds his ideas in *Sileni Alcibiadis* (from the 1515 edition of the *Adages*), a work which shows how creative an heir he is of Augustinian thought.[8] There Erasmus uses the figurine called a "Silenus" as the symbolic centrepiece of his argument. A "Silenus" was an image of a flute player, and upon opening it one found that the figurine concealed the form of a god. Erasmus proposes that history is variously patterned by men who resemble Sileni: externally unattractive, poor, socially insignificant, but transcendently wise and noble within. Whether Hebrew, Greek, or Roman such men exemplify richness of soul, and through their wisdom they seek to heal the spiritual illnesses of others, to enrich the spiritually poor. They form models of how the inner life is to be lived and of how wisdom is to function in the world. Antisthenes, Diogenes, Epictetus, the prophets of the Old Testament, the Apostles, Bishop Martin: all are Sileni. Erasmus' account of Socrates, one of his favourites, illustrates the public appearance and behaviour of the Sileni as well as their inner nature:

He took no care of his appearance, and his language was plain, unvarnished, and unpretentious, as befits a man who was always talking about charioteers, workmen fullers, and blacksmiths. For it was usually from these that he took the terms with which he pressed his arguments home.

[O]nce you have opened out this Silenus, absurd as it is, you find a god rather than a man, a great, lofty and truly philosophic soul . . . (p. 270)

"Saint Socrates, pray for us!" cries Nephalius in *The Godly*

Feast.[9] Erasmus implies that Socrates's life – like the lives of all the other Sileni – centres on a twofold accommodation: embodying a divine wisdom humbly; conveying that wisdom in plain and lowly speech. In other words, Socrates and his fellows are types of Christ, either prefiguring him or subsequently reflecting him. As Erasmus says:

> [I]s not Christ the most extraordinary Silenus of all?

> [I]f one may attain to a closer look at this Silenus-image, that is if he deigns to show himself to the purified eyes of the soul, what unspeakable riches you will find there ... (p. 272)

And just as Christ's appearance and inner nature are those of a Silenus, so is his speech:

> The parables of the Gospel, if you take them at face value – who would not think that they came from a simple ignorant man? And yet if you crack the nut, you find inside that profound wisdom, truly divine, a touch of something which is clearly like Christ himself. (p. 276)

> There are many things in the Gospel which come from the common people. Nor is this unworthy of Christ, but it is really in keeping, that just as he wished to take our body and become one of us, he should use the most familiar language, raising our humbleness to the height of his sublimity. (p. 27)

How Erasmus affirms and elaborates upon Augustine's thinking on the plain style thus comes into perspective. Like Augustine, Erasmus acknowledges the centrality of accommodation to Christ's redemptive role. But he sees that twofold principle as reshaping both our understanding of history as well as our understanding of rhetoric. According to Erasmus, Christ lies at the heart of a tradition of shabby heroes who have sought to redeem their different times and environments from Folly.[10] Christ is preeminent among a self-denying few who, rich in divine wisdom, have spent lowly, exemplary lives in the everyday world plainly conveying that wisdom to their contemporaries and trying to direct them away from material goods and the transient towards spiritual goods and the eternal. Erasmus complains that those who should be the Sileni of current times tend to be the reverse, glossy exteriors concealing worthlessness; he argues that one who desires now to communicate wisdom – and Christian wisdom is meant – should follow the example of the Sileni in both action and speech. As he has stressed that the tradition of the Sileni is Christocentric, Erasmus clearly implies that to be a Silenus in fact means to become an *imitatio Christi*. He later remarks in *Ciceronianus*: "Are not all our actions gauged by the rules of Christ from which if our speech departs we shall be neither good orators nor good men?"[11] So whilst the plain style is identified as the inevitable Christian rhetorical mode, for Erasmus it also forms part of history's inner pattern, the Silenus tradition. When he who seeks to teach divine wisdom uses the plain style he allies himself with the essential civilizing energies, as Erasmus sees them, in western culture – he takes sides with the foolishness of Socrates and with the folly of the cross against the Folly of the world.

The practice of the plain style in Tudor religious verse

As can be seen in the preceding discussion, when St Augustine and Erasmus advocate the plain style they are in fact referring to the Attic version of it: that form of the plain style which, as Cicero had described it, has a conversational immediacy of tone and informality of rhythm, a pellucid diction, a virtual lack of ornament (in the guise of the figures of speech) and, in keeping with that, a use of metaphor to crystallize meaning rather than to beautify (see *Orator*, 75–90). St Augustine distinctly indicates that the rhetorical model by which he judges plain speech is Cicero's description of the Attic plain style.[12] Erasmus, himself an admirer of Attic simplicity, puts forward Socrates as his type of the *orator humilis*, and as Socrates was a familiar Ciceronian exemplar of Attic plainness, Erasmus thereby reveals the affinity of his thinking with Augustine's on the nature of Christian stylistics.[13] It is not very surprising, then, to see the pervasiveness in Tudor religious verse of a plain style which can be more accurately called Attic than anything else. The long tradition of Augustinian influence on Christian rhetoric, the current prestige of this thought and its recent restatement by Erasmus, would seem enough to suggest why an Attic plainness should be a Tudor norm in Christian communication.

To illustrate something of the continuity and variety in the practice of that plain style as a religious mode by Tudor poets before Southwell, one can usefully focus on the writings of Surrey, Vaux, and Huggarde. Surrey illustrates the use of that plain style in scriptural paraphrase, Vaux its use in the religious lyric, and Huggarde its use in the poetry of religious debate.

Surrey paraphrased six of the psalms, numbers 8,31,51,55,73, and 88.[14] Metrical paraphrases of Scripture, especially of the psalms, were many in the sixteenth century; even so, three of Surrey's six paraphrases – his versions of psalms 88, 73, and 55, made during his last imprisonment – are unusual for a couple of reasons: first, they are rivalled in quality only by Wyatt's and Sidney's; second, they are highly personal, for they pointedly refer to a specific moment in Surrey's life and show him at once proclaiming divine truth and struggling to reconcile himself to it. In those later paraphrases, Surrey does not merely translate the psalmists' words into plain, contemporary speech; rather, he recreates the roles of the psalmists in terms of his own immediate circumstances. What results is conflict between theocentric and egocentric discourses. Surrey's voice echoes the words of men who, setting their misfortunes and aspirations in the context of God's will, proclaim God's justice and mercy; at the same time, he transforms their words into indignantly angry elaboration upon his sufferings. Preoccupation with the self struggles against the manifesting of divine truth; consciousness of the self contends against consciousness of God. Only in the last of those paraphrases does the self seem to become at one with the divine truth, and contrariety seem to end in harmony. Unfortunately there is not room here to trace that shifting dialectic to its apparent close. Discussion will focus, then, on Surrey's paraphrase of psalm 88, for that poem suggests both the usual practice of Tudor scriptural paraphrase (the fairly impersonal communication of biblical truth) and an unusual acknowledgement of personal difficulty in reconciling oneself to that truth. That is to say, the poem shows in microcosm how clear yet subtle, how unadorned yet sophisticated, the plain style can be in the retelling and reshaping of Scripture itself.

In his forty-four line paraphrase of that psalm Surrey departs from the *Vulgate* in at least twenty-five lines, sometimes adding single words or images (as in ll.3–4) and at others entire passages (as in ll.19–22).[15] With what effect he does so can be seen clearly enough in the poem's opening section (ll.1–8). Surrey designs those lines as a simple plea followed by a series of lucid, concessive statements – thereby imitating the original psalm:

> Oh Lorde, uppon whose will dependeth my welfare,
> To call uppon thy hollye name syns daye nor night I spare,
>   Graunt that the just request of this repentaunt mynd
> So perce thyne eares that in thy sight som favour it may find.
>   My soule is fraughted full with greif of follies past;
> My restles bodye doth consume and death approcheth fast;
>   Lyke them whose fatall threde thy hand hath cut in twayne,
> Of whome ther is no further brewte, which in their graves remayne.

Those lines declare their plainness and distinctly echo (see l.4) their scriptural model; however, they also reveal that Surrey sophisticatedly rewrites his original. Where, according to the *Vulgate*, the psalmist says merely, "*Intret in conspectu tuo oratio mea, / Inclina aurem tuam ad precem meam*" (v.3), Surrey asks for God's favourable attention to "the just request" of his "repentaunt mynd" (l.3, see l.4). The difference is marked and significant. The psalmist places the humble plea quoted above between his invocation of God (v.2) and his admission of suffering and/or sin (v.4); between Surrey's invocation of God (l.1) and admission of sin (l.5) stands out a plea which stresses the justice of his request and that the sinfulness to be subsequently admitted is a thing of the past (see l.5). In at once echoing and rewriting the words of the original, Surrey has radically altered the tactics of the psalmist's pleading: a deft change of rhetoric that contemporaries would have perceived as abandonment of *obsecratio* (a direct, earnest plea) for *purgatio* (a plea in which one's rights or merits are asserted). That alteration suggests how he transforms the tone and drama of the original. To begin with, the humble tone of the psalm – though of course still present in the paraphrase – becomes mingled with an argumentative righteousness (as the emphasis on "just" and "repentaunt" indicates). Moreover, from that moment begin to appear a flux and conflict of impulses within Surrey as he represents himself in the poem: submission to God's will (e.g. ll.11–18) fluctuating with self-assertion against being cast down (e.g. ll.19–22). The tone and psychological drama of the original become complicated by an intellectual and emotional self-division. For all its clarity of diction and syntax, for all its simplicity of image and statement, the opening section of Surrey's poem implies how finely nuanced the plain style can be as a Christian mode of communication.

The self-division expressed in the paraphrase of course reflects how the context of the original psalm has itself been transformed (ultimately by circumstance, if directly by Surrey). To the original's dialectic between individual suffering/sin and God's justice – the privately religious context – is added a dialectic between the individual's public uprightness and his social as well as political oppression (see ll.9, 15, 19–22, in conjunction with ll.3–5). Hence the poem's conflicting discourses come finally from that double dialectic. Here the interplay of those discourses need not be followed in detail. One could perhaps briefly mention the forceful rhetoric of contradiction shaping the poem's second section (ll.9–18), where the ostentatious *contrarium* – effected climactically at l.17 – draws attention to itself rather than to any emotional resolution the passage might seem to imply. But more revealing is the inconclusiveness of the poem's last section (ll.31–44). Surrey ends in humility (e.g. ll.31–34), echoing the psalmist's concluding lament; even so, his humility does not efface or subordinate the poem's discords. Rather it serves to heighten his expression of anguish at his twofold exile, from God's help and from those dearest to him. In the final couplet (ll.43–44) he evokes the psalmist's complaint at isolation from the people he loves. Just before doing so, however, he sums up all his misery in a climactic emblem which he takes only indirectly from the *Vulgate*: "Like to the roring waves the sunken shipp surrounde, / Great heaps of care did swallow me and I no succour found" (ll.41–42). Those last couplets epitomize the nature of Surrey's poem, for whilst he plainly evokes Scripture it does not encompass, or totally order, or sufficiently communicate his personal reflections: the two co-exist inharmoniously if creatively.

The theory of the plain style as a religious mode and Surrey's practice of it would seem, then, to be inconsistent in his later paraphrases of the psalms. There is indeed some inconsistency but it helps to illustrate the variety, as well as the continuity, of the religious use of the plain style before Southwell. Augustine and Erasmus imply that the plain stylist should not assert his individuality; he should adopt a humility in keeping with his lowliness of style and so become primarily a medium through which divine truth confronts his contemporaries. In the act of communicating divine truth he should become an *imitatio Christi*. Those ideas appear to govern most biblical paraphrase in the sixteenth century and afterwards, even Donne's. They govern Surrey's – but only at moments. His later paraphrases, in particular his version of psalm 88, show that the plain style can be used at once to embody divine truth (in accord with Augustinian and Erasmian thought) and to express the disturbance of an individual soul struggling for reconciliation to that truth. They show that in the one work a writer using the plain style can seem like, yet also not resemble, an *imitatio Christi*. Finally, here, Surrey's paraphrases show that as a religious mode the plain style can be flexible enough to convey transcendent, impersonal truth simply as well as intimately personal reflection with appropriate subtlety.

Introspection, if infrequent in biblical paraphrase, of course often shapes the religious lyric. In Vaux's "When I looke backe and in my selfe behold" one sees a meditative poem whose examining of the self – more comprehensive than in Surrey's poem – is traced in a plain style both uncompromisingly direct and oblique:

When I looke backe and in my selfe behold
The wandring wayes that youth could not descry:
And marke the fearful course that youth did hold,
And mette in mind, each steppe youth strayed awry;

> My knees I bowe, and from my hart I call, –
> O Lord, forget these faultes and follies all![16]

With their anecdotal tone (set by the opening verse), uncomplicated, biblically allusive imagery ("wandring wayes"), and
simple pleading (ll. 5–6), those lines could hardly be more lucid
or direct – or better represent Augustinian and Erasmian
notions of the plain style. For all their graceful plainness,
however, the lines are far from being simple. They imply that
Vaux bases his meditative poem on the familiar Augustinian
triad of memory, understanding, and love, which the saint
seems to have thought the soul's most important faculties.
Augustine had held that especially those faculties or "powers"
mark the human soul as being in God's image; moreover, as
will be discussed in detail below, Augustine had argued that
when the three faculties are concentrated upon God then the
soul achieves wisdom and moves toward perfecting itself as an
image of the Trinity. The lines quoted above reveal Vaux's
persona exercising memory (ll. 1–2), analysing his past to
understand it (ll. 3–4, especially "mette"), and turning his love
to God (ll. 5–6). They suggest an abandonment of youthful
error and blindly assertive will ("wandring wayes that youth
could not descry," l. 2) for the espousal of a wise submission to
God (ll. 5–6). Yet the self-examination in those lines tells us
more. Vaux's persona contrasts the futile movement of youth
(l. 2), the restlessness of its spiritual immaturity, with the stillness of spiritual adulthood (l. 5, cf. l. 1) – its *quies* as Augustine
might have called it. He also contrasts the selfish desire of
youth (implicit in l. 2) to the God-centred desire of maturity
(ll. 5–6, especially "from my hart I call"), an Augustinian
antithesis between *cupiditas* and *caritas*. Through a language at
once plain, simple and conceptually rich, Vaux both directly
presents and obliquely traces a re-orientation of the soul.

In the following two stanzas Vaux further traces the process
of that re-orientation, having his persona's self-examination
continue to unfold through contrasts. Whilst those oppositions still suggest the Augustinian categories which inform
the initial stanza, they now emphasize confession, contrition,
and repentance:

I doo confesse my faultes and all my ill,
And sorow sore for that I did offend,
   And with a mind repentant of all crimes,
   Pardon I aske for youth, ten thousand times. (ll.9–12)

From there, however, the poem leaves scrutiny of the self for prayer, in which the redirected personality asserts – and becomes set in the context of – divine truth. The poem's plain speech becomes even plainer as, in a litany, the persona appeals to God:

Thou that diddest graunt the wise king his request,
Thou that in Whale Thy prophet didst preserue,
Thou that forgauest the wounding of Thy brest,
Thou that didst saue the theefe in state to sterue:
   Thou onely God, the Giuer of all grace,
   Wipe out of mind, the path of youth's vaine race! (ll.19–24)

Yet even that very plain speech has its artfulness, for through his persona's successive evocations of Scripture Vaux argues that God's love shapes history. The allusion to Solomon (l.19) suggests God's love, and love of wisdom, at work in distant Old Testament times; Jonah (l.20) more recently illustrates God's love and serves to prefigure Christ, the embodiment of wisdom and love (ll.21–22) with whom the times of a new covenant have begun. Thus placing himself within God's encompassing love (ll.23–24), the persona turns to Christ as the cardinal manifestation of that love and appeals for renewal, forming his appeal wholly in terms of scriptural allusion (ll.25–30). He ends with a concentration of his love toward God ("Thee I only seeke to finde," l.33); once more he rejects his past foolishness and simply pleads for what Augustine would have seen as true wisdom (ll.35–36; cf. l.33). Vaux's lyric implies how finely the plain style – for all its lucid directness – can express the spiritual nuances of religious reflection.

The use of the plain style in the poetry of religious controversy needs only brief discussion. Myles Huggarde's *The Doctrine of the Eucharist* well illustrates a mingling of shrewdness

with crudity to be often found in such verse. In that poem one
reads:

> Who is more blind then those that wil not se
> What botes it to shew you any scripture
> Syth to no part therof ye wil agre
> Which to your reasone is harde or obscure
> But yet once a gayne to do you pleasure
> Ye shall heare if Christ made no relacion
> In scripture of the consecration . . .

> Christ at his last supper as I before saye
> Toke bread and blessed it and brake it truly
> Gave yt to his disciples and without stay
> Bad them take and eate this is my body
> Then to shew them what body he ment, truely
> He added these wordes to those he had spoken
> Saieng, which for your sinnes shalbe broken
> What body was broken for our trespas?
> No signe of a body I thinke ye wyl saye
> But even the same body which borne was . . .[17]

Huggarde was not unlettered and the lines are not naive. In
them he takes on the controversialist's familiar and useful role
of being someone forced by outrage to decry contemporary
violations of truth. He uses the role conventionally, putting
himself forward as a man eaten up by zeal for the house of the
Lord, as a man whose words confront the reader with blunt
truth in an argument not overly concerned with niceties of
style. The conceptual and stylistic crudity of his verse thus
functions as proof, as it were, of honest dealing and of a desire
primarily to make divine truth manifest. Huggarde plays that
representative role less skilfully than many other writers, but
he shows what verse results from it (for example Brereley, who
writes with a much more disciplined intelligence, differs from
Huggarde less in his satiric poems than might be thought).[18]
Huggarde also shows, one should finally point out here, that
the religious plain style can be various enough to express both

subtly inward spirituality and angry public argument about doctrine.

Aspects of Counter-Reformation poetic theory to 1649

Whilst the Catholic poets make significant use of the religious plain style, as do their Protestant contemporaries, they also draw on ideas of poetry in which the Protestant poets have little interest or to which they have distinctive counterparts. Those ideas derive from poetic theory and practice in the European Counter-Reformation, many being motifs in post-Tridentine discussion of poetry; they can be seen representatively in the critical writings of Pontanus, Tasso, and Gracián – two celebrated Jesuits, a more celebrated poet, and all of them influential. (Again, four of the poets considered below are Jesuits and three others write in apparently close contact with Jesuit thought; one would not want to deny, however, Marino's contributory influence on Crashaw.) Examining Pontanus's *Poeticarum Institutionum Libri Tres*, Tasso's *Discourses on the Heroic Poem*, and Gracián's *The Mind's Wit and Art* thus forms a useful guide to Counter-Reformation poetic theory to 1649, that is, until the death of Crashaw.

Before starting with Pontanus's *Libri Tres*, which well introduces the other works, one needs to say something of what his criticism – insofar as it is Jesuit – has in common with Gracián's criticism and that of other Jesuits.[19] During the Counter-Reformation the Society of Jesus resolved that literature and literary studies should be redirected to become truly Christian, that resolution epitomizing and enacting the Council of Trent's attitude to all the arts: as has been well documented, the Jesuit literary programme in fact magisterially expressed and disseminated the Council of Trent's view of the arts.[20] Pontanus's work clearly reflects that general concern, but with whatever degree of intent other Jesuit critical works may do so they nonetheless appear often to share with his a number of specific preoccupations. It can be reasonably said that, in essence, Jesuit poetic theory reworks the classical notion of literature as bringing both delight and instruction to the reader.[21] Through affective imagery and, more broadly speaking, the appealing cleverness of his artistry, the poet is to reveal to the mind and impress upon it the moral laws which should structure the individual's life and which can be discerned as organizing and informing the creation. From that imperative in Jesuit poetic theory emerge three things: first, that poetry is seen as manifesting an affective aesthetic (Jesuit opinions differ about precisely how poetry is affective); second, that the moral principles embodied in human art are considered as identical to those embodied in the divine art of the creation; finally, that true poetry is thought to achieve a reconciliation of pleasure and virtue (an old theme again being reworked). For all the inevitable differences within Jesuit poetic theory there is wide agreement on the nexus of ideas just described, and it is revealing to see how far Tasso's criticism accords with Jesuit thinking.

Those ideas are elemental to Pontanus's notion of poetry. Early in the *Libri Tres* he defines poetry as portraying the conduct of men, as setting it out (with overtones of interpretation) for the ordering of life.[22] Soon after he makes it quite clear that by "the ordering of life" – "*ad vitam instituendam*" – he means its moral ordering or regulation, for he explicitly links poetry to praise of good actions and blame of bad (1,4,15– 16; 1,5,16–17). The principles of morality to be inculcated will come from the great teachers of the past, especially the Socratics (1,5,17), and Pontanus indicates that those principles are ultimately the same as the ones at work in the divine regulation of the cosmos (2,32,173–177). But how is the moral ordering of the individual's life to be achieved? Pontanus warns that the poet should not attempt it by a direct appeal to the reader's reason, but by an appeal primarily to the reader's senses and thence emotions. The poet should reject divisions, definitions, calm reasoning, logical inquiry, and rely on the most euphonious (with overtones of being elaborate) diction, sensuously compelling images, to stir up the emotions and so entice the reader or carry him away.[23] Pontanus's words here are worth quoting in full:

[O]fficium docebit, ut divisiones, definitiones, ratiocinationes, interrogationes funditus repudiās, compositissima oratione, exem-

plisque pulcherrimis a se vel primũ excogitatis, vel ingeniosis fictio-
nibus amplificatis & illustratis, & quodammodo conditis, etiam
diversos animi motus misceat, & lectores sive spectatores vel alliciat,
vel rapiat quo placuerit. (1,5,17–18).

For Pontanus, then, poetry certainly instructs and delights but
he describes how it does so in ways that would have seemed
unusual to most readers of Sidney or Puttenham. Pontanus
advocates that poetry should sensuously impress moral
thought upon the reader, controlling the senses to achieve
control of the emotions: persuasion is seen as a matter of
directing the passions rather than in terms of logical acuteness.
(Of course the poet himself, Pontanus adds, should remain
distanced from the emotional texture of his work – he should
be tranquil and guided by judgment.) In putting forward that
view of poetry Pontanus seems to draw chiefly on the affective
Aristotelian concept of imagery familiar in the Renaissance and
to be found at once in Lomazzo and Descartes; he also draws
on the conventional Platonic notion of music's sensuous, emotive power. Thus the aesthetic within his theory of poetry
centres not on dialectic but on the senses and the "passions of
the soul" – and is primarily affective. Through being so it seeks
to unite inseparably sensuous and emotional pleasure with
virtue.

As will be presently argued, Pontanus's theory of poetry has
clear affinities with Tasso's and with Gracián's; however, in
larger terms, his theory is no less obviously connected with
those artistic categories which begin to pervade the arts after
1575 and which are called baroque. There is his emphasis on a
compelling appeal to the senses and on a manipulation of the
emotions, his interest in poetry's power to transport the reader
and in heightened psychological experience. Now admittedly
it is dangerous to use a label such as "the baroque" but such a
label can be helpful.

Recognizing Pontanus's theory of poetry as connected with
what we identify as the baroque means appreciating its relation
to (for example) the paintings of Annibale Carracci, Lan-
franco, and Pietro da Cortona – it also means appreciating how
alien his theory therefore is to English poetic theory and to
most English poetic practice until 1649. To suggest Pontanus's

affinities with the baroque is also, of course, to imply that if Tasso and Gracián significantly resemble him in their thinking on poetry then they too have links with the baroque. To propose that Tasso and Gracián are connected with that phenomenon is hardly startling; nonetheless, to identify Pontanus with them in a particular aesthetic context is to indicate an unusual homogeneity within Counter-Reformation poetic theory.

A consideration of Tasso's *Discourses on the Heroic Poem* reveals at once the resemblances of his thought to Pontanus's. There seem to be three main resemblances: Tasso's view on the true end of poetry; his notion of how that end is, in general terms, to be reached; and his stress on the persuasive force of the marvellous. Early in Book One of the *Discourses* Tasso defines poetry as "an imitation of human actions, fashioned to teach us how to live."[24] That is very like Pontanus's definition of poetry as "*Ars, hominum actiones effingẽs, easque ad vitam instituendam carminibus explicans*" (1,2,6 – "*vitam atque mores hominum effictos explanat*," as he says at 1,2,4). As for poetry's means of "teach[ing] us how to live," Tasso observes: "[P]oetry will deal with moral habit and with [*sententiae*]" (p. 10). He adds, discussing poetry's probable function both to delight and instruct ("pleasure directed to usefulness," p. 10): "We should at least grant that the end of poetry is not just any enjoyment [as Horace might be taken to imply] but only that which is coupled with virtue, since it is utterly unworthy of a good poet to give the pleasure of reading about base and dishonest deeds, but proper to give the pleasure of learning together with virtue" (p. 11). Pontanus of course makes a very similar point at 1,4,16. But still the question remains as to how "giving profit through delight" (p. 14) will be specifically achieved. Tasso's answer applies to the heroic poem; however, what he focuses on as most compelling in the highest form of poetry accords with what Pontanus says about the persuasiveness of poetry as a whole. Of "the delight [that] may get us to read more willingly and thus not lose the profit" (p. 14) Tasso remarks: "The epic poem ought therefore to afford its own delight with its own effect – which is perhaps to move wonder ..." (p. 15; "*e questa peraventura è il mover maraviglia ...*").[25] He emphasizes the emotionally persuasive power of poetry –

though he admits elsewhere (pp. 29–30) that poetry is related to dialectic and logic – as does Pontanus, who himself celebrates the force of wonder to move the reader (that occurs quite near the start of the *Libri Tres*, at 1,2,5). Tasso's stress on *"maraviglia"* also reveals the connection of his thought on poetry's persuasiveness with critical ideals such as *stupore*. Certainly the *Discourses* is a varied work to whose diversity a brief discussion can hardly do justice; even so, it can be fairly argued that Tasso's thinking on poetry, whilst inevitably diverging in a number of ways from that of Pontanus, yet has likenesses to Pontanus's thought that are both clear and elemental. The last of those resemblances, moreover, implies Tasso's affinity with the baroque.

Turning from Pontanus and Tasso to Gracián might seem at first to imply discontinuity, for the title of Gracián's work, *The Mind's Wit and Art*, suggests that he focuses upon the purely cerebral as those earlier critics do not. In fact, however, the similarities among the works of the three men are more striking and important than the differences. From the start of his work Gracián stresses the affective power of the creative intellect. He concentrates upon the conceit as the chief embodiment of the mind's wit and art, saying that "what beauty is for the eyes and harmony for the ears, the conceit is for the understanding."[26] He affirms that line of thought by remarking, soon after: "The imagination is not conte,t merely with truth, as wisdom is, but seeks for beauty" (2,96). Gracián seems to envisage the conceit as a verbal manifestation of affective conceptual beauty. The nature of that beauty – and thus essentially of the conceit, in which it is crystallized – Gracián observes as consisting "in an exquisite agreement, a harmonious correlation between two or three perceptible extremes, expressed by an act of the understanding" (2,97). He goes on: "Thus the conceit may be defined: it is an act of the understanding which vividly expresses the apt relation that is found between objects" (*ibid.*). The point there is that the understanding discerns then expresses the "apt relation"; the understanding does not invent the "relation."[27] In other words, the understanding surveys what surrounds it and perceives within its environs something of their informing pattern of relationships: the mind's wit and art reveal the creation's subtle interconnections (what Tesauro would call "*Divini concetti*").[28] So inasmuch as the conceit expresses those inner principles designing man's physical (and, by extension, social) or spiritual environments, then the moral values within human art will be identical to the ones by which God has shaped reality.[29] That would seem to be supported in particular when Gracián rhapsodizes: "[Producing wit] is a calling for cherubim, and exaltation of man's mind that carries us to the summit of a strange, fanciful hierarchy" (2,92). Producing wit, Gracián implies, makes the human mind resemble the angelic intelligence, which intuits – or directly perceives – and accurately manifests the inner and divine structure of things.[30] Moreover, the sense of wonder emanating from Gracián's words about wit's production helps to explain why his treatise so pervasively identifies wonder as an effect of wit.[31]

Gracián has much to say of what forms the conceit can take, but those matters will be referred to below in discussion of individual poems. More relevant here is consideration of the end toward which Gracián sees the affective conceptual beauty embodied in the conceit as working. To a degree he accepts the delight provoked by that beauty as an end in itself; unsurprisingly, though, he links that beauty firmly to moral persuasion. He associates "[p]leasurable moral criticism" (12,256) and "moral teaching" (12,258) with wit, an argument in fact developed throughout his twelfth and thirteenth discourses. But he puts the argument more emphatically in his twenty-second discourse: there he stresses the necessity of a forceful wit to move the will toward amendment (see in particular pp. 386–387). Wit's beauty may delight, yet for Gracián it cannot really be separated from moral usefulness.

Gracián's ideas on poetry harmonize well with the baroque thought of Pontanus and Tasso – especially with the thought of the former, from which he might seem likely to differ, given his preoccupation with cerebral art. Pontanus, after all, remarks in his *Libri Tres*: "*Sed quia dulce est hominibus ipsum artificium, quo quidem ad istiusmodi affectus volentes ac nolentes se impelli sentiunt*" (1,6,22). *The Mind's Wit and Art* implies Gracián's complete sympathy with such a view. Yet the poetic theories of the three men also, if unexpectedly, harmonize with the critical thought of St Augustine. As has been argued above,

Augustine posits the plain style as the truly Christian mode of discourse, for the first priority of Christian communication is a lucid conveying of divine truth. But he says as well that when telling the plain truth is not enough, then one must seek to delight and to move the reader (or listener, in the case of oratory) – an argument familiar from classical rhetorical theory. Pontanus, Tasso, and Gracián seek precisely that mingling of instruction with delight for the moving of the reader: their critical thought agrees with and complements that of Augustine. As can be clearly seen, the Catholic poets had available to them stylistic possibilities of a range quite distinct within religious writing of the English Renaissance.

Aspects of emblem theory and practice to 1649

The emblem (usually, the combination of a motto, picture, and poem) puts before the reader's eyes words and image focused on a conceit. Naturally enough, then, elements of how poetic imagery – especially the conceit – was thought of and practised in the Renaissance were immediately relevant to the contemporary theory and practice of the emblem, an interconnection to be seen frequently (though not, of course, exclusively) in the writings of the Catholic religious poets. Their verse shows them as drawing on, or as writing in harmony with, emblem theory and practice of broadly two kinds: the first, in general, secular; the second, not only Counter-Reformation but strongly Jesuit. Outlining a history of Renaissance emblems and emblematics will help to suggest how the emblem was available to the Catholic poets – and the way to start is with Plotinus.

Adopting Plato's distinction between icastic and fantastic art, Plotinus regards most pictures as fantastic shadows, as images having no substantial contact with reality.[32] But he also believes that it is indeed possible to discern within a picture something of an Idea "and so [be] called to recollection of the truth" (2,9,16; cf. 1,6,1–1,6,4). A striking instance of that for Plotinus is the Egyptian hieroglyphs; he considers them to be pictures centred upon absolute truth, ideal Forms (5,8,6). It is implicit in such accounts of icastic pictures or images that Plotinus thinks of icastic art as evoking meditation and drawing the contemplative mind from sensuous perception to spiritual insight. That implied linking of a visual image to meditation is to become consummately explicit in Counter-Reformation emblem books; however, for the moment it need be said only that Plotinus's account of the Egyptian hiero-glyphs becomes elemental to Renaissance emblematics.

When discussing the hieroglyphs, Ficino and many other Renaissance writers echo Plotinus's remarks on their import-ance as symbolic expressions of universal truths: the hiero-glyphs come in fact to be generally regarded as the source from which emblems derive, insofar as they are human artifacts. The *Hypnerotomachia* (1499) helps to spread that notion, and Tesauro, writing in the 1650s, still feels obliged to repeat the tale of the hieroglyphs.[33] Together with acceptance of the hieroglyphs' parentage of the emblem naturally goes a belief that emblems embody universal truths. Through association with the hieroglyphs emblems are thus identified with the orthodox neoplatonic concept of images as possible guides to the Ideal (a Christian version of such a view of the emblem being embodied in Montenay's Protestant *Emblemes, ou Devises Chrestiennes* of 1571). Not everyone in the English Renaissance of course takes so philosophical a view of em-blems. Puttenham airily dispenses with the niceties of emblem theory to assert merely that emblems either please or instruct, for they exist "to insinuat some secret, wittie, morall and braue purpose presented to the beholder, either to recreate his eye, or please his phantasie, or examine his iudgement, or occupie his braine or to manage his will either by hope or by dread...."[34] Even so, the more comprehensive European thinking on emb-lems is nonetheless taken seriously by Englishmen. Daniel translates Paolo Giovio but, more important, Blount translates Estienne in *The Art of Making Devises* (1646).[35] There the Egyptian hieroglyphs are discussed in some detail as being ancient repositories of "wisedome" (p. 2) from which the emblem has developed (pp. 1–3). A similarly neoplatonic point is made when it is observed that "the words of the *Embleme* may demonstrate things universall, and hold the rank of morall precepts ..." (p. 25). The reader therefore unsurprisingly learns that "The chiefe aime of the Embleme is, to instruct us ..." (p. 7). In brief, "the Embleme is properly a sweet and morall Symbole ... by which some weighty sentence is declared" (p. 7). *The Art of Making Devises* exactly describes the directing principles to be found in such representatively English emblem books as Whitney's *A Choice of Emblemes* (1586) and Peacham's *Minerva Britanna* (1612). *The Art* also epitomizes a notion of poetic imagery familiar in England throughout the sixteenth century and recurrent in the seventeenth.[36]

From such ways of thinking about, as well as designing, emblems the emblem theory and practice of the Counter-Reformation differ significantly (if by no means completely). At first one might not think so from a reading of Pontanus's *Libri Tres*. Pontanus says, conventionally: "[P]otestate & vi aliquid declarandi monendique emblemata metienda censemus" (30,10,229).[37] Whilst stressing the primarily moral function of emblems he also emphasizes their various power to delight: "*sitque vt emblema non possit nõ esse gratum, in quo & aures dulci carminum numero delectantur, animi pascuntur, & oculi pictura recreantur*" (3,10,228). Those remarks may show slightly more enthusiasm for the emblem, but what Pontanus says there does not greatly differ from Puttenham's account of the emblem, cited above. His remarks seem quite orthodox and uninspired (studiously he alludes elsewhere to the Egyptian hieroglyphs). But if Pontanus reveals no marked originality in his understanding of the emblem, other Jesuits do. For example, when discussing "learned erudition" (58,838) Gracián observes: 'Emblems, hieroglyphs, apologues, and impresas are the finery of precious stones set in the delicate gold of discourse" (58,841).[38] His imaginative words imply an understanding of the emblem unlike Pontanus's and not merely conventional. The association of emblems with hieroglyphs is familiar enough, but Gracián's brief celebration of the emblem goes beyond that. His hyperboles indicate the high value he sets on the emblem and hence his estimate of its literary importance. More than that, though, his tropes imply the emblem's compelling appeal, the superlatively affective beauty it can add to the already alluring beauty of well-wrought language. Gracián's understanding of the emblem accords naturally with his thoughts on the poetic conceit (something similar will later be found in Tesauro). His account of the emblem, in fact, harmonizes as well with Pontanus's ideas on poetic imagery, for all Pontanus's apparent indifference to the emblem as an iconic mode.

The resemblances among those accounts of emblem and poetic image imply that the affective, baroque aesthetic informing Counter-Reformation poetic theory may also be found in Counter-Reformation emblems. Even a glance at two of the major emblem books of the period shows that to be so, the works being Vaenius's *Amoris Divini Emblemata* (1615) and Hugo's *Pia Desideria* (1624). Vaenius's series of emblems traces the journey of *Anima*, when elevated by *Amor Divinus*, toward complete harmony with and fulfilment in the divine love – the emblems not only telling that tale, but becoming as it were a litany to the divine love itself. The second emblem, *"Incipiendum,"* clearly illustrates the baroque aesthetic variously manifested in the work as a whole (see figure 1).[39]

One immediately notices that the picture in *"Incipiendum"* is divided into realms of light and darkness. To the right of *Amor Divinus* (and so in keeping with biblical iconography) are the bright sky, the symmetrical architecture of a church, an ordered garden, a flourishing tree: light, order, peace, fertility. To his left lies the storm-vexed sea, in which symbols of worldly vanity are tossed by the waves and a *navis animae* seems near destruction.[40] To his left are obscurity, barrenness, and futile motion. Yet the interplay of light and darkness defining those symbolic realms also accentuates the robust solidity of the forms within them. For example, the stocky figures of *Amor Divinus* and *Anima*, the massy church and rocks, the sturdy tree are almost tangibly three-dimensional. With that solid realization of the larger, symbolic forms, moreover, can be seen prolific, substantial, and mostly symbolic detail such as the tree's luxuriant foliage, the flowers at its foot, the bird perched in the tree, and the furrows in the narrow pathway to the church. We are shown that in our world the physical and the spiritual merge or are contiguous, and perception of the spiritual – of its immediacy – is sensuously impressed upon us.

But Vaenius makes the picture affective not only in physical terms. The picture's centrepiece is the sudden and emotional encounter between *Amor Divinus* and *Anima*. The latter looks

Figure 1: "*Incipiendum*," from Vaenius's *Amoris Divini Emblemata*.

up in wonderment at the radiant, calm, beatific, and compassionate face of *Amor Divinus* who, reaching down to raise
Anima from the earth, points heavenwards toward her true
home. That is to say, then, that Vaenius's centrepiece emotively images the meeting of *agape* and *eros*. From there begins
his tale of the soul's upward journey, and he has shaped its start
as an encounter (that between his sacred romance's hero and
heroine) which seeks to convey holy truth affectively, mani-

festing a typically baroque concern with heightened emotions and with heightened psychological states. And one further point might be briefly made about the picture's centrepiece. The radiantly compassionate face of *Amor Divinus* has behind and above it the intense light of the sun: Vaenius sensuously emphasizes that the loving God is light – the real "light of the world."

The same concern for affectiveness can be seen in the texts accompanying the picture. For example, *"Surge, propera amica mea, columba mea, formosa mea, & veni . . .,"* one reads, and, *"Non enim antè anima Deo iungitur & sociatur, nisi omnis ex ea hyems perturbationum, ac vitiorum procella discesserit . . ."* Emotive, holy truth acts as the soul (to use an analogy familiar in emblem theory) to the body of the picture. Perceiving that relationship, one then recognizes how Vaenius's emblems finally work. The reader of the texts, made to contemplate holy truth, turns to the illustrative picture and finds that it is, as it were, a *compositio loci* which seeks to impress the truth sensuously and emotively upon him. Essential to that "impressing" is Vaenius's depiction of the human soul as being central to each picture's action: the reader sees an image of his spiritual self acting within the picture (and so enacting the holy truth of the texts) that he is scrutinizing analytically. To read Vaenius's emblems, as so many others produced in the Counter-Reformation, is thus to perform a series of meditations and so to realize Plotinus's implicit connection between meditation and icastic imagery.

Not all Vaenius's texts are as emotive as those of *"Incipiendum"*; even so, the pictures in his other emblems are insistently affective, using techniques identical to those through which the picture of *"Incipiendum"* seeks to be compelling. *"Ex Amore Adoptio"* shows a physically immediate, intensely personal, and awestruck confrontation with Christ himself; *"Amoris Merces Amplissima"* centres on the soul's ecstatic apprehension of the otherworldly and ecstatic anticipation of heavenly joys; *"Amoris Securitas"* focuses on the happy calm of the soul when, surrounded by vividly realized terrors, it clings to the Divine Love. Rather than going on to offer further examples, one might instead turn at this point to Hugo's *Pia Desideria* and suggest how well its aims and aesthetic accord with those of Vaenius's work. The pictures of *Pia Desideria* at once confirm the similarity; to illustrate that, the representative and beautiful picture in 2,2 need alone be examined (see figure 2).[41]

There dominates the conceit of "the world as labyrinth." The reader is shown *Anima* – that is, himself – standing in pilgrim dress at the centre of the labyrinth, the world in which she stands being intimidatingly depicted. The labyrinth has an austerely geometrical design yet one clearly beyond the comprehension of *Anima*, and indeed the reader's eye cannot make sense of it. Moreover, the paths of the labyrinth are bare, except for some scattered stones, and edged by black pits into which two men have already fallen (a blind man feels his way along the paths, guided by a small dog). The sensuously compelling detail of the picture impresses upon the reader how isolated he is within a sterile, dangerous, and confusing world. But the labyrinth/world is finite, for a wall and trees mark its boundaries. Now the wall and trees enclosing the labyrinth/world should be seen to define it as an inversion of the *hortus conclusus*, a type of paradise: it should be recognized as *locus non amoenus sed terribilis* – of which the labyrinth is a truly affective image. Part of the image of enclosure depicts, however, a way of possible escape. After all, the wall has an arched opening, from which leads a path to the tower of *Amor Divinus*, built on rock and displaying a beacon (all those details focused on *Amor Divinus* being familiar from the psalms or the gospels). To help *Anima* reach the archway a clue to the labyrinth runs from the hands of *Amor Divinus* to the grasp of the soul below, who stares fixedly at the radiant face in the tower not at the pathways (recalling 2 *Corinthians* 5,7). That second grouping of sensuous details, meeting with the first in the person of *Anima*, indicates that the picture is concerned to arouse at once strong and contradictory emotions: it evokes fear, confusion, a sense of claustrophobic entrapment, and hope, faith, relief. Through those heightened emotional responses the picture seeks most deeply to impress *contemptus mundi* and trust in God upon the reader, its affective aesthetic thus distinctly connecting (as do its *personae*) *Pia Desideria* with *Amoris Divini Emblemata*.

Hugo's verse – the soul of the accompanying picture – shows that the likeness is not fortuitous. One reads:

Figure 2: *Anima* in the labyrinth (from Hugo's *Pia Desideria*).

Qvo ferar? ambiguos aperit mihi semita calles;
    Semita non vno tramite secta vias.
Illa tenet dextram, partem tenet illa sinistram,
    Haec tumet in cliuos, vallibus illa cadit:
Haec faciles aditus, aditus habet illa malignos,
    Explicat illa vias, implicat illa dolos ... (ll.1–6)

Nec labirynthaei tanta est fallacia tecti,
    Curua licet varijs torqueat antra vijs.
Heu, grauiora meos cohibent discrimina gressus!
    En gemina dubiam parte pericla premunt. (ll.13–16)

With their sudden, counterbalancing contradictions, their anxious repetitions, their questioning and exclamatory tone, the lines vividly suggest the fear and confusion of *Anima* in the labyrinth. They trace her perception of an intimidating landscape and evoke the panic rising in her as she confronts both her surroundings and her inability to be guided by her own judgment (an as yet unresolved *divisio* working neatly with *incrementum*). That is to say, reading Hugo's verse reveals how aptly it and the picture complement each other, their harmony thoroughly affirming the connections between *Pia Desideria* and Vaenius's work. The same aesthetic does indeed inform each.

Aspects of meditative theory in the Counter-Reformation to 1649

The ideas on meditation formulated during the Counter-Reformation influence the Catholic poets no less significantly than do Counter-Reformation ideas on poetry and on the emblem. In particular the verse of the Catholic poets reflects the meditative theories of St Ignatius Loyola and of St Francis de Sales – the theory of the former because so many of the Catholic religious poets are either Jesuits or Jesuit-influenced; that of the latter because of his works' popularity at Little Gidding and fashionableness at the court of Henrietta Maria, wife of Charles I. Those meditative theories reveal the principles through which the Catholic poets so often image a creative ordering of spiritual experience; they also reveal an aesthetic which connects them to the notions of poetry and of the emblem that have just been discussed. In other words, to examine those meditative theories most favoured by the Catholic poets is to discern within them elements of a baroque aesthetic. Here, as in the preceding section, the way to begin is with Plotinus.

In the *Enneads* Plotinus argues that man is a triadic creature who perfects himself by contemplation of the Divine Triad, in whose likeness he has been made.[42] Plotinus's notion was to prove elemental to St Augustine's understanding of the human soul. Augustine proposes in *De Trinitate* that, since God made man in his image, the soul variously resembles the Holy Trinity. The soul is described as being in a number of ways triadic; however, for the art of meditation the most important of those was to be the soul's possession of memory, understanding, and love. To explain that, one has to consider for a moment what St Augustine says in *De Trinitate* about wisdom. He describes wisdom as "the intellectual cognizance of eternal things," requiring "a contemplative life."[43]

He goes on to say that when the soul focuses its memory, understanding, and love upon God (who alone is the eternal) then the soul achieves true wisdom – and at the same time moves toward perfecting itself as an image of the Trinity (14,12,15–14,16,22). Augustine thus associates the getting of wisdom, contemplation, concentrating the soul on God, and self-perfection.[44] Many of the heirs to his thought would do likewise, some of them doing so specifically in the context of meditative theory. That is true of St Bonaventure and of Walter Hilton to name but two; more to the point here, it is also true of St Ignatius Loyola.[45]

The meditative theory of St Ignatius, and its relation to the tradition of Augustinian thought, have been treated as familiar knowledge ever since Louis L. Martz's graceful *The Poetry of Meditation* (1954) first described each to students of Renaissance literature. But for all the carefulness of Martz's description – and innovative as his attempting it was – facets of Ignatian theory and of its Augustinian inheritance remain to be illuminated, especially in relation to the art of the Catholic poets. A reconsideration of St Ignatius' theory needs to begin with the question of his indebtedness to the Augustinian tradition. That there is indeed an indebtedness (whether incurred through the writings of St Bernard, St Bonaventure, or someone else) can be fairly assumed: early in *The Spiritual Exercises*, in fact in the third of the prefatory "Directions," Ignatius alludes to Augustinian faculty psychology; later, he explicitly bases his version of meditation on the Augustinian "three powers of the soul" (by which he means memory, understanding, and will – the latter to be exercised in love of God).[46] How Ignatius uses the Augustinian inheritance can be seen more clearly when one considers his design for meditation.

An Ignatian meditation starts with a preparatory prayer in which the self is subjected and offered to God. Following the prayer are two "preludes": the first, a *compositio loci* ("composition of place"); the second, a request for emotions in keeping with the theme of the meditation.[47] The *compositio loci*, or picturing to oneself of the scene and circumstances of what is being contemplated, has been much discussed in relation to the techniques of individual religious poets; for all that, the procedure itself needs closer attention than it has usually been given. To begin with, *compositio loci* acts within a meditation as the equivalent to *demonstratio* in literature: a formal, detailed, vivid description. St Ignatius' remarks on *compositio loci* stress the realism and physical immediacy that one's mental picturings should have: "[C]onsider the road from Bethany to Jerusalem, whether it is broad or narrow, whether it is level, *etc.* Consider likewise the room of the supper ..." (p. 91). Puttenham's account of *demonstratio* is neatly analogous, for he refers to it as description "in such sort as it should appeare [that things] were truly before our eyes though they were not present" (other accounts of *demonstratio* concur with his).[48] That mutual emphasis on realism and immediacy clearly indicates the equivalence between *compositio loci* and *demonstratio*, but Ignatius' remarks of course imply as well that the first prelude in a meditation will form an affective image solely of a sacred moment or spiritual truth. In initially describing composition of place St Ignatius makes its affective role quite apparent. Alluding to "meditations on subject matter that is not visible, [such as] meditation on sins," he says: "[T]he mental image will consist of imagining, and considering my soul imprisoned in its corruptible body, and my entire being in this vale of tears as an exile among brute beasts" (p. 54). His vivid and emotive (if conventional) words suggest that the aesthetic of Ignatian meditation has obvious affinities with the aesthetic common to Counter-Reformation poetic theory and emblematics. As will be argued below, subsequent Jesuit writers follow Ignatius in asserting the imagination's creatively affective role in meditation.

St Ignatius' remarks on the second prelude affirm what has just been observed of the first. He says that one should ask God for emotions in keeping with the meditation's "subject matter" (p. 54) – and thus with the preceding *compositio loci*: "[I]f the contemplation is on the Resurrection I shall ask for joy ..., if it is on the passion, I shall ask for pain, tears, and suffering with Christ" (p. 54; cf. especially p. 93). But whilst Ignatian *compositio loci* coincides with Pontanus's ideas on imagery, and functions in a meditation much as do Vaenius's pictures in *Amoris Divini Emblemata* (or those in *Pia Desideria* or in *Schola Cordis*), it also has elemental connections with Augustinian faculty psychology. St Ignatius indicates that the first of the preludes depends upon exercise of the memory, itself the first of St Augustine's three powers of the soul (p. 54). Now what Ignatius says of *compositio loci* reveals that through it the memory focuses, ultimately, on God. Therefore, in terms of the Augustinian principles informing Ignatian meditation, through *compositio loci* memory begins to lead the tripartite soul toward the parental Trinity – so directing the soul toward achieving self-perfection and wisdom.[49] Yet if *compositio loci* depends finally on the memory, the procedure is of course shaped directly by the imagination or *phantasia*. St Augustine describes the *phantasia* as having a dangerous instability and seductive vividness (*De Trinitate* 11,10,17; 12,8,13–9,14). However, concentrating it upon the sacred in composition of place, St Ignatius seeks to sanctify and control that mercurial faculty: for the length of a meditation the *phantasia* is organized into aiding the soul's quest for God. St Ignatius intends meditation to be a localized ordering – with lasting effects – of the entire personality: to be more exact, a Christocentric ordering of the personality.

The role of *compositio loci* in Ignatian meditation would seem, then, to be more subtle and important than has been generally allowed. The remainder of a meditation can in fact be seen as elaborating upon those spiritual and aesthetic themes initiated with the first of the preludes. That can be seen at once in what Ignatius says of the middle section of a meditation, which usually takes one of two forms, the first being a comprehensive and emotionally affecting analysis, or *distributio*, of the sacred topic under consideration. In the "first exercise," for example, St Ignatius remarks amidst the "points" of the analysis: "[M]y understanding is to be used to reason more in detail on the subject matter, and thereby move more deeply my affections through the use of the will" (p. 55). The second form which the middle section of a meditation can take is that of an analysis where different aspects of the sacred topic are related to the senses. That "application of the senses" uses the power of the imagination rather as it is used in composition of place. For instance, in a meditation on hell one is advised to analyse the nature of hell and "see in imagination the great fires, ... hear the wailing, the screaming, ... smell the smoke, ... taste

bitter things, ... feel how the flames surround and burn souls"
(p. 59). In this section of a meditation, then, St Ignatius naturally develops his Augustinian pattern, having exercise of the
understanding follow the exercise of memory in the preludes.
So the soul's movement toward self-perfection and wisdom
continues; so the *phantasia* again aids the soul's ascent. The
affective intent and, to a degree, method of the preludes persist.

The Augustinian pattern of a meditation is completed and its
affective intent brought to a climax in what follows – the
colloquy. There, in intimate address (usually to God alone)
one turns the will to God in deep, yet ordered, love: "The
colloquy is made properly by speaking as one friend speaks to
another, or as a servant speaks to his master ..." (p. 56; cf. p.
92). The experience is often to be intensified, according to St
Ignatius, through dramatic use of the imagination: "Imagine
Christ our Lord before you, hanging upon the cross. Speak
with him ..." (p. 56). The soul's three faculties have become
concentrated on God until, at the last, it finally confronts God
himself: the tripartite soul confronts its triune original. Thereafter a meditation closes simply in prayer.

Nothing more need be said here of the Augustinian elements
in Ignatian meditation, or of a meditation's affectiveness –
except for one thing. It has to be recognized that Ignatian
meditation, although designed solely for devotional ends, has
an aesthetic, one which distinctly associates St Ignatius'
thought with the poetics and emblematics of later Catholic
thinkers. Even a glance at some of the many later meditative
writers influenced by St Ignatius will suggest their acknowledgement of his affective aesthetic as a marked and essential
component of meditation. In the anonymous *Certayne deuout
Meditations* (1576), the author – who describes each meditation in terms of "points" on the Ignatian model – emphasizes
the affectiveness of meditative experience and advocates what
are in fact compositions of place as means of achieving intense
emotional identification with the suffering of Christ.[50] Just so,
the Jesuit Androzzi's *Meditations vppon the Passion of Ovr
Lord Iesvs Christ* (Englished in 1606) counsels that one imaginatively apprehend the life of Christ in order to imitate it,
meditation being initially if not exclusively characterized in
those terms of imagination and affectiveness.[51] Androzzi dis-

cusses both terms more specifically when examining "Representation" or *compositio loci* and "Consideration" (pp. 49–50).

Like the two works examined above, Berzetti's *The Practice of Meditating* (modelled on Ignatius' *Exercises* and translated by a Jesuit in 1613) stresses from the start the affective power of meditation, and when describing "the second Preamble," or composition of place, emphasizes its physical impressing of the sacred upon the contemplative mind:

> The way of framing such places shal be, either imagining that God in heauen doth shew them vnto him distinctly paynted in some fayre image: Yf with his imagination he was first transported thither.

> Which to performe more easely, and without daunger of wearying his head yt will help him not a litle, to haue before with attention beheld some image liuely representing the mistery, or to haue read, or heard, what authors haue written concerning those places, and in particuler to haue noted the distance from one place to another, the height of the hills where any mistery happened, where the city, castle, or village was scituated in which our saviour wrought his miracles.[52]

Finally, here, one might consider Puente's Jesuit *Meditations vpon the Mysteries of Ovr Faith* (as published in 1624).[53] Building on the topoi of the soul's three powers and likeness to God (pp. 1–2), Puente goes on to stress a meditation's affectiveness ("This meditation [no.x] hath a very great effect to moue a soule . . ." p. 23; cf. p. 11, p. 286). The nature and role of composition of place in contributing to that are revealed in all their subtlety when Puente discusses meditation on the passion of Christ. Writing of the "agony in the garden," Puente describes Christ's experience as one of meditative prayer. Christ is in fact described as meditating on his future pains through compositions of place – Puente, in translation, calls those compositions exercises of memory: "[T]he continuall memory, he had of the cruell torments, he was to suffer, . . . afflicted him . . ., as he testifyed in the prayer he made in the garden, where the only representation [i.e. *compositio loci*; cf. Berzetti cited above] of the pains he expected, caused him to sweet drops of bloud" (p. 287). Puente's insistence upon the immediacy and vividness of Christ's "representation" need hardly be pointed out, nor need its affectiveness.

What should rather be acknowledged is that Puente, in showing Christ as conforming to Jesuit ideas of meditative experience, unintentionally makes Christ the final authority for the affective aesthetic which informs Ignatian meditation: Puente's Christ reveals that the aesthetic of the *Exercises* acts as a valid part of true meditation. Understandably, then, when Christ's "agony in the garden" later appears as an actual theme for meditation (third week, no.xi) Puente counsels the reader "To consider, how [sin and its consequences for mankind] were presented altogeather before the minde of [Christ's] innocent soule, which we must imagine we see actually tormented . . ." (p. 321). The reader's contemplative mind is thus to become identified with the divine mind itself in meditation; the affective aesthetic of Ignatian meditation leads to imaginative apprehension of, emotional union with, the very soul of Christ. The aesthetic of the *Exercises* could seemingly take the reader no further than that – nor could its continuing importance be underestimated.

Given the strong Jesuit influence among the Catholic religious poets, much less need be said here of St Francis de Sales's *Introduction to the Devout Life* (1609) than of St Ignatius' *Exercises*. And there is another good reason for that. From the start of his *Introduction* St Francis admits to the various indebtedness of his work; allowing for the familiar rhetoric of modesty (the "inability" topos as *captatio benevolentiae*) and for his work's marked individuality, it is none the less clear that St Francis's thinking on meditation – to isolate that subject – owes much to St Ignatius.[54] The indebtedness, yet also the individuality and usefulness, of St Francis's thinking on meditation become apparent when one turns to the *Introduction* itself.

The structure of "Salesian" meditation immediately suggests St Francis's indebtedness to his predecessor, that structure comprising (pp. 44–45): preparations (putting oneself, as it were, in God's presence and asking for inspiration); considerations (analyses of the self in relation to God/of the specific topic for meditation); affections and resolutions (the emotional and intellectual results of the previous analyses); conclusion (turning the will to God in colloquy) and prayers. Here can be discerned a reworking of the Ignatian pattern already examined: prayers at the start as well as at the close; preludes, analysis, and colloquy in between. Moreover the Salesian structure, like the Ignatian, obviously depends upon exercise of the soul's "three powers." Composition of place is mentioned later, by name (p. 72), as a third "preparation" – though for St Francis too it can be fitted elsewhere into a meditation's design – and its affective power receives some strong emphasis (contrast p. 58, p. 72).[55] Salesian meditation departs, however, from its original in this striking way: it is fashioned for those who live much amidst the business and bustle of the world (p. 28) – hence its flexibility (not that Ignatian medittation can't be accommodating) and its refusal to make unnecessary demands upon the contemplative (see p. 72 once more). All in all, one might suggest finally here that if the Salesian form of meditation does not have the conceptual richness of its Ignatian model, its spiritual priorities and implicit aesthetic are still much the same as those informing *The Spiritual Exercises*.

The five traditions so influential upon the verse of the Catholic religious poets are not pigeonholes into which writers or their works can be snugly fitted. Nor do they form little maps of knowledge serving to mark out boundaries and to classify neatly everything thought to be, even in part, within them. They are instead clusters of living, various, interacting ideas and values which simultaneously shape and receive new shapes within the poets' verse. Being within that verse at once conventional and creatively restated, they combine with other traditions to form a religious poetry of unusual stylistic possibilities and distinctive religious sensibility in the English Renaissance. To demonstrate that, one must now turn to the works of the Catholic poets themselves.

CHAPTER TWO

St Robert Southwell

In his poems St Robert Southwell sets before the reader a comprehensive spiritual discipline, wherein one must especially consider two choices: that between an egocentric and a theocentric life; that between a self able to be expressed in merely human terms and a self which can find no expression without the Word.

Southwell confronts the reader with that discipline and its essential options by articulating a world-view, centred on the divine *agape* and on Christ, whose principles he expounds, celebrates, advocates, and (or) within which he explores the experience of evil, states of communion with God, and the manifestations of God's selfless love. In fashioning his poems to those ends, Southwell intermingles native with Counter-Reformation traditions and writes with a stylistic as well as psychological range, with a various aesthetic, unique in English religious verse of the sixteenth century. His poems are at once profoundly devout and aesthetically self-conscious; at their best, as in "The burning Babe" and *Saint Peters Complaint*, they have a sophistication and subtle inwardness that suggest why as demanding a critic as Jonson could praise Southwell so highly.

Little is known of the chronology of Southwell's poems, and nothing of the order in which he might have wished them to be printed.[1]

In what follows they are discussed in thematic groups which correspond approximately to those within the manuscript ordering of the poems, retained by Southwell's modern editors.[2] The aim in doing so is not to imply a neat unity to Southwell's poems but rather to clarify continuities within and among their thematic groups, thus illuminating Southwell's concerns and achievements. We may start by focusing on those poems, all early in the manuscript ordering, where he most clearly proposes his world-view.

Poems of agape *and accommodation*

In *The Sequence on the Virgin Mary and Christ*, Southwell argues that all interaction between man and God (in effect, between the natural and the spiritual) centres on the divine love that descends selflessly and unmerited to man: there as throughout his poems Southwell implies that God's *agape*, manifested in Christ through the Virgin Mary, lies at the heart of his world-view. He emphasizes that the Incarnation reveals accommodation (in St Augustine's sense) as the means by which the divine love expresses itself within the creation. Thus identified as elemental to human experience, accommodation becomes a basic principle of style in *The Sequence* – an Augustinian consequence.[3] For all that, Southwell is content in *The Sequence* neither with expounding and celebrating the divine *agape* and accommodation nor with urging response to them; in addition, to help put spiritual choices persuasively before the reader, he makes the reader not merely consider, but seem to encounter, the love of God. Where that most directly occurs in *The Sequence* has great significance, for there the reader imaginarily enters the life of Christ, yet the scope of such an event in Southwell's poems begins to appear when four further works are examined: "The burning Babe"; "A childe my Choyce"; "Sinnes heavie loade"; "Christs bloody sweat." To study *The Sequence* with those poems is to recognize much that is essential to the spiritual discipline offered by Southwell's verse.

Southwell textures *The Sequence on the Virgin Mary and Christ* with sacred paradox. He does so partly as a gesture toward the encompassing in language of mysteries beyond language or human logic, and partly to impress upon the reader a sense of wonder when considering the marvel of God's love (for example: "Beholde the father, is his daughters sonne: / The bird that built the nest, is hatched therein ..." 6,1–2). Sometimes he expresses his paradoxes in elaborate conceits meant not merely to evoke wonder but to dazzle with the marvellous, as where the slaughter of the Innocents is revealed

as the grotesque, the horrible, transformed to glory and
triumph because indirectly in God's service. Of the martyred
children Southwell writes, "With open throats and silent
mouthes you sing / His praise whom age permits you not to
name . . ." (10,15–16). But the frequent plainness, even at times
the homeliness, of Southwell's writing suggests that notions of
apprehension through paradox, of *meraviglia*, and of *stupore*
are accompanied by the idea of accommodating divine truths
to the reader. Even a glance at how Southwell has his speaker
narrate (e.g. 1,1–6; 7,13–18), expound (e.g. 1,13–18; 4,1–6),
and celebrate (e.g. 3,1–6; 14,1–6) those truths indicates that
The Sequence is pervaded by his desire for their plain, as well as
their arresting, expression. Their focus is, moreover, the Incarnation – the accommodation of the Logos to mankind (5,7–12;
6,1–6) – and so his *sermo humilis* enacts an imitation of Christ.
Southwell's exposition of the Incarnation and of the divine
truths connected with it defines what matters most both in *The
Sequence* and in his world-view.[4]

Southwell ends the fourth poem of *The Sequence* with an
interesting restatement of the *felix culpa* theme:

> With hauty minde to godhead man aspirde,
> And was by pride from place of pleasure chac'de,
> With loving minde our manhood God desired,
> And us by love in greater pleasure plac'de,
> Man labouring to ascend procurde our fall,
> God yeelding to discend cut off our thrall. (13–18)

He characterizes falling man as an overreacher mimicking
demonic ambition (l.13, l.17); he implies that ambition to be,
however, not so much a quest for self-elevation as a desire for
an importance equal to God's, for personal "godhead." In
other words, Southwell's account of the Fall stresses that
human nature has a primal desire to place itself at the apex of
existence and to rule – which Southwell of course identifies as
leading only to death (l.14 – see 2,12; 4,5; 6,7; 11,3). But if he
implies that human nature is fatally inclined to live egocentri-
cally (in fact, toward inhabiting an egocentric universe), he also
insists that God's unmerited love (l.18) has restored life to man
through the Incarnation: Southwell's emphasis on God's self-

lessly "loving minde" (l.15), regenerative "love" (l.16), and humbly "yeelding to discend" (l.18) indicates that the divine *agape* – accommodated to man through Christ (l.15, l.18) – has freed man from death ("cut off our thrall," l.18; see 4,5) and reunited creature with creator (l.16). Southwell suggests, then, that the divine love alone is the meeting-point between man and God; the world-view epitomized at the close of "The Virgins salutation" clearly has *agape* and Christ at its centre.

Southwell elaborates upon that world-view throughout *The Sequence*, mainly by tracing how the divine love perfects nature through grace. In stressing that fallen human nature's self-love has trapped man in death, Southwell refers to spiritual (2,12; 6,7) as well as to physical (4,5) death. It is from both decay of the spirit and bodily decay within mutability that God's *agape* has brought redemption. Southwell shows God to have redeemed man from a twofold death by a double perfecting of nature. First, God is seen to have imposed a sacred order, focused on the Incarnation, upon natural process (consider the typological imagery dominating the first four poems and the sacred chronology of *The Sequence* as a whole; one perceives secular time to be subordinate to the unfolding scheme of redemption – poems 10–12 are especially revealing in that context). Second, the Incarnation is variously interpreted as the manifestation of human nature's perfecting in Christ, he having descended into flesh through the virtually perfect humanity of his mother (see for example 1,7–8 and 7,3–4). Southwell constantly reminds the reader that the saving love expressed in those terms originates solely from God: man has not merited it, and it selflessly enters the temporal realm (1,11–12; 2,1–14; 3,7–8; 4,13–18; 5,13–18, 6, *passim*, and so on). As will become clearer below, the world-view thus proposed in *The Sequence* is essential to Southwell's verse.

Southwell does not allow the reader, however, merely to study the divine love and its accommodation to man; he seeks to make the reader experience something of them in imaginarily entering Christ's presence. In the ninth poem ("The Presentation") the reader seems through the figure of Simeon to come into close contact with the Christ child (9,7–12). Yet much more direct and important is Southwell's bringing the reader into attendance, as it were, at Christ's Nativity. At the point

where he does so in "The Nativitie of Christ" (poem 6),
Southwell raises the poem's rhetorical level from the middle
style of its opening stanza to a forcefully emotional high style:

> O dying soules, beholde your living spring:
> O dasled eyes, behold your sonne of grace;
> Dull eares, attend what word this word doth bring:
> Up heavie hartes: with joye your joye embrace.
> From death, from darke, from deafenesse, from dispaires:
> This life, this light, this word, this joy repaires.
>
> Gift better then himselfe, God doth not know:
> Gift better then his God, no man can see:
> This gift doth here the gever geven bestow:
> Gift to this gift let each receiver bee.
> God is my gift, himselfe he freely gave me:
> Gods gift am I, and none but God shall have me. (ll.7–18)

The reader, who at the poem's start has been made a mental
witness at Christ's birth and reminded of its being an act of
incomprehensible condescension ("Beholde the father, is his
daughters sonne ...," l.1), is now dramatically put in Christ's
presence (ll.7–8; ll.11–12) and is emotionally exhorted to
concentrate his whole being on Christ as his saviour. His
senses ("beholde," l.7; "behold," l.8; "attend," l.9), understanding ("attend what word this word doth bring," l.9), and
emotions ("Up heavie hartes: with joye your joye embrace,"
l.10) are directed to communion with Christ. At the climax of
the passages cited (ll.16–18), which would seem to form the
climax of the poem, Southwell's speaker decides to reciprocate
the divine love by offering gift for gift – donating himself to
God in a considered, if impassioned, act of love. That decision
implicitly involves the reader (l.16) and at once brings up the
question of whether the reader will likewise choose to become
a gift for God. In fact, through the speaker Southwell here puts
before the reader two antecedent choices, for a decision about
giving oneself to God can be made only after one has chosen
between an egocentric or a theocentric life, and (with the
Nativity as a context) between a self not expressible without
the Word or a self able to be expressed in merely human terms.
To urge on the reader, Southwell does not – as one might

expect from his poem's insistence on seeing – vividly depict the Christ child and his circumstances; rather, he fashions what Tesauro would later call "*concetti predicabili*." The "preachable conceit," according to Tesauro, "*è vn' Argutia leggiermente accennata dall' Ingegno Diuino: leggiadramente suelata dall' Ingegno humano: & rifermata con l'autorità di alcun sacro Scrittore.*"[5] He continues: "*Dico, ch'ella è vn' Argutezza Concettosa; cioè vn' argomento ingeniosamente prouante vna Propositione di materia Sacra, & persuasibile al Popolo: il cui Mezzotermine sia fondato in Metafora.*"[6] The first preachable conceit, that of the "gift" (ll.13–18), emphatically confronts the reader with an image of God's love, with the speaker's reciprocating donation of self, and with personal choices. The second, of God when incarnate therefore being "haye, the brutest sinner to refresh" (l.22), pervades the following lines (19–24) in what Tesauro would call an "urbane enthymeme," ingeniously to persuade the reader that God's love is indeed marvellous in its selflessness and humility. The reader's seeming encounter with the infant Christ distinctly illustrates both the presence and function of Counter-Reformation poetics in *The Sequence*, for when compelling the reader into mental attendance upon the Christ child, Southwell writes in the forming Jesuit literary tradition to promote the union of the reader with God.

The Sequence on the Virgin Mary and Christ has of course a number of purposes, not the least important of which is to define, by examining how the lives of Christ and the Virgin were interwoven, her role as *mediatrix* (see for example 1,1–6; 2,1–12, and so on) in relation to his greater role as mediator. In discussing the work, however, I have chosen to pay most attention to those aspects of it which illuminate Southwell's other poems – especially but not only his other poems of *agape* and accommodation. Having done so helps to suggest how various (rather than "Counter-Reformation" in some monolithic sense) are the designs and achievements of such major lyrics as "The burning Babe," where one can begin to see with what scope Southwell explores states of communion with God and manifestations of God's love.

Much that can be discerned in *The Sequence* can also be recognized in "The burning Babe," for example: the centrality

of *agape* and divine accommodation to the world-view informing the poem; the mingling of native with Counter-Reformation styles. But in "The burning Babe" those elements are so
compacted with many not to be found in *The Sequence* that the
poem forms, at more than one level, a curious instance of
multum in parvo. The poem recalls a moment of dialectic, the
encounter between an "I" profane of consciousness (the narrator's past self) and the "I" who is Christ, the oppositions and
interplay between the profane "I" and his divine counterpart
being subtly diverse. Focusing initially on the languages
through which those opposed identities appear, leads naturally
into the complexities of their dialectical relationship. The profane "I" recreated in the poem's opening lines is revealed
through a language dominated, understandably enough, by
sensuous detail: "As I in hoarie Winters night / Stoode shiver-
ing in the snow ..." (ll.1–2). Yet the lines are emblematic
rather than merely realistic, for the cold, isolation, and darkness that they evoke suggest a condition of consciousness, an
awareness preoccupied with sensuous experience and alive
only to the mundane. Their language suggests, as the reader
soon perceives, the state of a soul without Christ. The abrupt
unsettling of consciousness then indicated in that profane "I"
is conveyed by the transition from a language implicitly internal to one increasingly interior: "Surpris'd I was with sodaine
heate, / Which made my hart to glow ..." (ll.3–4). The lines
register more than the startling of a mundane mind by an
intrusion of the marvellous (the narrator now using words for
physical sensation to describe spiritual experience). Through
his narrator Southwell signals that the profane "I" has person-
ally encountered – through no merit or quest of his own – the
love of God and thereby entered a new dimension of existence.
The "sodaine heate" (l.3) is not metaphoric, even though the
preceding references to cold are metaphoric as well as literal: it
marks the experiencing of an archetypal spiritual phenomenon, so that the language of the couplet implies the profane
"I" to be unexpectedly, and as yet unknowingly, progressing
from a secular perception of reality to a recognition of reality as
manifesting continual interaction between the physical and the
spiritual. The point is affirmed by Southwell's *S. Mary Magdalens Fvnerall Teares* and Walter Hilton's *The Ladder of Perfec-*

tion. In the latter, Hilton says: "[T]he ... experience of God [becomes] not merely a fire, but a glowing fire in [the] heart ..."[7] Reflecting on Christ's remark to Mary Magdalen's sister "that *Mary had chosen the best part, which should not be taken from her*," Southwell speculates: "But thy [Christ's] meaning happily was, that though it be taken from her eyes, yet it should neuer be taken from her hart, and it may be thy inward presence supplieth thine outward absence: yet I can hardly thinke, but that if *S. Mary* had thee within her, she could feele it, and if she felt it, she would neuer seeke thee. Thou art too hoat a fire to be in her bosome, and not to burne her ..."[8] Aptly enough, the language tracing the encounter of the profane "I" with God's love continues to emphasize his confusion, fear, and wonder (ll. 5–8).

If the spiritual awakening of the profane "I," even when he is still in quite indirect contact with God, reveals the disparities between nature and grace, the mundane and the otherworldly, creature and creator, then those disparities are revealed more tellingly when he fully focuses on the vision of Christ:

Who scorched with excessive heate,
   Such floods of teares did shed,
As though his floods should quench his flames,
   Which with his teares were fed ... (ll.9–12)

The symbolic language of the stanza is violent and paradoxical because to human perception (although the profane "I" does not yet understand what he sees) the divine love manifested in the world through Christ must be viewed as supranaturally powerful and beyond logic.[9] That further transformation of the poem's language suggests, then, the continuing transformation of the profane "I": the heightening (unknown to him in his incomprehension of the vision) of his spiritual sensitivity; the intensification of his confusion and wonder. In subsequently having the vision of Christ speak in self-explication, Southwell shrewdly extends the dialectic between the poem's opposed identities.[10] The language of the sacred "I," unlike that recreating his enfeebled counterpart, expresses a greater than human self: its pervasion by *catachresis* and paradox implies the vastness of the distance between Christ's perfect human nature – shown to be sacrificial and universal in love – and what we consider usual. Moreover, as the speech of the "Babe" proceeds one sees that his language is centred on timeless absolutes ("Love," "Justice," "Mercie," and his own faultlessness) whereas the language recreating the conscious- ness of the profane "I," and hence of all who are without Christ, has been indicated as linked to mutability. The lan- guage of the "Babe" is to be recognized as of both our world and eternity.

An examination of the two languages of the poem reveals basic contrasts between the vision of Christ and the mundane figure whom he confronts, but that dialectic has in fact far more sophistication than has yet been suggested. To begin with, the context of the profane "I" is secular time, Becoming (ll.1–2); the vision of Christ, fusing Nativity with Passion, reveals secular time to be reorganized and encompassed by the divine patterning of history, at whose core is God's *agape* embodied in Christ. Southwell thus doubly stresses accommo- dation in his poem, for he identifies it as essential to God's intervention in history and to God's mediating of his truth to man (the vision's self-explication is accommodation). South- well's contrast between secular time and its sacred reorganiza- tion has, however, another aspect. Through the vision of Christ, the reader, as well as the profane "I," is of course invited to accept the offered love of God and so to become part of history's redemptive scheme. That in effect asks both the reader and the profane "I" to progress from self-centred (cf. ll.1–2) to theocentric experience – and the demand is made in specific terms. Confronted by the vision, one is asked to live Christocentrically, to have no life apart from the Word (see the "harts" image of l.15). One is asked to choose between Chris- tocentrism and nothingness. In so defining the inner nature of the Christian life (cf. *Galatians* 2,20), Southwell simul- taneously implies what is the inner nature of Christian verse: it too must be Logocentric or nothing.[11] With that notion neither Lok nor Herbert would disagree.

In that context one can trace the poem's various dialectic into its style. Southwell frames his poem with the profane "I" and a shifting plain style; at its centre he writes in a Jesuit poetic to manifest the persuasive presence of the vision. A plain style of sensuous, then emotional specifics helps initially to characterize the profane "I". A plainness stating two facts (ll.29–32), both about spiritual events, characterizes him at the last and indicates his development from a mundane to a devout consciousness. Between those contrasts lies an antithesis to them both, an icon through which Southwell seeks to make divine truth sensuously compelling. At the centre of his poem, then, he places an icon anticipatory of Pontanus's ideas on poetic imagery (see "In fierie heates I frie," l.14, "warme their harts," l.15, "feele my fire," l.16, in conjunction with ll.9–12). But in that this icon is an affective symbolic image which explains itself to the reader, it also accords with Counter-Reformation emblematics. Moreover, since the icon is fashioned for contemplation by the reader, it acts as a composition of place, a focus for meditation. Having diverse, if interrelated, functions (to make truth sensuously compelling, to teach it affectively, to realize it vividly), the icon has affinities with diverse Counter-Reformation modes. Those resemblances are affirmed by even a glance at the aesthetic informing the icon. It has been argued above that Jesuit poetics, Counter-Reformation emblematics, and Jesuit meditative theory are pervaded by a baroque aesthetic. Southwell's concern in the icon to picture extreme physical sensations, to simulate and to evoke heightened psychological experience, and to reveal the marvellous, identify it as a baroque centrepiece to his poem. One can reasonably suggest, therefore, that the icon is elementally connected with the Counter-Reformation modes to which it seems related. Yet there is another aspect to the centre of Southwell's poem. If there he draws on an aesthetic unfamiliar in contemporary English religious verse in order to impress the truths of divine love on his readers, he also draws on it there to explore how beyond reason, how incomprehensible in its intensity (cf. ll.13–14), and how terrible, as well as beautiful, is the *agape* manifested in Christ. The stylistic contrasts in "The burning Babe" express an astute interplay of the native with the Counter-Reformation.[12]

No less astute a strategy in "The burning Babe" is Southwell's implication, through the nature of the vision that he sets before the profane "I" and the reader, of how far his text points beyond its narrative boundaries. That strategy becomes clear when the poem is set in the context of some observations by St Thomas on knowledge and vision. In his *Summa Theologica* Thomas remarks that "[w]e see and judge of all things in the light of the first truth ..."[13] That implies how privileged the profane "I" has in fact been, for in a visionary moment he has been allowed to understand himself "in the light of the first truth" – as, at a couple of removes, has the reader. The visionary moment recalled in the poem does indeed manifest *agape*. But more significant are remarks by Thomas concerning vision itself. He asserts in *Summa Contra Gentiles* "that man's ultimate happiness [without which man cannot truly find rest] consists solely in the contemplation of God ..."[14] He also observes in *Summa Theologica*: "Final and perfect happiness can consist in nothing else than the vision of the Divine Essence."[15] The vision of Christ in "The burning Babe" does not of course indicate the "Divine Essence", but God at work in the world; it is a vision to redirect or encourage man toward beatitude (it redirects the profane "I" by letting him perceive himself in relation to the divine love), and so a vision for the church militant. Through a partial vision, in other words, Southwell's poem points beyond its boundaries to man's fulfilment in the supreme vision.

With its elaborate interaction of the native and the Counter-Reformation, "The burning Babe" implies rather more forcefully than *The Sequence on the Virgin Mary and Christ* that Southwell is unique in sixteenth-century English religious verse. Nonetheless, not all his poems affirm his uniqueness by containing such interaction, even though they do tend to affirm his skill as a writer; rather, being almost if not entirely native – or similarly Counter-Reformation – some indicate his singularity as a religious poet only when they are considered as contributions to an aesthetically diverse canon. That can be seen from an examination of the remarkable and quite familiarly English "A childe my Choyce." The poem is related to lyrics such as Vaux's "When I looke backe ...," and like "The burning Babe" it explores a state of communion with God, the manifesting of God's love, within a world view centred on *agape* and its accommodation to man (here again Southwell concentrates on *agape* and accommodation as manifested in the Incarnation). A major difference between "The burning

Babe" and this poem is, however, that in "A child my Choyce" one listens to the professions of a resolved soul, not to the voice of a now-resolved soul recalling its spiritual transformation:

> Let folly praise that fancie loves, I praise and love that child,
> Whose hart, no thought: whose tong, no word: whose hand no deed defiled.
> I praise him most, I love him best, all praise and love is his:
> While him I love, in him I live, and cannot live amisse. (ll.1–4).

Those lines indicate that the poem, being focused on the Nativity, decorously celebrates and explores the nature of the Christ child – as well as the speaker's responses to him – in a plain style; for all that, the rhetoric of its plain speech is unusually complex.

The rhetoric of the poem is strikingly terse and, as can be seen from the representative lines quoted above, has a number of interconnected functions: to achieve brevity and compression (*contrarium* – with *concessio* – l.1; *adjunctio*, l.2; *dissolutio*, ll.2–3; *comprehensio*, ll.1–2, ll.3–4); to insist and elaborate (*disjunctio*, ll.3–4; *frequentatio*, l.3; *repetitio*, *passim*); to indicate the true way and to express union with Christ (*incrementum*, ll.1–4; *allusio*, l.4; *chiasmus*, l.4). The first two functions clearly reinforce the third. The poem's rhetoric enacts, then, the speaker's assertion that his existence is identified with Christ (ll.3–4) – though at one point it also helps to qualify what it affirms, stressing the ambivalence of the speaker's claim, "While him I love, in him I live ... (l.4)." In effect the textual strategies of the first three stanzas thus enact *New Testament* dicta (for example, *Galatians* 2,20 and *John* 15,2–11) which postulate that the Christian life is a life of unity with Christ.[16] Yet the complex rhetoric which suggests that concept also helps to explicate it by tracing the speaker's reflections on, and responses to, the Christ child.[17] Reflecting on the Christ child, the speaker delightedly explores his nature and stresses that he embodies a love, *agape*, which is central to human experience ("He mine, by gift...," l.7; "his love, doth cherish all ...," l.11). Not only is the Christ child considered as the manifestation of divine love, however, for the speaker studies him cumulatively to imply that he is every aspect of the Good and in that sense *non multum sed omnia in parvo*: the Christ child is, to cite merely several instances, absolutely "[un]defiled" (l.2); "Loves sweetest mark, Lawdes highest theme, mans most desired light" (l.5); "life" (l.6); "delight" (l.6); "First friend ... best friend" (l.8); always "true" (l.8).[18] Hence the poem's rhetoric of unity aptly tells both of Christ and of the speaker. Southwell does not allow the reader to forget, nonetheless, that even so thoughtfully and fervently resolved a soul will somehow fail in its faithfulness. In the poem's final stanza the speaker prays: "Almightie babe, whose tender armes can force all foes to flie: / Correct my faultes, protect my life, direct me when I die" (ll.15–16). There he confesses that, whilst he identifies his life with Christ, he has "faultes" which prevent a complete identification; in other words, his closing prayer makes explicit his earlier, oblique admission that, for all its eagerness, his fidelity to Christ is flawed. (That admission is made, of course, in hopeful submission to the Christ child's power and love.[19]) Southwell's study of the divine love's manifestation in the infant Christ, and of the speaker's response to it, is the shrewder for his underlining the necessary inconsistency within, as well as the wisdom and joy of, considered commitment to Christ.

"A childe my Choyce" puts before the reader a model of the Christian consciousness but does not vicariously offer the reader spiritual choices, as does "The burning Babe." Much the same can be said of two other poems of *agape* and accommodation, "Sinnes heavie loade" and "Christs bloody sweat," which focus on the Passion rather than on the Nativity. Concentrating on the selfless love embodied in Christ at its time of climactic expression, both poems place *agape* and accommodation at the centre of time, space, and human experience. Both poems, moreover, explore Christ's love and loving responses to it, unfolding as meditations textured by dialectic.

"Sinnes heavie loade" opens with a brief composition of place which it relates immediately to the life of the poem's everyman persona:

O Lord my sinne doth over-charge thy brest,
  The poyse therof doth force thy knees to bow;
  Yea flat thou fallest with my faults opprest,

And bloody sweat runs trickling from thy brow:
But had they not to earth thus pressed thee,
Much more they would in hell have pestred mee. (ll.1–6)

That image of Christ as "fall[ing]" under sin's weight emphasizes his role as the second Adam who, condescending through
love to bear sin's load for man, falls only to rise and to undo the
weakness of the first Adam – hence the subsequent stress on
individual indebtedness to Christ. Just as *agape* and accommodation are there implied to be central to individual human
experience, so they are later indicated to be central to space
(ll.19–20, ll.31–32) and time (ll.27–28, ll.37–42). But when the
conceit of sin's heaviness and its effect on God himself is
examined in the points of the following analysis, one perceives
that Christ's fall has another aspect. The dialectic informing
the analysis opposes the old Adam to the second Adam (ll.17–
18), God's fatherhood of the soul to earth's motherhood of the
flesh (ll.29–30), and the Virgin as mother of life to the earth as
mother of corruption (ll.29–36). Within those oppositions
Christ's fall is revealed as a fortunate one for mankind, a
second descent (ll.21–22) which brings creator and creation
(ll.22–25), Being and Becoming (ll.29–30) together in peace.
The divine love manifested in that act is interpreted, then, as
reconciling the opposites surrounding it; in exploring the
divine love through his awed persona, Southwell shows it as
reunifying the fragmented world. The colloquy which closes
the meditation, and so the poem, of course conveys the persona's responses to the analysis of Christ's fall and thus allows
Southwell to end in exploration of devout responses to, and
communion with, God's love. Southwell brings out two particularly interesting things. First, having declared (ll.1–6) that
his sins have been transferred to Christ, the persona now
pleads for life to be transferred the other way (ll.37–38).
Second, in his faithful prayer the persona seeks oneness with
Christ; his last words rework *Romans* 6,5–11 and so repeat
Southwell's emphasis on the *New Testament* themes – an
essential element of his verse – of there being no self expressible
without the Word, no life outside a theo(Logo)centric
universe.

"Christs bloody sweat," whilst similar in its meditative

design and identical in its world-view to "Sinnes heavie loade,"
nonetheless differs from it markedly. For a start, the elaborate
composition of place opening the poem forms a highly stylized
image of Christ's agony in the garden: Christ's sweat of
anguish is pictured through symmetrically disposed and
extreme conceits, appearing as beneficently fertile for man
(virtually, in fact, as a *locus amoenus*). Christ's pain is shown to
be expressive not of confusion but of creative order:

> Fat soile, full spring, sweete olive, grape of blisse,
> That yeelds, that streams, that pours, that dost distil,
> Untild, undrawne, unstampt, untoucht of presse,
> Deare fruit, cleare brookes, faire oile, sweete wine at will:
> Thus Christ unforst prevents in shedding blood
> The whips, the thornes, the nailes, the speare, and roode. (ll. 1–6)

The following emblematic (ll. 7–12) and typological (ll. 13–18)
analysis of Christ's agony is equally elaborate. By means of its
striking, familiar conceits (l. 7, l. 13) Southwell's persona examines the wonder of God's love within a dialectic between
creator and creation, omnipotence and powerlessness. In the
colloquy (ll. 19–24), the persona then manifests himself as an
epitome of that dialectic – exploring his minimal existence, and
his need of transformation, through definition of himself as a
correlative type of the materials burnt by "Elias." He implies
that without the divine love, without a life focused on Christ,
he is virtually nothing. It is interesting that, though the persona
here alludes directly to *1 Kings*, Southwell also has him echo
Romans 12, 1–2 – just as the preceding poem is made by
Southwell to end in a reworking of verses from *Romans* – with
its advocacy of oneness with God.[20]

To look at the poems discussed above and at their fellows is
to recognize that the divine *agape* and accommodation are
important to Southwell's world-view because he perceives
them as having redefined (and as still redefining) human experience. As has just been argued, he shows them to have
renewed and still to be renewing individual human life through
the person of Christ; he shows them to have imposed, through
Christ, a redemptive pattern on human history. Yet since the
Incarnation, the poems also suggest, notions and expressions

of political power must be interpreted in the context of the omnipotent God's choice to redeem mankind through the force of self-abasing and unmerited love (see *The Sequence on the Virgin Mary and Christ*, 6 and 10; "New heaven, new warre," ll.1–6, ll.25–30; "New Prince, new pompe," ll.9–28; cf. "A holy Hymme," ll.19–24). Just so, conventional ideas of value have to be revised since the Incarnation because thereby God manifested himself in poverty and demonstrated that true worth has nothing to do with possessions or status (*The Sequence on the Virgin Mary and Christ*, 5–9; "New heaven, new warre"; "New Prince, new pompe"). The poems clearly imply, moreover, that "love" is to be understood essentially in terms of the divine love and the response that it does or should evoke from man.

Poems of wisdom – Poems of repentance

Southwell's poems of wisdom advise how one must act to hold to a God-centred existence, to keep within a God-centred universe. His poems of repentance consider what it means to place self at the heart of things, and focus on the abandonment of that folly; in other words (as "God is love"), they study the rejection of divine love and the subsequent awareness that one cannot endure separation from it. Through the poems of both groups Southwell confronts the reader with the same choices and possibilities as he does in the poems of *agape* and accommodation. Here, however, he writes with an even broader aesthetic and stylistic range in order to do so.

The wisdom poems have much in common. They are almost always in the mid-century plain style of Gascoigne, Googe, and their peers – hence they tend to be descended from the medieval lyric of moral analysis and counsel, instances of which include Chaucer's "Balade de Bon Conseil," the anonymous "Alas! deceite that in truste is nowe," and thereafter poems by Thomas More.[21] In keeping with that, they tend to seem relatively emotionless and to be impersonally declared – as it were – rather than spoken by an individualized persona. (The poems of complaint, leaving aside those of complaint in repentance, are of course much more emotional even though they strongly resemble the wisdom poems in their attitudes and values.) Two examples will illustrate what they have in common and suggest, also, the subtle differences among them, indicating how the poems function: "Losse in delaies" and "Looke home."

"Losse in delaies" appears to counsel action which is prudent. Textured by common-sense maxims, proverbs, familiar emblems, and *exempla* adducing natural law, it urges the reader to follow the conventional and prudent courses of *carpe tempus, festina lente*: "Shun delaies, they breede remorse: / Take thy time, while time doth serve thee ..." (ll.1–2); / "Seeke not time, when time is past, / Sober speede is wisedomes leasure ..." (ll.9–10). Yet in fact the poem exhorts the reader to a prudence which is really sapience – that is the wisdom it proposes. The poem does not counsel "seizing the time" or "hastening slowly" in secular senses, but rather in the sense of doing so to crush sins while yet small (ll.25–42) and thus to find spiritual health (ll.19–22). The reader is advised to act wisely in temporal terms that refer not to temporal things (such advice would then counsel *prudentia*) but to things eternal (hence counselling *sapientia*). Moreover, the natural reason of the poem's argumentation seems to depend on, as well as to complement, the revealed truth of James 1,15. The same sophistication can be seen in the impersonal, declarative plainness of Southwell's verse. For example the opening line, quoted above, catches the reader's attention by the strangeness of its conceit, "breede." The conceit is uncomplicated, its meaning clear, and yet the process which it identifies is a weird intermingling of inaction, action, and reaction. Just so, the final couplet ("Happie man that soone doth knocke, / Bable babes against the rocke") bizarrely juxtaposes "Happie" with "knocke, / Bable babes," and hence contentment with ugly violence to end the poem in a grotesque but rationally devout image of spiritual well-being.[22]

"Looke home," drawing on a neoplatonic theology familiar from St Augustine and St Bonaventure (and perhaps making use of Ficino), advocates that the reader know himself and recognize that he can seek true happiness through contemplation of the soul, for thereby he will come ultimately to "look home" to God. The poem counsels, then, the pursuit of *sapientia*; however, it departs from neoplatonic convention by not arguing that the contemplative way is the one way to wisdom. Here it appears as a valid way, but as no more than that. The poem is content to emphasize man's need for acknowledgement of, and for seeking enlightenment through, his kinship to God.[23] In accord with that moderation are the unassertiveness and indirectness of the poem's counsel. The poem implicitly advises the reader amidst an analytic celebration of the soul's dignity; necessarily lacking the brusqueness and urgency of "Losse in delaies," it offers its counsel with a graceful plainness which is deliberate and yet without any markedly individual inflection. Southwell was not of course the first Catholic religious poet to have written wisdom poems in a strongly English manner, but his are the most accomplished to have survived.

If the wisdom poems advise how one must act to hold to a theocentric existence, the poems of repentance explore the experience of an egocentric life (that is to say, of evil) and of a reawakened desire for God. Those poems are important in the Southwell canon not merely because of their own merits, nor merely because they are obviously essential to the spiritual discipline which his poems as a whole set forth, but also because they form an essential introduction to his greatest work: his extended repentance poem *Saint Peters Complaint*. Nevertheless before they can be examined there is in turn a preliminary to them, those poems that dwell on betrayal of the divine yet do not as well deal with repentance.

"Christs sleeping friends" and "Josephs Amazement" will serve to set the poems of repentance in perspective. The former is a typological warning against unresponsiveness to Christ's suffering, thence against failure to watch and pray, and so against failure to lead an absolutely God-centred life. The poem uses "*Jonas*" as a type ambivalently but, for all the interest of that, the immediate relevance of "Christs sleeping friends" lies in what it implies about God's capacity to forgive. The reader knows that, unresponsive to Christ and therefore self-endangering as the disciples are, their virtual betrayal of their master through weakness and impercipience will be forgiven by him in his encompassing love (in connection with which see l.7, ll.33–34). Christ can forgive betrayal even by those closest to him. (Southwell remarks of God's faithfulness, in *S. Mary Magdalens Fvnerall Teares*: "It is vndoubtedly true, that thou neuer leauest those that loue thee ..."[24]) "Josephs Amazement" considers St Joseph's doubts about the Virgin's pregnancy (his imagining of betrayal by her) and his impulse to forsake her – which would in fact be betrayal of the Virgin and of Christ. Drawing on the rhetoric of Petrarch, the poem images Joseph as a lover trapped between paradoxes: trust and suspicion; love of the Virgin and desire to reject her. He is "amazed" in his predicament; like so many others whose loving can be described in Petrarchan terms, he stands irresolute. Southwell's choice of a secular rhetoric to describe Joseph's experience of love suggests, however, precisely why Joseph finds himself in "a maze of doubtfull ende" (l.79). It suggests that, although drawn by a spiritual beauty (for the Virgin is indicated to be the ideal Petrarchan lady, as Petrarch's *Vergine bella, che di sol vestita* had already implied) and himself capable of spiritual love (ll.40–52), Joseph nonetheless loves and reasons humanly (ll.79–84 suggest Wyatt at least twice). Pondering imagined betrayal by the Virgin and on the edge of betraying her and Christ, Joseph will not be reconciled with both by either human emotion or human reason. He will be reconciled to them, as the reader knows, by an angel: the poem points to reconciliation with the divine as being effected ultimately by God. In "Christs sleeping friends" and "Josephs Amazement," Southwell's concern respectively with God's capacity to forgive and with God's final power to reconcile prepares one to understand what repentance actually involves in the poems which focus on it.

Southwell's studies of repentance stress the extent and power of divine mercy; they are poems which, though certainly making use of English devotional and literary traditions, can also strikingly exemplify those of the Counter-Reformation. An apt instance is "Saint Peters Complaynte" (the earlier and shorter of the two works bearing that name).[25] It seems to develop from poems such as More's "A ruful lamentacion ..." or such as are familiar from *A Mirror for Magistrates*: elaborate and monitory laments at personal misfortune. Yet if it is akin to them it is, even so, informed by strategies that one would associate rather with the poetic theories of Pontanus and his successors. The poem's third stanza well illustrates its style and introduces its preoccupations:

> If tyrans bloody thretts had me dismay'd:
> Or smart of cruell torments made me yelde,
> There had bene some pretence to be afray'de,
> I should have fought before I lost the feilde.
> But o infamous foyle: a maydens breathe
> Did blowe me downe, and blast my soule to death. (ll.13–18)

The grand manner of the verse suits the gravity of its matter and gives a violent immediacy to St Peter's almost incredulous self-analysis. More to the point, the declamatory and elaborately schematic rhetoric of that grand manner (see ll.13–16) suggests the English origins of Southwell's poem. Yet on the other hand the strange conceits of the final couplet ("breathe," "blowe me," "blast my soule" – punning interplays of *transmutatio*, *dementiens*, and *abusio*) have affinities with Counter-Reformation poetics and aesthetics. In their curious and forceful physicality the conceits look toward the poetics of Pontanus; in their wittily unusual logic they anticipate the poetics of Gracián and of Tesauro. Southwell uses them to fashion a grotesque and psychologically appropriate image in which he depicts the terrible, the marvellous. Within the third stanza, as throughout the poem, Southwell cunningly brings together the native and the alien.

Through the grand and various style of the poem Southwell seeks to convey the extreme, ambivalent emotions of Peter in order to explore his experience and rejection of evil. Southwell carefully probes the sin that Peter has committed and now lamentingly repudiates. Peter reveals that, ruled by self-love, he has fatuously boasted of his unique adherence to Christ (ll.7–10) and divorced himself from Christ (ll.13–24), defying natural law in fear of death for his master (ll.25–30) and speaking the un-Word (ll.35–66, especially ll.59–64; cf. *James* 1 and 3). Hence he has abandoned a Logocentric for an egocentric existence – which is of course no existence at all, as "I am ... the life" (cf. l.1 and ll.29–30) – aligning himself with a tradition of traitors: Satan (ll.5–6, l.10, cf. ll.65–66); Adam (ll.41–42); the Jews (l.34); Judas (l.35). That is to say, by

abandoning devotion to Christ for love of self, he has lost Life
and Hope (ll.1–2); thereby, moreover, he has departed from
his telos (ll.19–24, ll.43–48). Southwell's complex and
thorough exploration of Peter's self-love shows wherein lies
the misery of evil, a misery still apparent in Peter's confession.
The close of the poem interestingly depicts the final stage in his
rejecting of his sin. Peter ends his violently contrite confession
with calm, plainly worded prayer in hope of reunion with the
Word (ll.67–72). Humbly submitting himself at the last to
Christ's capacity to forgive and power to reconcile, he completes his returning to Logocentric being. Southwell forms
Peter into an icon of betrayal transcended through repentance
and confronts the reader with elemental spiritual decisions
about the self's relation to the Word.

"Saint Peters Complaynte" ends without, but does not lack,
resolution: what Peter cannot know about his forgiveness and
his future loyalty to Christ the reader of course knows well.
Using the reader's knowledge of divine truth to resolve narrative is a favourite strategy of Southwell in his poems of betrayal
and of repentance. In those poems, furthermore, the strategy
functions to make the reader infer that one cannot perceive, yet
should not doubt, the outcome of a quest in true faith for
reunion with God (cf. *1 John* 1,9). The inference seems inevitable in "Saint Peters Complaynte," and in drawing it one
acknowledges again the subtlety of Southwell as a spiritual
director in his poems.

In exploring the experience and rejection of evil, only
"Davids Peccavi" – among the shorter poems of repentance –
rivals the complexity of "Saint Peters Complaynte." Southwell
unfolds David's lament with a deft and cunning plainness; as
can be seen at once, the poem is very English in style and has
virtually nothing in it of Counter-Reformation poetics.

In eaves, sole Sparrowe sits not more alone,
    Nor mourning Pellican in Desert wilde:
Then silly I, that solitarie mone,
    From highest hopes to hardest hap exilde:
Sometime (ô blisful time) was vertues meede,
Ayme to my thoughts, guide to my word and deede. (ll.1–6)

The poem opens upon scenes which suggest David's isolation and desolation when separated from God, and amidst those scenes are, in effect, emblems ("Sparrowe," "Pellican," drawn, like a number of the poem's images, from psalm 102) which indicate the alternatives between which he now stands: lust, and likeness to Christ. Between those contraries develops the dialectic that shapes the poem, for throughout it the reader follows simultaneously David's reflecting on his experience of evil and his repudiation of evil. The beginnings of that dialectic are apparent in the lines quoted above. David identifies his sinful self as irrational ("silly I," l.3), reveals that in being both he has become an outcast from the divine ("exilde," l.4; see l.5), and admits to the abandonment of his telos ("Ayme to my thoughts," l.6). He implies that in experiencing evil the self is displaced physically (ll.1–3), psychologically and spiritually (ll.4–6). Inseparable from David's analysis of his plight is, of course, his contritional movement toward God ("thoughts, ... word and deede," l.6).

Thereafter, Southwell develops the poem's dialectic not merely through contradictions, as he does explicitly in l.4 and implicitly in ll.5–6, but through paradoxes and equivocations (*allusio* occurring often). From this there follow two implications. When David says, "But feares now are my Pheares, griefe my delight, / My teares my drink, my famisht thoughts my bread ..." (ll.7–8), one recalls the politicized Petrarchan rhetoric of Wyatt's "Sighs are my food, drink are my tears," and the similar rhetoric of Tichborne's elegy, wherein paradoxes suggest – as they do here – a confusion of the natural order within, as well as outside, the speakers' lives. Here, however, the paradoxes of David's lament suggest a radically profound confusion in and around him; as he subsequently reveals, his sinful self has chosen (by, one remembers, preferring lust and murder to divine love) to inhabit an egocentric world (cf. ll.1–4) which is a world of unnatural process and death ("[K]ill'd with murd'ring pangues, I cannot die," l.12 – see ll.7–11). Hence David also and unsurprisingly reveals later that the sinful self in fact feels self-hatred because of its self-love (ll.13–18). The same phenomenon can be seen distinctly in "Saint Peters Complaynte". The second implication of the paradoxical and equivocating form of the dialectic is that

Southwell can thereby indicate David's extreme psychological disturbance as he seeks reunion with God, part of that disturbance significantly being – as David is a religious poet – his struggle to reunite his words with the divine (ll.15–16), for with him they have been separated from God by a corrupt *phantasia* ("Fansie," l.25; cf. ll.18–30). The struggle to connect human words with the divine, though important here, predictably becomes of greater moment in *Saint Peters Complaint*.

The poem ends with David's resolve to correct his life (ll.29–30), its contritional movement concluding much as does that of "Saint Peters Complaynte," since David apparently trusts in God's capacity to forgive and power to reconcile. Thus David too has been fashioned into an icon of betrayal transcended through repentance, and also confronts the reader with spiritual decisions about a theocentric or an egocentric existence. Southwell's fashioning of both icons indirectly stresses, one might finally point out, that to live theocentrically/Logocentrically is to inhabit a world centred on *agape*.

The two poems just considered form a useful introduction to Southwell's greatest poem, *Saint Peters Complaint*, but before it is examined another poem has to be looked at, even if briefly. "A vale of teares" is a repentance poem which affirms how astutely Southwell can intermingle the native with the Counter-Reformation and, which is particularly important to an understanding of *Saint Peters Complaint*, emphasizes how aesthetically self-conscious his writing indeed is. The poem has a medieval ancestor, "In the vaile of restles mynd," and like its ancestor it alternates between plainness and *ornatus*.[26] It pictures in sensuously compelling detail what is at once a physical environment and a landscape of the mind (see l.33), inviting the reader's meditative participation in the speaker's perceptions and emotions. The contritional experience of the speaker has various elements: dominant among them is a melancholy interwoven with fear and wonder (ll.17–24; ll.29–32), which Southwell conveys not only through the speaker's unfolding of the *topothesia/locus mentis* but also through pointed allusions to contemporary aesthetic categories. In other words, Southwell's poem at once communicates its speaker's experience and identifies its own artistic values as a meditative composition of place:

Yet natures worke it is of arte untoucht,
So strait indeed, so vast unto the eie,
With such disordred order strangely coucht,
And so with pleasing horror low and hie,

That who it viewes must needs remaine agast,
Much at the worke, more at the makers might,
And muse how Nature such a plot could cast,
Where nothing seemed wrong, yet nothing right . . . (ll.25–32).

Said to be "untoucht" by human "arte" (l.25 – though pervasively it draws attention to its existence as just that, an instance
of human devotional art) the "vale" has nonetheless, in fictional terms, been made by nature (ll.30–31), which means that it
is God's art. The aesthetics manifested in the "vale" are thus
supposedly planned by God to reflect and to stimulate the
intense emotional states of contrition. God's artistry has
created the terrible (l.24), the pathetic (ll.53–60), and evokes
wonder (ll.29–30) at the *concordia discors* (ll.27–28) of both the
landscape's melancholy design and its paradoxical emotional
attraction, part of which is violent. (One is compelled, moreover, to acknowledge the landscape's overwhelming dimensions.) What results is that Southwell's self-reflexive fiction at
once conveys contritional emotions, in doing so defines the
emotions typifying contrition, and implies – by allusion as well
as by enactment – the agreement between Counter-Reformation aesthetics and archetypal religious experience. It implies
too the uniformity of those aesthetics with the principles of the
divine art. From "A vale of teares," then, one turns naturally to
Southwell's extended study of the contrite Saint Peter.

Saint Peters Complaint

Saint Peters Complaint should not be seen merely as amplifying its brief counterpart, but as interweaving with great
sophistication the concerns and strategies of virtually all
Southwell's other verse. The poem considers the dialectic
between egocentrism and theocentrism, between self-love and
agape; it examines both the manifesting of God's selfless love
and communion with God; it focuses minutely on the experi-

ence and repudiation of evil, revealing the necessity of faith in God's capacity to forgive and power to reconcile. Consonant with the scope and complexity of the poem's concerns are its extraordinary range and subtlety of style. One could thus reasonably suggest that the poem relates to Southwell's other verse much as *Upon Appleton House* does to Marvell's other verse prior to 1654. Yet for all the attractions of that comparison, not least among which are its ironies, another made for some different reasons is more illuminating; as will be argued below, a doubly closer analogue to *Saint Peters Complaint* can be seen in Ralegh's *Ocean to Scinthia*. At the moment, however, one might propose at least this: to associate Southwell's poem with Marvell's and Ralegh's is to indicate something of the status which it merits, but has never been granted.

The lament of Saint Peter opens in a grand manner meant to convey both the magnitude of his sin and the violence of his remorse.[27] Southwell begins the poem, in other words, as he does "Saint Peters Complaynte" – except that here he starts with a crowded and disturbed allegory:

> Launche foorth my Soul into a maine of teares,
> Full fraught with grief the traffick of thy mind:
> Torne sailes will serve, thoughtes rent with guilty feares:
> Give care, the sterne: use sighes in lieu of wind:
> Remorse, the Pilot: thy misdeede, the Carde:
> Torment, thy Haven: Shipwracke, thy best reward.
>
> Shun not the shelfe of most deserved shame:
> Sticke in the sandes of agonizing dread:
> Content thee to be stormes and billowes game:
> Divorc'd from grace thy soule to pennance wed:
> Flie not from forreine evils, flie from thy hart:
> Worse then the worst of evils is that thou art. (ll.1–12)

Those lines reveal in microcosm Southwell's characterization of Peter throughout the poem. Recreating the *navis animae* topos (perhaps rewriting *"Passa la nave"*) they suggest that Peter is an exile from Being (l.10, cf. l.16) who now seeks it in a spiritual journey through and toward the intensities, the violences of contrition.[28] The lines allude to "grief" (l.2), to "feares" (l.3), and so on; more important, however, they indicate the self-hatred in Peter's "[re]morse" (l.5, ll.11–12), the obsessiveness and anguish with which he anatomizes himself, and his vulnerability. They imply that his quest for Being is indeed to lead through frenetic spiritual process. Southwell's strategy in thus characterizing Peter would seem to be twofold. First, the dramatic and emotive images in which he is presented apparently invite the reader's pity for Peter in his extreme and wretched experience of evil – as an historical event his sin was, after all, nearly unique. Finally, the emotionally compelling presentation of Peter also apparently invites the reader's sympathy with him; that is reasonable, as in sinning all have denied Christ and so have at times variously resembled the fallen apostle. Southwell in fact implies in *An Epistle of a Religious Priest vnto His Father* that Peter's sin typifies every betrayal of Christ. Citing "*S. Ciprians* lesson" he observes: "Lett no mans contrition be lesse then his crime. Thinkest thou that our Lord can be so soone appeased, whō with perfidious words thou hast denied ... [?]"[29] The end of Southwell's strategy can be inferred readily enough and is, in any case, generally indicated in "The Author to the Reader": "Learne by [Peter's] faultes, what in thine owne to mend" (l.6).

As has been suggested above, *Saint Peters Complaint* encompasses much that can be found in Southwell's other verse. Nonetheless, its central concern is of course to explore (for the purpose of spiritual direction) Peter's experience and repudiation of evil. If, to begin that exploration, Southwell focuses directly on Peter himself (ll.1–30), he continues it by gradually broadening his focus to convey how Peter – having separated himself from Christ – perceives and undergoes existence in a Christless world. Southwell emphasizes that, through the frightened self-love which prompted denial of Christ, Peter has entered an egocentric world deprived of Life (see l.49), pervaded by his unnaturalness (e.g. ll.79–82, ll.103–114), and where he has no place (e.g. ll.55–60, ll.83–84): a shadow world, where the commonplaces of *contemptus mundi* are proven true and writ large; the world as evoked in "Saint Peters Complaynte" and in "Davids Peccavi." Here, connecting himself with Satan (ll.59–64), Judas (l.99), "Caiphas" (l.100), and the Jews (l.127), Peter speaks in effect a discourse of nothingness.

Whilst that discourse derives from the choice, and expresses the misery, of a self-centred existence Southwell goes on to identify more precisely what has generated it. In the set-piece on the treachery of Peter's tongue (ll.121–144; cf. *James* 1 and 3, as for "Saint Peters Complaynte"), Southwell has Peter reveal that when he denied Christ he lost both the Spirit and the Word, being left merely with the letter, with human words. Peter cries, "Ah wretch, why was I nam'd, sonne of a dove, / Whose speeches voyded spight, and breathed gall? / No kin I am unto the bird of love ..." (ll.121–123). Soon after he asks how his tongue could be "stain'd with such detesting wordes, / That every word was to [Christ's] hart a wound" (ll.134–135). The allusions to Peter's name perhaps obliquely associate him with the Holy Spirit, yet more significant are the conceits between those allusions. Through them Peter implies unknowingly that his words of denial were filled with an unholy *pneuma*, an unSpirit of venomous hostility ("voyded spight," "breathed gall" – cf. *James* 3,7–10). Later, again referring to the "spite" of his denial (l.138), he compares his speech to demonic utterance. Aptly, then, in the other lines cited above he describes his denial of Christ as a speaking of words against the Word: an unsaying of the Word/a saying of the unWord (cf. l.130 and especially ll.185–186).[30] Peter's account of how he manifested his traitorous self-love thus helps to explain, not only the tone of his monologue, but also its movement and so Southwell's unfolding of the poem.

Southwell composes *Saint Peters Complaint* from a biblical narrative (that of Peter's betrayal) into which he incorporates further biblical narratives (such as typological episodes from the *Old Testament*, or examples from the *New Testament* of faithfulness to Christ) and extra-biblical materials (*sermocinatio*, *demonstratio*, and so on). He disposes the whole as a sequence of interconnected set-pieces; as one would particularly expect from a Jesuit poet, and as has been already indicated, those interconnections can be logical as well as emotional. But it would be wrong to over-emphasize the poem's rational congruences, for in having Peter reveal that he has spoken the unWord in the unSpirit Southwell points to the irrationality within Peter's monologue. (Moreover the poem's emotional continuity, of disordered and violent states of mind, is obviously linked to the unreason following necessarily from denial of the Logos.) Peter has not, of course, lost all rational control of his thoughts: he can sometimes analyse himself and his actions with logical exactness (e.g. ll.631–636); as was suggested above, the phases of his monologue can be logically interconnected (e.g. ll.247–249, ll.349–354). Nonetheless his analyses are often flawed (e.g. ll.49–60, ll.79–84) and, whether logical or not, insistently imply the powerlessness of self-analysis as such to solve his plight. That appears strikingly in a passage (ll.217–228) where Peter analyses his treachery through compacted antitheses and paradoxes which tell of his anguish, yet in themselves are impotent. The poem's set-pieces, too, frequently either lack reasoned association (e.g. ll.217–258, especially ll.223–234 and ll.247–258; ll.289–330, especially ll.313–330) or are interconnected by logic which is insubstantial if not impaired (e.g. ll.547–564, ll.595–630). The compounding of reason with unreason in Peter's monologue can thus be seen to shape the *Complaint* not merely in its parts but as a whole, and recognition that it does so illuminates the poem's twofold movement. On the one hand, the poem moves in circles centred on Peter's remorse and emptiness without Christ, his obsessive self-analysis, varying but not progressing. Peter's denial of the Logos and of the Spirit in favour of a self-centred existence has meant, ironically, that his defective human words cannot lead anywhere – they focus on his misery and then, iterating his wretchedness, turn in prayer to Christ. On the other hand, paradoxically, the poem does move forward, because Peter's self-analysis is made in submission to Christ and forms part of the process of his repentance: his self-analysis continuously, if not always rationally, searches his conscience, denounces his sin, and so heads – despite its circl-ing and intrinsic powerlessness – toward reunion with the Word.[31] Southwell affirms that only through submission to the Word (see ll.325–480, ll.751–792) can the fallen human personality and its defective self-expression begin to approach wholeness and true meaning.

In that context one can at last suggest the likenesses and significant dissimilarity between Southwell's poem and Ralegh's *Ocean to Scinthia*. The latter poem focuses upon the helpless misery of the Ralegh persona, who laments his separ-ation from the principle of order, of life itself (as he understands them in his world): Cynthia/Queen Elizabeth. Now cut off from that idealized figure, the Ralegh persona laments the emptiness of his life in a complaint that oscillates between minute examination of his misery and the studying of different aspects of his paradoxical mistress. His words propose no consolation and move toward no resolution; abruptly stopping, they end, but do not conclude. The broad resemblance of the Ralegh persona to Southwell's Peter seems clear, and so does the similarity between the unfolding of the poems in which each appears. Both poems repeatedly scrutinize the plights of their central personae, avoid lucid progression, and contain no resolution. In brief, the poems are alike in personae, structure, tone, and emotional range. As it happens, they are also close in times of composition.[32] Yet the essential dissimilarity between them seems no less clear. Ralegh's poem relies, for all its mythologizing of Elizabeth, finally on the uncertainties of human love and forgiveness; Southwell's looks to the certainties of Christ's love and compassion. Then, too, the outcome of Ralegh's complaint could not be foreseen when he wrote it, whilst the course of Peter's history was known.[33]

Having had Peter reveal his repudiation of the Word and of the Spirit, Southwell goes on to present the environment of that act, Caiaphas's court, as a place where the unWord is institutionalized among men – an outpost of hell on earth (l.229, ll.233–234). There, "rayling mouthes with blasphemies did swell, / With taynted breath infecting all resort" (ll.231–232).[34] Peter remarks on the court as being both physically cold and a place where the inhabitants' hearts are frozen against charity and grace, his description bringing to mind the depths of Dante's hell: "Sharpe was the weather in that stormy place, / Best suting hearts benumbed with hellish frost, / Whose crusted malice could admit no grace ..." (ll.247–249). Peter subsequently acknowledges that, having denied Christ in such surroundings, he was bodily in a type of hell and also experiencing a hell within (ll.331–334): he had in effect translated the court's blasphemy and failure to love into his inner life. Much at that point, moreover, one comes to what is arguably the dramatic centre of Southwell's poem. When Peter recalls his meeting with Christ in the courtyard (ll.325–444) he recollects it as an encounter between hell (ll.331–334, cf. l.229 and so on) and heaven (l.332, l.338, ll.379–381), death and life (ll.331–333). He describes a meeting of utter contraries, and his memories – as well as his reflections springing from them – are pervaded by violently contrary emotions: awe, wonder, love, evoked by Christ; remorse, misery, self-hatred, evoked by his sinfulness.

But in that episode, of course, both Peter's memories and his reflections form an extended meditation on the eyes of Christ.[35] What in fact dominates that meditation, and so the essential drama of it, is the emphasis on Christ as the embodiment of God's selfless love. Southwell has Peter doubly stress that Christ manifests the divine *agape*. Celebrating Christ's eyes as "[G]racious spheres, where love the Center is, / A native place for our selfe-loaden soules" (ll.403–404), Peter images them and the desire (*eros*) that they beget (cf. l.408) in familiar neoplatonic terms; underlying the neoplatonic imagery is, however, the premise that Christ's eyes express representatively the divine love's accommodation to man through the Incarnation, for they are shown to be "Spheres of love, whose Center, cope and motion, / Is love of us ..." (ll.407–408), manifestations of a perfect love which has condescended to enter the flesh entirely because of its own compassion for humanity (cf. ll.337–342, ll.427–432). More specifically, Peter stresses that Christ's glancing (l.356) at him was an act of completely selfless love which re-established contact between master and traitor, making possible – through no merit of Peter's – his return to Christ: "O sacred eyes, the springs of living light, / The earthly heavens, where Angels joy to dwell: / How could you deigne to view my deathfull plight, / Or let your heavenly beames looke on my hell?" (ll.331–334); "The matchles eies matchd onely each by other, / Were pleasd on my ill matched eyes to glaunce" (ll.355–356). The love expressed through Christ's eyes bestowed, appropriately enough, the gift of tears on Peter (ll.355–364).[36]

One result of Peter's past and present sensitivity to the divine love has been that it has intensified his experience of evil. When glanced at by Christ in the courtyard, Peter suddenly recognized the hell of his sinfulness (ll.326–330, cf. l.334); now, as he meditates on the "Spheres of love" (l.407), those "[L]ittle worldes, the summes of all the best, / Where glory, heaven, God, sunne: all vertues, starres" (ll.409–410), Peter thereby studies the cost of his sinfulness and heightens his sense of Christlessness (see notably ll.421–426).[37] Another result of Peter's sensitivity to the divine love is that here, as he meditatively communes with the eyes of Christ, the relations between elements of Southwell's writing in the poem and Counter-Reformation stylistics become especially distinct. Peter's meditation is the first instance of his leaping beyond what seems virtually a discourse of nothingness toward the Word. Southwell forms the meditation as a sequence of striking images wherein Peter insistently traces correspondences between the Logos and his creation. Diversely iterating the principle of *concordia discors*, those images imply that the unity of the universe lies ultimately in Christ (see particularly ll.409–415). Through them Peter's ecstatic (though also distressed) play of mind clearly agrees with Jesuit practice of – and anticipates Jesuit theorizing on – the conceit, anticipates later Counter-Reformation emblematics, and crystallizes Jesuit ideas on composition of place (interestingly foreshadowing Puente) as well as on application of the senses. Southwell's point in thus presenting the meditation appears to be the concentration of sensuously and conceptually elaborate icons to locate compellingly at his poem's centre a celebration of, and yearning for, the absent Christ, represented not only as the goal of Peter's desire, but also in order to evoke desire in the reader. At the poem's dramatic centre, then, Southwell places Counter-Reformation icons which variously suggest the divine *agape* (embodied in Christ), holy *eros* fulfilled (in the redeemed, e.g. ll.338–340), holy *eros* unfulfilled (in Peter, see ll.397–402 and so on), and a holy *eros* to be summoned forth (in the reader): the poem's centre is in effect a *theatrum amoris*.[38] Southwell's exploration of Peter's troubled communing with the eyes of Christ reveals in little both how astutely he can use Counter-Reformation strategies in his poem and how important to it such strategies are.[39]

After his sudden leap toward the Word, Peter is shown as continuing uninterruptedly (except for a brief anatomizing of sin, which he subsequently relates to his plight) his obsessive and anguished self-analysis. To define and to castigate his sinfulness he mirrors himself in Scripture and in the lives of those who have been faithful to Christ or who have singularly escaped faithlessness. Accordingly, he considers that David and Anna are mourners whom he should surpass (ll.487–492). He decides that his sinfulness has surpassed Adam's (ll.511–516), Cain's (ll.523–528), and Absolon's (ll.541–552), making him unworthy to confront Mary and the friends of Christ (ll.577–606). He counts fortunate the slaughtered Innocents (ll.553–570) and the young man of *Mark* 14,51–52 (ll.571–576). Elsewhere he depicts himself as an actor in a strange drama of his own making (ll.703–714). Perhaps the most arresting thing is that whilst a moment earlier Peter was seeing reflections of his master throughout the creation, now "all thinges Characters are to spell [his own] fall" (l.680). It is true that he hopes to atone for betrayal of Christ through Christ's gift of tears (ll.355–366; ll.439–468), yet even so he says, "[C]irckling griefes runne round without an end" (l.678): he is at once engaged in the process of penitence and still, in himself, circling powerless to resolve his separation from Christ.

Thereupon Peter turns directly to Christ in search of that resolution, his self-analysis through fallen words ceasing in his prayer to the Word. The resolution of his plight of course occurs outside the boundaries of *Saint Peters Complaint*, taking place in the reader's memory of Scripture, and by so ending the poem Southwell interestingly concludes both Peter's lament and the reader's experiencing of it. At the end of his psychologically intense narrative Southwell thereby impresses on the reader that even profound treachery against Christ can be forgiven if one will repent in faith, trusting in the selfless divine love. Southwell's ending of the poem is very Jesuit in its strategy.

Saint Peters Complaint encompasses the concerns of nearly all Southwell's other poems, and in it the intermingling of native with Counter-Reformation devotional and literary traditions, so recurrent in his verse, is subtle indeed. How the concerns of his other poems are present in *Saint Peters Complaint* has been discussed in some detail above; now a few remarks may perhaps further clarify the nature of its diverse style and hence its achievement as a whole. A predominantly, if not exclusively, English grand manner pervades much of the poem. (Nonetheless, in harmony with Cicero's and with St

Augustine's ideas on rhetorical mastery, it ranges from lofty to ornate to plain speech. Some of the ornate and all of the plain are native in manner.) A significant portion of the poem is, however, textured by images – conceits, emblems, compositions of place – born of the Counter-Reformation. What results is a thematically and psychologically intricate poem which forms at once a monument to the writings of Southwell's Tudor predecessors and a substantial introduction of the devout aspect of the baroque into Tudor poetry (an introduction buttressed by works such as *The Sequence*, "The burning Babe," and so on). What results is, in other words, one of the greatest English religious poems of the sixteenth century.

Southwell's poems and his introductions to them (two of which are of course poems) imply his preoccupation with the instability of the *phantasia*, especially with its vulnerability to misdirection. For example, in "The Author to his loving Cosen" he condemns the "idle fansies" demonically inspired in "most Poets" (l.19; see l.3 and ll.16–23); in "Davids Peccavi" he warns against allowing uncontrolled "Fansie" (l.25; see ll.25–30) to dominate one's life.[40] Yet his poems and their introductions also suggest his desire to sanctify the *phantasia* and so to correct its waywardness. Southwell predominantly indicates that wish in "The Author to his loving Cosen" where he identifies God as the source of true poetry and associates it emphatically with the Word (ll.4–16). By informing his poems with sacred truth and with human judgments which follow or complement that truth Southwell seeks to rouse at least some of his fellow poets to sacred rather than profane "fansies"; thus, too, he seeks to guide the imaginations of his readers in general (see "The Author ...," ll.23–27; "To the Reader," *passim*; "Davids Peccavi," ll.25–30; "A Phansie turned to a sinners complaint," ll.145–152). The latter and broader aim seems fundamental to Southwell's poems as a whole, and not merely to his sacred parodies.[41] Southwell writes for a Catholic people virtually without their priests, and through his poems he appears to take on for them the role of spiritual counsellor or director.[42] He centres his poems on the divine *agape* and on Christ, constantly assuring his readers – directly or indirectly – of God's selfless love. He celebrates and interprets that love, exploring its manifestations; he persuasively teaches the other truths dependent on that central one, affirms the doctrinal emphases of Trent, exhorts his readers to amendment. He fashions icons which allow him to explore the experience and rejection of evil, thereby tracing consolingly, if uncompromisingly, for his readers the process of repentance.[43] In doing those things he mingles the culture of post-Tridentine Europe with that of his homeland, a consequence being that he accommodates the Counter-Reformation to his readers and renews or recontextualizes those devotional and literary traditions with which they are more familiar. He stands out as a poet whose scope and astuteness of psychology, of style, mark him as a unique and major presence in the English religious verse of his century.

CHAPTER THREE

Henry Constable
and William Alabaster

Only two of Southwell's Catholic contemporaries could approach his sophistication and insight as a religious poet. Henry Constable wrote his *Spirituall Sonnettes* after 1589, though exactly when is not known; the *Divine Meditations* of William Alabaster were written between 1596 and 1598.[1] Constable's *Spirituall Sonnettes* proclaim and celebrate tenets of the Church. Often, as they put forward Church teaching, they form or end as prayers for spiritual renewal. Their main – though by no means their only – achievement is that in doing so they shrewdly depict an abandonment of profane for sacred *eros*, wherein courtiership and the male experience of desire (preoccupations in Constable's secular verse) are redefined, and wherein many of the values (if not all the ideas or the rhetorical norms) in his secular verse are denied. It is remarkable, moreover, that although the *Spirituall Sonnettes* clearly bear the doctrinal impress of the Council of Trent, they are otherwise virtually independent of the Counter-Reformation. Alabaster's poems are less concerned than Constable's with putting forward Church teaching, but they, too, strongly reveal the doctrinal influence of Trent. Furthermore, whilst his poems have natively English elements of style, as do those of Constable, they are also diversely related in style to the devotional literary traditions of the Counter-Reformation. His *Divine Meditations* offer perceptive studies of major themes in the spiritual life: purgation; illumination; penitence; wonder at God's love; conversion; human nature's capacity for perfection by grace or for dissolution in sin. His poems are perhaps most successful when considering purgation, illuminative ecstasy, and human nature's capacity for elevation or for fragmentation. Neither Constable nor Alabaster could be called a major poet, yet each wrote some discerning, stylistically astute, and moving poems.

Henry Constable

Throughout the *Spirituall Sonnettes* many tenets of the Church are distinctly stated, at times being asserted with a post-Tridentine emphasis. The doctrine of the Trinity, for example, is enunciated with careful orthodoxy ("To God the Father," ll.1–8; "To God the Sonne," ll.1–2; "To God the Holy-ghost," ll.1–4), but there is insistence upon the physical presence of Christ in the Blessed Sacrament ("To the blessed Sacrament," *passim*), the unique and honoured position of the Virgin ("To our blessed Lady," [1], *passim*; "To our blessed Lady," [4], ll.1–5), the unique truth and holiness of the Catholic Church ("To St Mychaell the Archangell," ll.9–14), the spiritual primacy of Rome and the Pope ("To St Peter *and* St Paul," ll.9–14). The influence of the Counter-Reformation on the poems is of course also indicated by their emphatic honouring of the saints. For all that, in putting forward Church teaching – and in imaging response to it – Constable's poems draw on concepts and styles either natively English or so familiar in England as not to appear alien. They draw on Scripture, details from hagiology, ideas and language from neoplatonic theology, the religious plain style – the dominant style throughout the *Spirituall Sonnettes* – ideas and language from the neoplatonic love lore and verse fashionable at court (among that verse being Constable's secular love poems), and a flamboyantly analytic use of the conceit, much as Donne sometimes uses it. His poems seem to have almost no stylistic connection to the Counter-Reformation. Those concerns and tactics appear from the start of the *Spirituall Sonnettes* (according to the order of the Harleian manuscript), and from their start, too, one is introduced to their main achievement: depiction of a radical commitment to sacred *eros*.

In the initial quatrain of "To God the Father" Constable's persona epitomizes Church doctrine lucidly and epigrammatically, that accommodation of sacred truth suggesting how gracefully Constable can write in the religious plain style:

> Greate God: within whose symple essence, wee
> nothyng but that, which ys thy self can fynde:
> when on thyself thou dydd'st reflect thy mynde,
> thy thought was God, which tooke the forme of thee. . . .
>
> (ll. 1–4)

The lines of the following quatrain are the same, until the appearance of something quite unexpected:

> And when this God thus borne, thou lov'st, & hee
> lov'd thee agayne, with passion of lyke kynde,
> (as lovers syghes, which meete, become one wynde,)
> both breath'd one spryght of aequall deitye. (ll. 5–8)

The simile in the seventh line is surprising because it brings into theological exposition an allusion to human love. It represents that love in physical terms, offering a rarefied yet material image of union in mutual devotion. The following line then curiously sets that image in perspective. There the love between the Father and the Son is described as a spiritual union, for in their mutual devotion they "breath'd one spryght": the Holy Spirit. Constable's persona implies that the love between Father and Son is the transcendent fulfilment of the neoplatonic idea, familiar in courtly circles, that those truly (and hence nobly) in love join souls, mingle "that inward breath which itself is even called soul" (cf. "To God the Holy-ghost," ll. 1–2).[2] Thus at the climax of the octave the persona plays discriminatingly on *"spiritus"* ("syghes," "wynde," "spryght"), at once creating a solely material image of union in human love and deftly transferring an idea about spiritual union in human love – about its joining souls, not sighs – to consideration of the perfectly spiritual love within the Trinity. In expounding doctrine he emphasizes that human love exists only as an attractive, infinitely inferior, type of the divine. Thereafter, in response to the doctrine that he has proclaimed and celebrated, he prays to become truly godlike (ll. 9–14), asking for a mind in constant possession of "heavenly [rather than earthly] knowledge" (l. 11) and for a heart filled with "holy [rather than profane] Love" (l. 13).

Even a glance at "To God the Father" indicates, then,

something of that interplay between doctrinal and other concepts which can be seen to pervade the *Spirituall Sonnettes*. Moreover that interplay introduces, in conjunction with the prayer ending the poem, the abandonment of lower for higher *eros* which is depicted in most of the other poems. No less typical is the interaction of styles in the sonnet. In it the persona rises at one point from plainness to ornateness: where he aptly conveys an idea from the love lore of courtly neoplatonism in a style resembling that of courtly love verse (l.8 – often his ornateness is more explicitly courtly in the other religious sonnets). The dramatic change illustrates, in part, not only the various styles within the *Spirituall Sonnettes* – and the dominance of the plain style – but also the astuteness with which they are interwoven, for it suggests the frequent connection in the poems between shifts in style and the transferring (as well as transforming) of concepts. If "To God the Father" reveals, however, many of the tactics and concerns in Constable's religious verse, his scope and achievement as a religious poet can better be seen in other early poems, "To God the Holy-ghost" and "To the blessed Sacrament."

In those poems Constable's persona reflects on the manifesting of divine love and seeks to be made anew by its power. "To God the Holy-ghost" begins with an elaborate account of both the divine love itself and its workings:

> Aeternall spryght: which art in heaven the Love
>   with which God, and his sonne ech other kysse:
>   and who, to shewe who Goddes beloved ys,
>   the shape, and wynges, took'st of a loving dove:
> When Chryste ascendyng sent the from above
>   in fyery tongues, thow cam'st downe vnto hys
>   that skyll in vtteryng heavenly mysteryes
>   by heate of zeale, both faith & love myght move.... (ll. 1–8)

The poem opens in sacred parody (ll. 1–2), describing the Holy Spirit through a courtly neoplatonism and with a courtly elegance of style. The persona alludes to the same neoplatonic concept as he does in "To God the Father" (ll. 7–8), and to much the same effect: a fashionable idea about the spirituality – and dignity – of human love is transferred to consideration of the love between the Father and the Son. Thus the courtly style embodying the idea (see especially the conceit, *audacia*, ending l.2) also becomes transferred from the secular to the divine. In effect, the love between the Father and the Son, expressed in the Holy Spirit (l.1), is presented as transcendently fulfilling what secular thought and language can best tell of human love. The importance of that for the valuing of human love is then shrewdly heightened. Throughout the rest of the octave the persona goes on to examine the divine love expressed in the Holy Spirit, developing his reference to its transcendence. He reveals that the Holy Spirit has diversely affirmed and enacted the *agape* of the Trinity. First, the Holy Spirit descended into the world to identify Christ, about to enter upon his ministry, as the beloved Son incarnate among men: the divine love descended, in a symbolically declarative form, to disclose another manifestation of divine love descended. In affirming Christ's identity the Spirit affirmed the divine *agape* (ll.3–4, especially "shewe" and "beloved"). Second, not only did the Holy Spirit thus identify Christ; the Spirit again descended, at Christ's behest, to promote the Kingdom (ll.5–8). The persona, himself descending from the courtly elegance of the sonnet's opening, plainly rehearses and deftly explicates sacred truth, examining the divine love expressed in the Holy Spirit and showing that love as in fact twofold. In heaven, as the initial couplet asserts, the Holy Spirit expresses the oneness in love of the Father and the Son. On earth, as is then complementarily revealed, the Spirit has helped to reunite man with God. Hence the poem's octave takes the courtly idea of spiritual union in human love – an idea in which Castiglione (like other courtly writers) posits what he thinks human love truly and nobly is – and reveals that the divine love which is the Holy Spirit so transcends and encompasses it as to make human love seem almost insignificant.[3]

Where the persona's contemplation of the Holy Spirit leads him appears dramatically in the sestet:

> True God of Love: from whom all true love sprynges,
>   bestowe vpon my Love, thy wynges & fyre
>   my sowle a spyrytt ys, and with thy wynges
> May lyke an Anngell fly from earths desyre:

and with thy fyre a hart inflam'd may beare,
and in thy syght a Seraphin appeare. (ll.9–14)

Having suggested that the Holy Spirit supremely manifests the
principle of union in love, the persona now declares the Spirit
to be the "True God of Love" and "all true love['s]" source
(l.9). His assertion does not necessarily deny value to "true"
human love, but of course it denies the authority of blind
Cupid (cf. l.12) and so the value of profane *eros*. (The persona
has already implied, after all, the infinite inferiority of human
love – in even its highest secular form – to the divine love.)[4]
With that simultaneous declaration and denial the sonnet
moves toward a climax at once subtle and resplendent. The
sestet is radiant with sacred *eros*, with yearning for ascent to the
Spirit; it expresses ideas typical of neoplatonic theology in
conceits formed from that theology's fervent imagery and
diction. It recalls, for example, the way in which St Bonaventure describes the burning desire of the soul for God.[5] In other
words, after alluding parodically to courtly neoplatonism in
the style of fashionable love verse (ll.1–2), then telling in a plain
style of God's love come down to man (ll.3–8), the persona
ends the sonnet in a return to ornateness – yet in rising from the
plain style he does not end as he began, for he ends beyond
sacred parody.

"To God the Holy-ghost" is remarkable for the astuteness
of its stylistic interplay, for its discerning study of love's
variety, and for the ardent spirituality of its conclusion. The
poem finely suggests not only the scope of Constable's
religious verse but also how substantial, interesting, and well-
wrought that verse can be. And the poem suggests something
more: in representing an abandonment of profane for sacred
eros it indicates how many of the values in Constable's secular
love verse (such as physical beauty, sexual fulfilment, and so
on) are meant to be acknowledged as worthless, when set in the
contexts of the divine love and of eternity.[6]

Consideration of "To God the Holy-ghost" leads naturally
to the groups of poems to the Virgin and to St Mary Magdalen,
wherein one sees rejection of lower for higher *eros* involving
redefinition of courtiership and of the male experience of
desire. Yet to go straight to those poems might seem to imply a

degree of sameness within the *Spirituall Sonnettes* that they do not have.⁷ There are indeed distinct and strong continuities among the poems but there are, too, some revealing divergences from dominant concerns and ways of writing. "To the blessed Sacrament," a poem which diverges in part from the concerns and styles pervading the *Spirituall Sonnettes*, shows that not all Constable's most significant poems make use of fashionable courtly discourses or the discourses of neoplatonic theology, though the poem does emphasize the rejection of profane *eros*.

In "To the blessed Sacrament" the persona seeks to have sacred history recreated within himself. He seeks to internalize, through the physical presence of Christ in the Eucharist, the Harrowing of Hell: he desires renewal of his life by an experience such as the souls in Limbo underwent when they were freed by Christ. The poem, well worth quoting in full, is as follows:

> When thee (O holy sacrificed Lambe)
>   in severed sygnes I whyte & liquide see:
>   as on thy body slayne I thynke on thee,
>   which pale by sheddyng of thy bloode became.
> And when agayne I doe beholde the same
>   vayled in whyte to be receav'd of mee:
>   thou seemest in thy syndon wrap't to bee
>   lyke to a corse, whose monument I am.
> Buryed in me, vnto my sowle appeare
>   pryson'd in earth, & bannish't from thy syght,
>   lyke our forefathers, who in Lymbo were.
> Cleere thow my thoughtes, as thou did'st gyve the light:
>   And as thou others freed from purgyng fyre
>   quenche in my hart, the flames of badd desyre.

The sonnet is a cunning harmony of contrasts. Contemplative stillness becomes united to passionate outcry; plain speech is textured with ostentatious conceits.⁸ Moreover through those conceits careful theological discrimination (e.g. "severed sygnes," l.2; "vayled," l.6) mingles with precise analysis of the self (e.g. "monument," l.8; "pryson'd," l.10); familiar Petrine texts evoke a quite different Pauline commonplace (ll.8–11. See: 1 *Peter* 3,19 and 4,6; *Romans* 7,24); the persona's death-in-life is set against Christ's triumphant life-in-death (ll.8–14). Nor is that the only interesting aspect of the sonnet. First, if the poem does not draw on some of the discourses so recurrent in the *Spirituall Sonnettes* it has instead a tortuous plain speaking and an ingenious drama suggestive of Donne's religious verse. Furthermore, like many of the *Spirituall Sonnettes* the poem images unresolved desire. The persona prays in faith and hope, but has to await the deliverance for which he asks; the poem ends forcefully but can be concluded only from without.

"To God the Holy-ghost" and "To the blessed Sacrament" indicate the stylistic scope and skill of Constable's religious verse, the continuities and divarications of its concerns. The grouped poems to the Virgin and to St Mary Magdalen suggest as well what most notably lies within the main concern of his *Spirituall Sonnettes*. It seems best to start with the triad of sonnets to the Virgin, for she is the more important figure (in her own right and throughout the *Spirituall Sonnettes*) and the matters considered in the poems to her are broader than those in the poems to Mary Magdalen.[9]

The poems to the Virgin depict a rejection of lower for higher *eros* but, intriguingly, they do so with a political emphasis. They stress that the Virgin is a queen, in fact the "Sovereigne of Queenes" ("To our blessed Lady," [2], l.1; see also "To our blessed Lady," [1], *passim*), and imply that abandoning the love of earthly beauty and power to love her, and thereby Christ ("To our blessed Lady," [4], *passim*), involves redefining courtiership. The profession of courtiership was not unfamiliar to Constable. A number of his secular poems imply, and the events of his life make explicit, that he was persistently and busily a courtier.[10] He seems to have sought favour at several courts, working hard to advance schemes which finally came to nothing.[11] Perhaps our knowing that he was not a successful courtier illuminates the poems by him which devoutly redefine the courtier's way. Far more helpful, however, is an insight into the literary strategies of his courtiership. Especially two of Constable's political sonnets, "To the Queene touching the cruell effects of her perfections," and "To the K: of Scots vpon occasion of his longe stay in Denmarke . . .," tell much of the poems to the Virgin. The former poem celebrates Elizabeth I as uniting transcendent political authority with transcendent personal beauty: "Proude hast thow made thy land of such a Queene / Thy neighboures enviouse of thy happie dayes" (ll.3–4); "[H]e whose eyes thy eyes but once haue seene / A thowsand signes of burning thoughts bewrayes" (ll.7–8). As those lines suggest, the sonnet is an act of Petrarchan courtiership. Naturally then, and as the second of the couplets cited above implies, a dominant motif in the sonnet's celebration of the Queen is the love, *eros*, supposedly directed to her. That represented desire is sexual or, at the least, sexually intense (see ll.7–8 and ll.10–11); at the same time it is more than that, for the poem of course images Elizabeth as having the allure of a spiritual perfection correspondent to her perfect physical beauty (ll.12–14). Thus, if not wholly profane, the *eros* represented in the poem, and essential to its Petrarchan strategy, is certainly secular. The poem "To the K: of Scots" has a strategy similar to that just considered and is also informed by *eros*. There the King and his wife are reverenced as godlike figures (ll.10–14) in terms recalling the praise given Elizabeth ("To the Queene," ll.5–6). There, too, royal perfection evokes love – though *eros* which is secular rather than profane. "If I durst loue as heertofore I haue / Or that my heart durst flame as it doth burne / The ice should not so longe stay youre [the King's] returne [from Denmark] ..." (ll.1–3), says Constable's persona. In that last line one can see the poem's humour: its wish to amuse, as well as to give due honour, through hyperbolic wit. Nonetheless its humour, like its reverence, centres on the persona's loudly asserted love for the distant King. As acts of courtiership, the poem to Elizabeth and that to James have within their allied strategies *eros* which the poems to the Virgin condemn.[12]

The first of the grouped sonnets "To our blessed Lady" forms an elaborate image of grace perfecting nature, and at the centre of that image is the Virgin. Constable's persona sees the moral order that he desires in his life as realizable by grace mediated through the Virgin – for of course its origin lies in God (see ll.1–4) – perfecting his unstable personality. Through her he seeks to confirm his abandonment of mundane courtiership and of lower *eros*: he asks her, should his resolve waver, to remind him that true courtiership focuses on God (ll.1–4, ll.9–11) and that the love of female beauty will find its true fulfilment in the beauty of her spiritual radiance (ll.5–8, ll.12–14). Yet the persona's image of a perfected self is neither simple nor unproblematic. To begin with, at the same time as the persona separately considers his rejection of profane for sacred *eros*, of secular for devout courtly service, he implies that the former not only accords with the latter but in fact involves perceiving and defining courtiership anew. The sonnet is a plea to the Virgin, addressing her as "Sovereigne of Queenes" (l.1); if that plea in part explicitly considers courtiership, it is also entirely an act of courtiership wherein the persona's devotion to the Virgin, and in particular his celebration of her spiritual beauty, expresses a sacred love which seeks to evoke aid from her as a divine political authority. In performing that act of courtly service the persona offers a new perspective on courtiership itself. He necessarily points out that not temporal, but eternal power governs the devout courtier (ll.1–4). He also indicates that the devout courtier should seek not arbitrary esteem or favour ("grace," l.2) but divine grace and honour (ll.2–4, l.11), should primarily fear not external but internal mutability (l.1, l.5, l.9, l.12), should direct passion not according to courtly ideas of love, but by a sacred revision of them (ll.6–8, ll.12–14), and should hope to rise, not through ambition, but through self-abasement (l.1, ll.9–11). In other words, the persona implies that a commitment to sacred *eros* involves redefining the psychology and contexts of courtiership. Of course his concept of devout courtiership is, however, one that he wishes to realize rather than one that he now fully embodies. The poem forms a proleptic image of grace perfecting nature.[13]

The following sonnet, for all its agreement with its predecessor, nonetheless differs from it markedly. An obvious difference is that, whereas the preceding sonnet separates lower *eros* and mundane courtiership (the two being closely connected in Constable's political verse) and does the same to their opposites whilst at the same time implicitly linking them, this poem clearly associates earthly love with mundane courtiership, sacred love with devout courtiership ("why should I any love O queene but thee?" asks the persona initially; see ll.2–8, especially l.5 and l.7). Furthermore, when the persona has turned from love and courtly service that are merely of the world (ll.1–8) he then celebrates the Virgin in terms from neoplatonic theology – he turns too from the courtly lore and language of love and does not use them even in sacred parody (as he does in the foregoing poem). But most important is that the sonnet's redefinition of courtiership seems much less developed than that in the previous poem, if still in harmony with its main ideas: looking to divine rather than to temporal and arbitrary "grace" (ll.5–8); fearing inner rather than exterior change (ll.1–4); the need for humility (ll.1–4). The poem, even so, inverts the sonnet on the "cruell effects" of Elizabeth's "perfections."

The last of the grouped sonnets "To our blessed Lady" interestingly illuminates the other two, for it implies where devout courtiership may lead. The beginning of the sonnet appears to elaborate on the neoplatonic celebration of the Virgin which ends the second poem of the group. In the octave the persona reveals that, drawn in sacred *eros* to the Virgin and become her courtier ("Sweete Queene . . . lett me . . .," l.1 and l.3), he hopes for elevation by her to a mystical apprehension of Christ. Here, as in the other sonnets, the persona stresses the Virgin's mediating role, and suggests that entry into her service has enabled him to enter God's (see ll.3–8). The sestet of the sonnet offers an affective image of the contemplative ecstasy, the beatitude, to which he hopes his devout courtiership may lead – an image that recalls the accounts by St Bonaventure of such experience.[14] In ending with the fervid language, the emotional and sensuous intensity, of neoplatonic theology, the poem emphasizes not only that sacred *eros* indeed transforms the idea of courtiership, but that devout courtiership utterly transcends the lore and language of temporal courts. In so ending, moreover, the poem suggests that the grouped sonnets to the Virgin identify true courtiership with each of the three mystical ways. Filled with sacred *eros* and desiring to be, ultimately, God's courtier, the sonnets' persona seeks freedom from mundane loves and concerns (see the first two of the sonnets), hopes for a constant sensitivity to the divine (as all the poems indicate), and yearns for oneness at the last with Christ (as the third sonnet indicates). Having set out upon the ways, he formulates anew what courtly service is.[15]

The persona in those sonnets speaks from amidst the way of

purgation as one who looks beyond it to the illuminative and
unitive ways. So too does the persona of the sonnets to St Mary
Magdalen, but he places a special emphasis on the unitive way,
the Spiritual Marriage. The emphasis is telling, for in the triad
of sonnets his rejection of profane for sacred *eros* involves a
redefining of how desire is experienced by a man. The nature of
that redefinition can best be seen in the first sonnet:

> Blessed Offendour: who thyselfe haist try'd,
> > how farr a synner differs from a Saynt
> > ioyne thy wett eyes, with teares of my complaint,
> > while I sighe for that grave, for which thow cry'd.
> No longer let my synfull sowle, abyde
> > in feaver of thy fyrst desyres faynte:
> > but lett that love which last thy hart did taynt
> > with panges of thy repentance, pierce my syde.
> So shall my sowle, no foolysh vyrgyn bee
> > with empty lampe: but lyke a Magdalen, beere
> > for oyntment boxe, a breast with oyle of grace:
> And so the zeale, which then shall burne in mee,
> > may make my hart, lyke to a lampe appere
> > and in my spouses pallace gyve me place.

Constable's persona draws on the topos of the soul's femininity to depict himself as an androgyne, yet he does so to
suggest neither the completeness and harmony of his identity,
nor his confusion and elemental division. He seems poised
between those alternatives. (His body and soul act together,
but lack tranquility within themselves; he has determined to
forsake profane for sacred *eros*, but the success of his resolve
cannot be foretold.) He represents himself as an androgyne, it
would appear, in order to distinguish his spirituality from his
gender, to suggest the otherness of the soul. Now the persona
certainly images soul and body acting together: contrition is
expressed in tears, and so on. Nonetheless, through portrayal
of his soul as female he implies its distinct difference from his
body; in particular, he stresses that its experience of desire
differs from the body's as much as woman does (biologically)
from man.[16] He heightens the contrast between his soul and
body, moreover, by focusing on the soul rather than on its
partnership with the flesh (in fact, all his references to the body

or to physical processes serve to identify spiritual states and processes), and by his indicating that the soul is where desire is essentially experienced (whether of earthly or of heavenly love – see ll.5–14). What results from the contrast is that the male experience of desire seems doubly to transcend masculinity: it lies essentially in the "femininity," the otherness, of the soul and thus transcends the physical limitation of gender; further-more, being so located it is an experience in which male roles or types (or, as the sixth line and the sestet imply also, responses that might be considered specifically male) have no special importance, if any – the close of the eighth line suggesting an obvious and supremely important exception. In declaring and reflecting upon his abandonment of lower for higher *eros*, in seeking to become a counterpart to Mary Magdalen and, at a remove, Christlike (l.8), the persona so redefines the male experience of desire as virtually to deny its unique maleness. He indicates that what maleness the experience does possess only covers aspects of it that go beyond the exclusively masculine.

The two subsequent poems share almost all the concerns of their predecessor. For example, in both the persona seeks to become a counterpart to Mary Magdalen, and in both the male experience of desire seems to be redefined as it is in the first poem. Yet the subsequent poems are nonetheless quite indivi-dual.The second creates a landscape of the self – a *locus non amoenus* (ll.3–7) – and interplays that dominant topos with four others in particular: solitary repentance in the wilderness (ll.1–4); nature's perfection by grace (ll.8–11); the paradise within (l.3, ll.8–11); and blind/seeing Cupid (ll.12–14). The final poem develops into an ecstatic image of the Spiritual Marriage (ll.7–14), ending: "My sowle vncloth'd, shall rest from labors past: / and clasped in the armes of God, inioye / by sweete coniunction, everlastyng ioye" (ll.12–14). Both poems are attractive and interesting; even so, they lack the intellectual and stylistic richness of the first sonnet in the group.

Constable's religious and secular sonnets have a number of common elements, perhaps most notably a passion for rhetori-cal symmetry and a fascination with *eros*. But the religious sonnets seek to build their rhetoric on the Word – they are centred on Scripture, Tridentine doctrine, and the plain style.

They abandon or condemn lower *eros* in favour of higher. It is not that the sacred poems are narrowly devout or merely renunciatory: they astutely interweave many discourses; they acknowledge (if they do no more) the claims and worths of things not sacred. It is rather that they correct the secular poems, putting human life and art, and thus of course the fashionable sonnet form, in the context of the eternal. In doing so they reveal themselves (for the most part) as subtle and substantial creations – seldom equalled by their secular counterparts – and Constable as no insignificant religious poet.

William Alabaster

Unlike the religious verse of Constable, that of Alabaster not only reflects the doctrinal influence of Trent but also shows distinct affinities with the devotional literary traditions of the Counter-Reformation. That is not to deny his poems' connections with the medieval religious lyric, particularly through their use of typology, or their drawing on the Petrarchan psychology and rhetoric of contemporary love verse (especially as, like Constable, he diverts the sonnet form from secular to devout purposes).[17] Nor is it to underplay the significance of the plain style or of the strong-lined style in his poems, but it is to suggest their frequent harmony with Counter-Reformation poetics and emblematics, their frequent use of meditative strategies that are either Ignatian or in accord with Ignatian thought. In his mingling of the natively English with the (apparently) continental and baroque, Alabaster has some resemblance to Southwell, and though his poems lack the stylistic and psychological range of Southwell's, seeming rarely, moreover, to have a sustained excellence, their achievement is nonetheless at times remarkable. The scope of that achievement can best be seen when one considers how they treat of major themes in the spiritual life: purgation; illumination; penitence; wonder at God's love; conversion; human nature's capacity for perfection by grace or for dissolution in sin. As nothing is known that dictates an order for the discussion of Alabaster's sonnets, a useful way to begin might be to focus on the sonnets about the experience of purgation, for they suggest both the spiritual and social environments in which Alabaster wrote.

Alabaster's *Divine Meditations* on Christ's Passion (sonnets 1–11) form his most thorough examination of experiencing the purgative way, for they study the public as well as private demands that the purgative way could make on an Elizabethan Catholic.[18] The sonnets are spoken by a persona convinced that he is about to face persecution for his faith. In them he meditates anticipatorily on a twofold purgation, considering purification of the self for Christ but recognizing that as the prelude to a further act of denial for his sake: acceptance of public humiliation and execution – of martyrdom – in imitation of Christ's self-denial for mankind through his Passion (see particularly sonnets 1–3, 7 and 9). Hence the sonnets are proleptic studies of suffering; yet at the same time, as their speaker believes, they signal the start to his physical confrontation of it (l.12–14), just as Christ's contemplative "hymn" (1,3–8) acted as the announcement of *his* Passion's beginning. The poem's examination of the purgative way thus centres on the Gospel accounts of the Passion and on those texts from the Epistles which postulate our oneness with Christ's sufferings, the especially relevant texts here being *Romans* 6,5–11, 2 *Corinthians* 5,15, and *Galatians* 2,20 (*John* 15,1–5 linking with them in 5,9–14). With the example of Christ before him, Alabaster's persona encourages himself as he is about to enter the way of pain (1,9–14 and so on); with the same example and that of his own determination, with repeated exhortations drawing on Scripture, he encourages the contemporary Catholic reader not to avoid it (see sonnets 3, 4 and 10).

As the poems scrutinize that doubly purgative experience open to the Elizabethan Catholic, they make apparent not only Alabaster's new allegiance to Catholicism but also the Tridentine spirit typical of his *Divine Meditations* as a whole. The Council of Trent's iteration that the Catholic Church is Christ's mystical body within which alone salvation can be found, and that it is the unique bearer of Apostolic tradition, receives vehement affirmation. The poems argue that no Protestant has been able to stay on the way of purgation through martyrdom trodden by Christ in his Passion and followed thereafter by members of his Church (sonnets 5 and 6, *passim*;

cf. sonnet 8): Protestants have been able, at best, to achieve only pseudo-martyrdom (5,9–14), an idea subsequently inverted by Donne.[19] At one point (in the ninth sonnet), it is suggested emphatically that Protestants have spurned the legacy of divine truth passed on from St Peter, who knew Christ, for the legacy of doctrines made by Luther, who knew demons. The sonnets on the Passion express distinctly the Tridentine temper of Alabaster's religious verse.

Yet whilst the sonnets on Christ's Passion are Alabaster's most comprehensive studies of the purgative way and clearly bear the doctrinal impress of Trent, they are nonetheless not – with one or two exceptions – among his most accomplished poems, nor in style do they apparently owe anything to the Counter-Reformation, although they do suggest something of his other poems' affinities with its devotional literary traditions. The sonnets are very unequal in achievement and natively English in style. A glance at the first of them reveals the English traditions and modes on which they draw (and which are present in so much of Alabaster's verse); it also reveals how shrewdly those traditions and modes can be used by him. The poem is one of his most admired:

> The night, the starless night of passion,
> From heaven began, on heaven beneath to fall,
> When Christ did sound the onset martial,
> A sacred hymn, upon his foes to run;
> That with the fiery contemplation
> Of love and joy, his soul and senses all
> Surcharged might not dread the bitter thrall
> Of pain and grief and torments all in one.
> Then since my holy vows have undertook
> To take the portrait of Christ's death in me,
> Then let my love with sonnets fill this book,
> With hymns to give the onset as did he,
> That thoughts inflamed with such heavenly muse,
> The coldest ice of fear may not refuse.

The sonnet follows an Augustinian pattern of meditation to be seen practised or recommended in the writings of Hilton, Vaux, and many others: its speaker focuses his memory (ll.1–4), understanding (ll.5–8), and love (ll.9–14) on Christ. That

the plain and strong-lined styles pervade the sonnet is no less
familiarly English; sacred parody (ll.13–14), too, is an English
presence. Here Alabaster uses those native elements as astutely
as he does in any of his poems.

Alabaster recreates that Augustinian form of meditation
with imaginative freedom. The sonnet's opening quatrain,
with its haunting first verse, offers not merely a recollection of
the moment when Christ announced, in effect, the start of his
Passion, but a symbolic image of Christ as the cardinal point
between heaven and earth ("heaven ..., heaven beneath," l.2),
as the embodiment of a new heroic virtue defined by endurance
and self-sacrifice ("the onset martial, / A sacred hymn, upon
his foes to run ...," ll.3–4). Just so, whilst the subsequent
quatrain interprets the initial sign of Christ's heroism – his
"sacred hymn" (l.4) – as implying the spiritual intensity
necessary for entry upon a way of self-denial such as his (ll.7–
8), it also seeks to convey something of, or to arouse sympathy
with, Christ's spiritual state prior to his sufferings. In that
respect Alabaster's meditative strategy resembles the Ignatian,
and indicates his receptiveness to *The Spiritual Exercizes*.[20]
Furthermore the sestet represents a concentration of love on
Christ and, in doing so, suggests aesthetic aspects of the purgative way. First, the conceit of "tak[ing] the portrait of Christ's
death" (l.10) in oneself inevitably points to purification, and
hence perfection, of the self as an aesthetic act. (It evokes in
aesthetic terms, moreover, the topos that faithful imitation of
Christ restores the image of God – *imago Dei* – in man.)
Second, the conceit also implies that truly to follow the purgative way not only inspires art (cf. "heavenly muse," l.13) but
purifies art as well as the self, for it too becomes Christocentric
(as ll.11–12 affirm, and sacred parody in the final couplet
indicates). And inseparable from Alabaster's creative, flexible
use of that Augustinian meditative pattern is his flexibility of
style. Initially, adapting the newly fashionable strong-lined
style to devout ends, he writes in a series of analytic tropes and
paradoxes; his verse unites dialectic with devotional fervour
(ll.1–4). It then modulates suddenly into a plain style that is, of
course, less elaborate rhetorically, yet far more emotive (ll.5–
8). Thereafter his verse returns to being strong-lined, but ends
in sacred parody of Petrarchan rhetoric (ll.9–12; ll.13–14). The

sonnet, shrewd in its exercise of English traditions and modes no less than in its analysis of the purgative experience, deserves all the praise that has been given it.[21]

Whilst Alabaster's sonnets on Christ's Passion focus upon self-purification in connection with martyrdom, his other sonnets concerning purgation examine it in juxtaposition or connection with illumination – and in a quite different style. The three sonnets "Upon the Crucifix," the sonnets "Upon St Paul to the Corinthians" and *"Ego Sum Vitis,"* in *Upon the Ensigns of Christ's Crucifying* (30–34), image either the desire to purge the self through participation in Christ's final sufferings or fellowship with Christ following from identification with them.[22] Hence the poems, sharing an emphasis on both Christ's death and the achievement of a oneness with him, study complementary spiritual states. As Evelyn Underhill observes: "[T]hey [purgation and illumination] ... often exist side by side in the individual experience."[23] In style, furthermore, the sonnets are baroque rather than natively English.

The first two sonnets "Upon the Crucifix" and "Upon St Paul ...," which examine the experience of purgation, express their speaker's yearning to have physical sensation of and to internalize Christ's sufferings on the cross. The speaker asks Christ to "print those wounds which did thy feet torment, / On [his] affections ..." ("Upon the Crucifix (I)," ll.5–6). "And let my mouth savour of thy distaste," he also pleads (*ibid.*, l.11). Just so, in "Upon St Paul ..." he says of the blood and water which poured from Christ's side: "All faithful souls must drink this potion, / Where pain to passion is ingredient" (ll.5–6). He concludes: "Lord, let me feel the tartness of thy pain, / Or drink mine own heart's blood to relish thine" (ll.13–14). In "Upon the Crucifix (2)" the speaker says, referring to Christ's blood: "Drink, drink apace, my soul, that sovereign rain / By which heaven is into my spirit infused" (ll.11–12). And that yearning, which lies at the heart of the poems, is linked to many other extreme, at times violent, emotions, for inseparable from the speaker's longing are his feelings of amazement, passionate love, complete submissiveness, and unwavering determination. The heightened emotional state of the speaker, however, suggests not only the spiritual intensity of purgative experience but also that its spiritual intensity is not confined by, but can transcend, mundane reason. For example, in the initial "Crucifix" sonnet the speaker prays that Christ's wounds and pain be imprinted on his "soul and body" (l.2, see l.5). Throughout the poem he usually specifies what he seeks in terms of logical correspondences; the imagery of the opening quatrain, where he first reveals his desire, alludes, after all, to the logic of natural law. Yet at times the correspondences which express his longing are indifferent to logic (ll.5–6) or rise above it, as in the poem's last line: "And in thy Cross mine honour to esteem." There it can be seen that the speaker's longing to experience Christ's suffering necessarily leads him to transcend mundane reason for, gesturing toward *Galatians* 6,14, he ends by identifying himself with "the folly of the cross". Moreover his espousal of "the foolishness of God" (1 *Corinthians* 1,25) denies worldly wisdom, *prudentia*. The same elements of unreason can be seen in the two other sonnets. In "Upon St. Paul . . .," the speaker excitedly ignores and goes beyond worldly reason in embracing the paradoxes of the cross (ll.5–10). There, too, he abandons prudence: "Lord, let me feel the tartness of thy pain, / Or drink mine own heart's blood to relish thine" (ll.13–14). At the end of the second "Crucifix" sonnet he denies the logic of moderation, telling his soul: "O drink [of Christ's blood] to thirst, and thirst to drink that treasure, / Where the only danger is to keep a measure." The sonnets represent purgative experience as the delighted rejection of all conformity to the world, and as the eager embracing of the Passion.

"*Ego Sum Vitis*" and the third sonnet "Upon the Crucifix" study the experience of illumination, suggesting what it is to pass beyond purgation and to enter fellowship with Christ. The former poem, based of course on *John* 15,5, begins with the speaker announcing his retreat from the "midday heat" (l.1) of mundane passion to "cool repose" (l.5) under the "vine whose arms with wandering spire / Do climb upon the Cross" (ll.3–4) and "Whose leaves are intertwist with love entire" (l.6). His abandonment of profane for divine love by identifying himself with Christ crucified necessarily implies his self-purification. He clearly alludes to that (ll.2–4 and especially ll.9–10) but he focuses rather on the experience of a oneness with Christ following from purification of the self.[24] In developing the "vine" image from St John's gospel, the poem celebrates Christ – as the embodiment of divine love – in pastoral terms: the emblem of the cross covered with the luxuriant vine indicates Christ to be the true *locus amoenus*, the earthly paradise made once more available to man and able to renew him (ll.3–10). The speaker tells of his fellowship with Christ, then, as the happiness – the ecstasy – of paradise regained. Rapturously he says, in what is the climax to the sonnet: "List, list, the ditties of sublimed fame, / Which in the closet of those leaves the choir / Of heavenly birds do warble to his name. / O where was I that was not where I am?" (ll.11–14). "Upon the Crucifix (3)" offers an interesting counterpart to that experience of illumination. There the speaker tells not of seeking and finding, but of having achieved fellowship with Christ: "Now I have found thee, I will evermore / Embrace this standard where thou sitst above" (ll.1–2). He then suggests, through natural imagery which inverts that of *"Ego Sum Vitis,"* the ecstasy he feels:

O that I were transformed into love,
And as a plant might spring upon this flower;
Like wandering ivy or sweet honeysuckle,
How would I with my twine about it buckle,
And kiss his feet with my ambitious boughs,
And climb along upon his sacred breast,
And make a garland for his wounded brows. (ll.7–13)

In *"Ego Sum Vitis"* Christ was the vine about the cross; here, the speaker wishes to cling like "ivy" or "honeysuckle" about the cross and Christ. The contrast reflects the different, if related, concepts of illuminative experience that are developed in the poems. The natural imagery of both poems, of course, implies and seeks to communicate the ecstasy of fellowship with Christ; in addition, the imagery of the former poem represents Christ as the soul's Edenic refuge, and the imagery of this poem depicts his cross as the support of the soul (that is, as the support of the vine-like love which the speaker wishes he could become). But whereas the vine emblem in *"Ego Sum Vitis"* presents fellowship with Christ as the ecstasy of paradise regained, here another vine emblem presents that oneness with

Christ as an ecstasy which expresses itself particularly in the desire always to reverence and to celebrate him – in other words, within the experience of illumination it emphasizes acting for Christ, serving him, and the desire for spiritual union with him.[25] A further important difference between the sonnets' versions of illuminative experience is that the third "Crucifix" poem stresses how far from certain one's possession of illumination may be, and how dependent it is on grace. At the end of the sonnet the speaker concludes the statement of his wish to be transformed (ll.7–13) with the prayer, "Lord, so I am if here my thoughts might rest" – a careful qualification of his first enthusiastic assertion of constancy ("I will evermore / Embrace this standard …," ll.1–2). Alabaster's discerning studies of illumination do not exclude acknowledgement of human nature's disruptive instability.

The five sonnets just considered represent heightened, and at times violent, religious emotions in language which is elaborately conceited, dramatic, and insistently sensuous. In doing so they reveal intriguing harmonies with the Counter-Reformation baroque. To begin with, as meditations the sonnets unfold their spiritual dramas through strategies that are perhaps indebted (given that Alabaster read The Spiritual Exercises), but certainly akin, to those of Ignatian meditation: each poem employs what St Ignatius would have recognized as composition of place, analysis, and colloquy.[26] But if those strategies are familiar from The Spiritual Exercises onwards, Alabaster's use of them is not quite conventionally Ignatian. He uses strikingly realized emblems (the crucifix, the blood and water from Christ's side, the grapevine, the vine of ivy or honeysuckle) as compositions of place; as might be expected, analysis in the meditations becomes the persona's explications of the emblems or applications of them to his experience. To have emblems function as compositions of place, and be subsequently analysed, is unusual neither in The Spiritual Exercises nor in works by Ignatius's successors. Much less usual, however, is having meditations closely related to or on the Ignatian model open and continue in colloquy, for according to Ignatian convention the colloquy concludes a meditation. Alabaster begins each of his sonnets with the persona talking to himself or to someone else, and so the sonnets continue, their colloquies changing rhetorical forms: Alabaster draws on *obsecratio, adhortatio, praeparatio, constantia, aversio, optatio, ominatio, interrogatio*. Hence his unconventional (by Ignatian standards) use of colloquy constantly adds to, and broadly shapes, the spiritual dramas unfolding in the poems. The details of those dramas he of course presents through the emblems and their dependent tropes. And if his using emblem to effect composition of place and analysis is not unusual, his emblems themselves sometimes are. Alabaster can not only develop his emblems imaginatively (if still conventionally), as when he makes the crucifix the immediate focus of meditation on psychological, as well as physical, reception of the stigmata ("Upon the Crucifix (I)"), but startlingly recreate them, as when he makes the grapevine come to suggest both the concept and the experience of paradise regained (*"Ego Sum Vitis"*). Finally, one might suggest that the physically affective and elaborate tropes through which he develops and sometimes puts forward his emblems (and which indicate – more than anything else in the poems – the emotional and intellectual fervour arising from the sensuous apprehension of Christ in purgative or illuminative experience) imply that his sonnets have connections not only with Jesuit meditative technique but, in their more local strategies, with Jesuit poetics.

Stylistic affinities between Alabaster's verse and the Counter-Reformation baroque can also be seen in the sonnets on penitence (12–18) and in the sonnet beginning "Jesu, thy love within me is so main" (19). The former, in studying penitence, focus on the gift of tears. They suggest the efficacy of that gift by presenting tears of repentance as supranatural mediators between Alabaster's speaker and Christ. The speaker envisages that his tears will "run" to Christ and overcome all objections to his forgiveness (12; see ll.4–7); his tears, he believes, will be "turned in heaven to grace" (13; see l.14); they first fall in "humility" to the earth then rise to heaven (14,9–14); they curiously mingle water with the fire of love for Christ (18). To image the tears in their dramatic role, Alabaster uses an affective rhetoric: his speaker pleads, commands, exclaims, and queries; the tears are at times personified; they are celebrated and analysed in vividly sensuous tropes, especially hyperbole, and in paradox. For example, the speaker commands his tears to "run, O run / Out of [his] eyes ... / One after other run for [his] soul's sake ... / Until [they] come before [Christ's] heavenly throne" (12,4–6 and 8). He tells of his tears as a "shower" paradoxically like, yet unlike, a shower of rain (13,9–14; cf. the elaborate conceits of the sonnet's octave). In a paradoxical allegory he describes them as the "april showers" of an inner universe (15 – see l.14); in another, more dramatic allegory he pictures them as "pearls" to "spangle" his impoverished soul, and then compares them to "drops of amber" richly entombing a "fly" (17,6 and 9–11). Counter-Reformation in style no less than in doctrine, the sonnets have among them some of Alabaster's best (12 and 17), poems which, with 30, 33 and 34 from *Upon the Ensigns*, imply his mastery of a baroque as well as of a native manner.[27]

The sonnet "Jesu, thy love within me is so main" (19) also illustrates how successfully Alabaster can write in a baroque style. An emblematic poem, it works paradoxical variations on the familiar conceit of Jesus acting on the human heart – a conceit thoroughly explored in Luzvic's *The Devout Heart* (1626). It shrewdly examines the self-defeating desire to understand, to encompass, the divine love and illuminative experience. The poem ends in both submission to Christ and wonder at the infinity of his love, Alabaster's speaker concluding with: "[M]y heart holds not thee [Christ], hold thou my heart." That note of wonder is no insignificant element of Alabaster's verse; it is in fact sounded pervasively and strongly throughout his sonnets. Many of his sonnets are marvelling contemplations of God's love (that is, of the divine *agape*). Nearly all of them can be seen in *Upon the Ensigns of Christ's Crucifying* and *The Incarnation* (nearly all, moreover, are natively English in style). In "Upon the Crown of Thorns (I)," for example, from *Upon the Ensigns*, the speaker tries to discover why, in *The Song of Solomon*, Christ seemed to connect his crown of thorns with "glory" (l.4 – see *The Song*, 3,11 and ll.3–6, l.9 of the poem). Bewildered, the speaker finally says in yet greater bafflement:

...[W]herein doth that hidden glory rest,
Which mortal dimness cannot apprehend?
Was it the merit of his pain increased,

Which he for purchase of the world did spend?
It may be, but my thoughts cannot attain
What pleasure 'tis to smart for others' gain. (ll.9–14)

To the speaker, Christ's crowning with thorns is a paradox
(ll.1–2), his prefiguration of it in *The Song of Solomon* is
another (ll.3–8), and the redemptive love that it expresses is the
greatest of all (ll.9–14).[28] In "Another of the Same (2)" Alabaster's speaker tells, in imagery of thorn trees made thornless and
enabled to bear roses lacking thorns, of human nature's perfection by grace through the "purple tincture of [Christ's] blood"
(l.9), for thereby Christ "hath transformed us thorns from
baser wood, / To raise our nature and odious strain, / That we,
who with our thorny sins did wound him, / Hereafter should
with roseal virtues crown him" (ll.11–14).[29] Narrating history
in terms of pastoral and anti-pastoral, the speaker wonders at
the love which has raised fallen humanity and changed its
ugliness to beauty.

Throughout Alabaster's sonnets on the Incarnation, his
speaker repeatedly marvels at the incomprehensible love
informing that mystery. Even a few passages will suggest the
tone and rhetoric of amazement in the poems. "But see the
violent diffusive pleasure / Of goodness, that left not till God
had spent / Himself by giving us himself, his treasure, / In
making man a God omnipotent[,]" exclaims the speaker in
"*Incarnatio est Maximum Dei Donum*" (ll.9–12). His wonder
is expressed in a vehement language shaped primarily by sacred
paradox, the latter not only helping to reveal his amazement at
God's love, but also implying his necessary limitations in
explicating it. Sacred paradox recurs throughout the sonnets to
suggest both things, in accord with elements of its traditional
role in Christian rhetoric, namely, to indicate the wonder of
the human at, and to indicate the incomprehensibility of, the
divine (the two often being inseparable). "*Incarnationis Pro-
fundum Mysterium*" has an equally paradoxical rhetoric and
emphatic language (see especially ll.9–14), but "*Incarnatio
Divini Amoris Argumentum*" illustrates other, no less recurrent, features of the sonnets' tone and rhetoric of wonder.
There the speaker begins: "God was in love with man, and
sued then / To get return of love by all those ways / Which

lovers use to compass in their praise" (ll. 1–3). That opening initiates a formal comparison of great things with small, and exemplifies the frequent presence of *comparatio* (including *icon, similitudo,* as well as other figures) and allegory in the sonnets. Their speaker, trying to come to terms with the complexities of the Incarnation and of the love it manifests, often studies those complexities through analogies with the worldly and familiar. His doing so, however, tends at once to defamiliarize the familiar, the mundane, and to make the divine apprehensible whilst also stressing its otherness (see, for example: 56,1–8; 59,1–8; 61, *passim*). Hence his use of analogy implies the immediacy but transcendence, the intelligibility but incomprehensibility, of the divine love embodied in Christ, and constantly expresses his awe as he confronts it (cf. 66, especially ll. 13–14). The sonnet illustrates, too, something of that quiet wonder before sacred mystery which mingles in the poems with startled, exclamatory amazement.

Informing the poems of wonder at God's love is the idea that through Christ new life has been made possible to man; the poems on illuminative experience are informed by the idea that, for the individual, new life lies in fellowship with Christ. The poems on purgative experience and on penitence examine death to sin (by sharing in Christ's Passion) or the abandonment of it. One can reasonably suggest, then, that Alabaster's sonnets on major themes in the spiritual life tend, as a whole, to express the topos of death to sin and resurrection with Christ – the topos central to so many of Southwell's poems. That suggestion finds support both in Alabaster's sonnets on his conversion, and in those where he studies human nature's capacity for perfection by grace or for dissolution in sin.

The sonnets apparently connected with Alabaster's conversion (46–51) focus on the troubles evoked by denying the established Church and on the determination born of a commitment to the Old Faith. In one poem Alabaster represents his conversion as a return from life-denying Protestantism to the *alma mater* of the soul: he likens Reformers to malign fairies who "after baptism did us steal, / And starved us with their enchanted bread" (49,11–12), and tells of the joy in returning to "Our Mother Church" who "of Christ's treasure hath the seal, / And with sweet junkets doth her table spread"

(l. 10, ll. 13–14). But it is on the threats to remaining with "Our Mother Church" and on resolved loyalty to her that the other sonnets mainly concentrate, and they stress more strongly that the goal of loyalty to her is God, and new life in Christ (46,9–14; 47,9–14; 48 *passim*; 50,9–14, though obliquely; 51,1–4). One very perceptive sonnet, "Away, fear, with thy projects, no false fire" (46), indicates their concerns and styles:

> Away, fear, with thy projects, no false fire
> Which thou dost make can ought my courage quail,
> Or cause me leeward run or strike my sail.
> What if the world do frown at my retire,
> What if denial dash my wished desire,
> And purblind pity do my state bewail,
> And wonder cross itself and free speech rail,
> And greatness take it not and death show nigher!
> Tell them, my soul, the fears that make me quake,
> The smouldering brimstone and the burning lake,
> Life feeding death, death ever life devouring,
> Torments not moved, unheard, yet still roaring,
> God lost, hell found, – ever, never begun:
> Now bid me into flame from smoke to run!

Fashioning an emblem of his predicament, Alabaster begins with the *navis animae* motif and implies that adherence to Catholicism is like continuance in a dangerous sea voyage (ll. 1–3). The subsequent *contrarium* (ll. 4–13) explicates the image that opens the sonnet through two further images: one, a composite likeness of Elizabethan society (ll. 4–8); the other, a picture of hell (ll. 9–13). Alabaster suggests that within Elizabethan society (and hence the temporal world) he is threatened with social and political hostility ending, quite possibly, in the first death (see especially l. 8) if he remains a Catholic; yet to repudiate his conversion will, he then argues, subject him to a self-imposed second death (l. 11) within eternity. Thus the sonnet forms a personal emblem of a spiritual journey both seemingly toward the first death and certainly away from the second – toward Being (in despite of physical death's approach) and from Nothingness. The emblem's drama, it should be added, is heightened by Alabaster's interweaving of styles. Alabaster writes mainly in the plain style, using emotive commonplaces and the rhythms of urgent speech (see, for example, ll.1–4, ll.7–8. l.10, l.14). But toward the end of the sonnet he writes briefly in a different and more powerfully emotive style. Amid the sestet (ll.10–13) he fashions a composition of place (or, at the least, a *demonstratio* with the same function) that depicts hell.The picture is introduced in sensuously specific terms and in the plain style (ll.9–10); however, Alabaster then goes beyond the terms and style of that introduction by depicting hell through processes which seem sensuously apprehensible, yet which frighteningly transcend the laws of physical process ("feeding . . . devouring," "not moved, unheard, . . . still roaring," "lost . . . found"). Alabaster creates a composition of place whose effect comes not only from specific physical detail but also from forceful allusion to, and at the same time, transcendence of the physical.His sonnet momentarily and climactically becomes baroque in style.

The sonnets examining human nature's capacity for perfection by grace or for dissolution in sin at least match in stylistic interest, but surpass in intellectual scope, those connected with Alabaster's conversion. They contain some of the most ambitious and successful writing in his *Divine Meditations*; they indicate, furthermore, how comprehensively (as well as strongly) he was once influenced by the Counter-Reformation. His paradigmatic study of the soul's dissolution in sin is "Shall I confess my sins?" (52):

Shall I confess my sins? Then help me tell:
In lust I scorch, and drown in riot, pine
With envy, and with looseness moulder, shine
In easy fortunes, and in harder quell.
I shrink with baseness, and with pride I swell,
Fear makes me stoop, detraction repine,
With avarice I twist, and do untwine
With largess, heaven I buy with wish, but sell
My soul for pleasure, with ambition
I overreach, with shame I sneak, dissention
Doth rend asunder, kindness not content me,
Repose doth slow my mind, and study break,
Knowledge doth cloy, and ignorance torment me.
Shall I confess my sins? Then help me speak.

The poem is framed by appeals which seem directed to the Logos, for Alabaster's persona requests help to catalogue and to ask pardon for his sins (l.1, l.14): presumably, without Christ's aid the persona cannot identify his own offenses against Christ or speak in penitence. Within that framework, the persona lists the seven deadly sins and his other failures in faith, hope, and charity. (The greater part of the poem resembles an Ignatian examination of conscience.) What one sees, as he does so, is an image – *notatio* – of a restless, contradictory, and fragmented personality. The rhetoric through which Alabaster creates that strong-lined portrait is shrewd, if neither unusual nor complex. The pervasive antitheses of course suggest that sin constantly divides the persona's soul against itself, fragmenting it. The tropes alluding to physical actions imply the experience of extreme psychological states. The denial of order to the catalogue of sins implies that evil subjects the persona to meaningless spiritual flux. One of the most famous Renaissance commonplaces is that which proclaims man to be a protean creature, a being capable of infinite self-transformation; here, Alabaster vividly images self-transformation into spiritual anarchy – a self-unfashioning.

The counterpart to "Shall I confess my sins?" is the ambitious *"Exaltatio Humanae Naturae"* (57). There Alabaster studies the perfection of human nature by grace as embodied in Christ and as made possible through him:

> Humanity, the field of miseries,
> Nature's abortive table of mischance,
> Stage of complaint, the fair that doth enhance
> The price of error and of vanities,
> Whither? who seeth it? whither doth it rise?
> Or do I see, or am I in a trance?
> I see it far above the clouds advance,
> And under it to tread the starry skies.
> My dazling thoughts do hold this sight for pain,
> Vouchsafe me, Christ, to look: see, now again
> Above the angels it hath distance won,
> And left the winged cherubins behind,
> And is within God's secret curtain gone,
> And still it soareth: gaze no more my mind!

The sonnet offers two images of human nature, beginning with a various image of its weakness and self-love (ll.1–4), then depicting its virtual apotheosis (ll.5–14). The first restates the themes of *contemptus hominis*. The second implies that with the Incarnation human nature has been raised by grace to participation in godhead; it also implies that grace to perfect human nature comes through Christ, for through Christ's aid the persona seeks to retain his ecstatic, almost unendurable, vision (see ll.9–10) of "Humanity" exalted. The image of human nature perfected by grace triumphantly transcends the preceding one of "Humanity" as flawed and frail; however, the second image does not negate the first. Both are true, and neither displaces the other. Alabaster pictures what human nature has become in Christ, which indicates something of what it may subsequently become in Christ's followers, yet he does not repudiate, nor is the reader intended to forget, his initial *contemptus hominis*.

But Alabaster's image of human nature perfected by grace does repudiate, if it does not do so deliberately, the picture of humanity apotheosized that Vives creates in *A Fable about Man*. There Vives writes:

> The gods were not expecting to see [man-the-actor assume] more shapes when, behold, he was remade into one of their own race, surpassing the nature of man and relying entirely upon a very wise mind.... [T]here was an unbelievable outburst of applause, and they prevented that great player from acting any longer. They begged Juno to let him into the stalls of the gods, unmasked, and to make of him a spectator rather than an actor. She was already eagerly going about obtaining this of her husband, when, at that very moment, man came out upholding the great Jupiter, the worthiest of gods, and with marvellous and indescribable gestures impersonating his father. He had transcended the characters of the lower gods and was piercing into that inaccessible light surrounded by darkness where Jupiter dwells, of kings and gods the king.[30]

The contradiction between the two images (like that between Alabaster's version of protean man in "Shall I confess...?" and Pico's in his *Oration*) suggests how thoroughly the Counter-Reformation influenced Alabaster, for the sonnet implies a post-Tridentine revaluation of familiar Humanist notions of human potential.

"*Exaltatio Humanae Naturae*" is a useful poem with which to end discussion of Alabaster's *Divine Meditations*, both because in its perceptiveness, emotional force, and rhetorical astuteness it is among his most successful poems, and because it tells significantly of his relationship to the Counter-Reformation. That is to say, it exemplifies the considerable skill with which Alabaster often wrote, and it indicates the breadth of his relationship to the dominant context of his religious verse. All in all, the sonnet affirms an opinion that if Alabaster's religious verse can occasionally be clumsy, opaque, and banal, at times it can almost rival the finest verse of Southwell. Alabaster's achievement as a poet also resembles that of Southwell because each brings the baroque, in its sacred guise, into Tudor poetry. Southwell may do so on a much larger scale and more elaborately than does Alabaster, but the latter's introduction of a baroque style into the sonnet is no insignificant feat. Such a comparison of course invites a further one, between Alabaster and Constable, especially as the two poets have just been considered side by side. Some specific comparisons between them have already been made; here, by way of general comparison, it would seem enough to suggest that whilst Alabaster is often clearly the greater poet he is also often, and no less clearly, the worse. What seems more valuable than comparison of Alabaster and Constable, however, is consideration of their importance as Tudor religious poets.[31] If they are not Southwell's equals (it has been argued above that Southwell wrote some of the most sophisticated and various English religious verse of his century) then they are nonetheless among the few truly outstanding religious poets of Tudor times, because of their poems' frequent intensity of devotion, acuteness of perception and of style – and intellectual as well as stylistic daring. Perhaps that view may be too generous, yet, even so, its main implication seems easily defensible: that they were among the prominent contributors to what remains of interest in sixteenth-century English religious verse.

CHAPTER FOUR

Sir John Beaumont, William Habington, and Some Others

Of the Catholic religious poets writing before Crashaw in Stuart times, the most interesting are Sir John Beaumont, essentially a Jacobean author, and William Habington, Crashaw's near contemporary and a cavalier.[1] Beaumont wrote devout lyrics whose lucid design and plainness of style suggest the influence both of the Christian traditions of plain speaking and of Ben Jonson. His lyrics differ widely in achievement: the majority of them could not be called impressive, but the best celebrate God and analyse sppiritual issues with an epigrammatic, graceful, and sophisticated wit. It is mainly as a lyrist that Beaumont is now remembered, yet in fact he aspired beyond that poetic role. He also wrote a sacred epic, *The Crowne of Thornes*, which unfolds a Christocentric vision of the universe. Like most of his lyrics, that more ambitious work is very markedly uneven; one of its intriguing aspects is, however, that (in contrast to the native Englishness of his short poems) its style is frequently baroque, suggesting the influence of the Counter-Reformation. In particular, the work reveals an indebtedness to, or at the least distinct affinities with, Ignatian meditative technique. When uniting the meditation and the grand manner, Beaumont's epic can become spectacularly baroque.[2] Unlike Beaumont's religious verse, that of Habington consists of lyrics and verse epistles. Habington may have lacked Beaumont's aspiration to epic, but certainly as a maker of short poems he is Beaumont's superior, writing more evenly and, at times, with greater intellectual and stylistic astuteness. His verse sometimes resembles that of Donne's satires, epistles, and elegies, but at others appears closer to that of his fellow cavaliers. It is also verse whose thematic range is narrow – much more so than that of Beaumont's verse: *contemptus hominis* and *contemptus mundi* are its preoccupations. Habington's various use of those themes seems, nonetheless, to be sufficient compensation for his constant concern with them, as is suggested especially by the images of spiritual transformation and of sanctity, and by the neostoic accounts of retirement, that he fashions as he reflects on them. Beaumont and Habington having been discussed, there follows a brief account of those Catholic religious poets of the English Renaissance who could not be considered at length in this book, but whom it would be wrong to ignore.

Sir John Beaumont

Beaumont's lyrics are pervaded by elemental Christian antitheses, such as those between spirit and flesh, love of the Creator and love of his creatures, desolation of spirit and spiritual consolation, man's wretchedness and Christ's redemptive love. Just so, elemental Christian motifs such as that of the *navis animae*, and that of the spiritual shipwreck, recur throughout his poems. Yet Beaumont seems infrequently to present those antitheses in other than quite familiar terms, and often he makes the great Christian commonplaces appear merely commonplace. For example, in "An Act of Contrition" one reads:

Lord, from Thy wrath my soule appeales, and flyes
To gracious beames of those indulgent eyes,
Which brought me first from nothing, and sustaine
My life, lest it to nothing turne againe,
Which in Thy Sonne's blood washt my parents' sinne,
And taught me waies eternall blisse to winne.
The starres which guide my bark with heau'nly calls,
My boords in shipwrack after many falls:
In these I trust, and wing'd with pleasing hope,
Attempt new flight to come to Thee, my scope,
Whom I esteeme a thousand times more deare,
Then worldly things which faire and sweet appeare. (ll.21–32)

Perhaps the *navis animae* topos (l.27) is given some vitality through its use as Petrarchan parody (cf. "*Passa la nave ...*," l.12); more striking is Beaumont's presentation of spiritual antitheses in an harmoniously contrapositive rhetoric which can make his couplets seem faintly anticipatory of Pope's (see especially ll.29–30) – though the heroic couplet is his favourite measure and that rhetoric, with its occasional intimations of Augustan style, recurs throughout his verse.[3] For all that, in their unremarkable competence the lines represent much of his writing in his lyrics.

Beaumont can, of course, write more imaginatively and sophisticatedly than that – he does so elsewhere in "An Act of Contrition" itself (see ll.1–4 and ll.41–44) – and "A Dialogue Betweene the World, a Pilgrim, and Vertue" illustrates his writing in his shorter poems at its best. "A Dialogue" is a debate poem in which Christian topoi and primary contradictions in Christian experience are studied through the interplay of dramatic emblems, identified in the poem's title. The poem opens with a speech by the Pilgrim:

> What darknes clouds my senses? Hath the day
> Forgot his season, and the sunne his way?
> Doth God withdraw His all-sustaining might,
> And works no more with His faire creature Light?
> While heau'n and earth for such a losse complaine,
> And turne to rude vnformèd heapes againe?
> My paces with intangling briers are bound,
> And all this forrest in deepe silence drownd;
> Here must my labour and my journey cease,
> By which in vaine I sought for rest and peace:
> But now perceiue that man's vnquiet mind
> In all his waies can only darkenesse find.
> Here must I starue and die, vnlesse some light
> Point out the passage from this dismall night. (ll.1–14)

Certainly Beaumont's verse in that passage has a subtlety of rhythm, a vividness, and an analytic astuteness not equalled in the verse quoted from "An Act of Contrition": the lines "My paces with intangling briers are bound, / And all this forrest in deepe silence drownd" (ll.7–8) and "But now perceiue that man's vnquiet mind / In all his waies can only darkenesse find"

(ll.11–12) have no counterparts there.[4] The verse beginning "A
Dialogue" and that cited from "An Act of Contrition" are
chiefly different, however, because Beaumont has the Pilgrim
reflect upon his experience in apparently Augustinian terms.
When climactically considering his predicament the Pilgrim
says that, having laboured and journeyed "in vaine" to find
"rest and peace" (ll.9–10), he "now perceiue[s] that man's
vnquiet mind / In all his waies can only darkenesse find" (ll.11–
12). The remark seems an allusion to St Augustine's idea that
mankind primarily desires and constantly seeks *quies*, which it
can find solely in God. As the saint observes in his *Confessions*:
"For thou hast created us for thyself, and our heart cannot be
quieted till it may find repose in thee" ("*[Q]uia fecisti nos ad te
et inquietum est cor nostrum, donec requiescat in te*").[5] Thus
the contradictions that the Pilgrim reveals himself as experiencing, and which are focused by his evocation of the *selva
oscura*/wood of error topos, seem to express the Augustinian
contradictions between *cupiditas* and *caritas*, between *frui* and
uti – between, that is to say, nothingness and Being. The speech
of the Pilgrim, it would appear, implies an Augustinian interpretation of humanity's relations to the Creator and to the
creation.

Those Augustinian contradictions seem to shape the debate
that then takes place between the World and Vertue. The
former offers the Pilgrim a "resting place" (l.22) in her "glitt'r-
ing palace" (l.20), an existence without "strife" (l.37), and tells
of Vertue's making "men draw vnquiet breath" (l.49); she
identifies herself as his *telos* ("I am thine end, Felicity my name
...," l.27); she promises him "Pleasures, Riches, Fame" (l.28)
and one of the "triumphant crownes" (l.35) in her gift: she
offers the Pilgrim *quies*, but *quies* to be gained from mutability
and inseparable from fear of time – founded in the self-centred
enjoyment of earthly goods. As she says:

> In my left hand delicious fruits I hold,
> To feede them who with mirth and ease grow old;
> Afraid to lose the fleeting dayes and nights,
> They seaze on times, and spend it in delights. (ll.31–34).

Vertue, on the other hand, also reveals her "house" (l.42) to the

Pilgrim as the site of "repose" (l.41). In doing so she reveals to him that the goods off the World are only transient and that the World's peace is in fact misery ((ll.43–44). She indicates the unity of *cupiditas*, enjoyment of the World, and unquiet when she demands of her opponent:

> Heare this my challenge, one example bring
> Of such perfection; let him be the king
> Of all the world, fearing no outward check,
> And guiding others by his voice or beck:
> Yet shall this man at eu'ry moment find
> More gall then hony in his restlesse mind. (ll.53–58)

Offering the Pilgrim a thorny crown, as distinct from the World's offer to him of one of her "triumphant crownes" (l.35), Vertue gives him the opportunity to espouse *caritas* (cf. ll.39–44), use – rather than enjoyment – of earthly goods, and thence to gain beatitude throughout eternity:

> Within these folds lie hidden no deceits,
> No golden lures, on which perdition waites:
> But when thine eyes the prickly thornes haue past,
> See in the circle boundlesse ioyes at last. (ll.65–68)[6]

The Pilgrim's acceptance of that crown (ll.69–72) is the start of a journey toward *quies*.

"A Dialogue Betweene the World, a Pilgrim, and Vertue" illustrates both the elegant conciseness with which Beaumont can use the plain style in his lyrics and the sophisticated wit that he can display in them.[7] One instance of his wit in the poem is particularly significant. The emblem of the thorny crown brings together Christ's crown of thorns and the crowns mentioned in *James* 1,12 ("Blessed is the man who endures trial, for when he has stood the test he will receive the crown of life which God has promised to those who love him" – cf. verses 13–15 and l.72 of the poem) and in *Revelation* 2,10 ("Do not fear what you are about to suffer.... Be faithful unto death, and I will give you the crown of life." Cf. 1 *Peter* 5,4 and l.71 of the poem); through that emblem Beaumont indicates what *quies* is, how it is to be achieved, and so completes his (apparently) Augustinian analysis of the Christian life. The emblem is, of course, the climactic image of "A Dialogue," and it is unique in Beaumont's shorter religious verse. Even so, it tellingly interacts with other images in his lyrics. In "Of the Transfiguration of Our Lord," the persona associates Christ's crown of thorns and the purgative way, saying: "But ye are blest, when being trodden downe, / Ye taste His cup and weare His thorny Crowne" (ll.35–36). In "Against Inordinate Loue of Creatures," to take another example, Beaumont's speaker describes the fallen world as "a thorny waste" (l.18). "An Expression of [the] Sibyll's Acrostichs" offers a similar view of the fallen world, for it alludes to Christ as the one who will "[r]edeeme the world from thornes and barren taints" (l.8 – cf. "Virgil. Eclog. IV," l.35). The emblem of the thorny crown in "A Dialogue," then, not only brings that poem to a climax, but joins with other images to imply Beaumont's close association of thorns with both the individual's quest for beatitude and that quest's mundane environment. Beaumont's connecting of those things is confirmed, and the extent of his doing so becomes clearer, when one considers his epic *The Crowne of Thornes*.

As was suggested earlier, Beaumont's *The Crowne of Thornes* unfolds a Christocentric vision of the universe (see Book 5, *passim*) in a style that is frequently, and sometimes resplendently, baroque. Leaving aside, for the moment, scrutiny of the epic's various style, one can describe the unfolding of its vision in these terms. The work initially studies the Passion (Books 1–4). Thereafter it considers Christ's making of, and more broadly examines his physical presence in, the world (Books 5–8). It ends in study of his continued spiritual presence on earth through his followers, expressing the hope that the true Church will be restored to England (Books 9–12).[8] Christ's crown of thorns provides at once the work's title and dominant image, being used as an emblem that suggests, primarily, the cardinal importance of the Passion to the divine pattern of history and also to the individual's search for spiritual union with Christ. The Christ-centredness of Beaumont's epic, and a foreshadowing of the crown of thorns' appearance in it as an emblem, can be seen in his introduction:

> I sing of thornes transform'd in bloody springs
> To pearles, and rais'd aboue all earthly things:
> Which hauing dwelt below, dare now aspire
> To crowne his forehead, whom the heauens admire.
> My hand through forrests hewes mine entrance plaine
> To narrow gates, which spacious ioyes containe.
>   Eternall, boundlesse, vndependent Might,
> Whose pallace is beyond accesse or sight,
> Thou life of creatures, to whose piercing eye
> Intangled thickets smooth and open lye,
> Since thou with humane nature would'st combine
> The heauenly lustre of thy rayes diuine,
> Let firy drops of thy redeeming blood
> Secure my paces through this shady wood,
> Where I haue ventured from the prickly Thorne
> To gather flowers, which yet no Muse hath worne. (ll. 1–16)

Those lines, in which the narrator states the epic's argument and invokes Christ, imply from the start Beaumont's centreing of his poem on Christ and his intent to use Christ's crown of thorns emblematically. In the opening couplet his narrator identifies the crown of thorns as the subject of the poem and thereby indicates Christ's centrality to it; in so doing, furthermore, the narrator describes the crown of thorns through spectacularly sensuous conceits which present the crown as a sign of the glory of Christ's Passion and of his Passion's power to transform, to exalt, fallen nature – thus he indicates at the outset that the crown has an emblematic role in the poem.[9] Yet whilst the introduction begins by suggesting those things, it goes on to do more: to attest to Beaumont's perception of the world as "a thorny waste." Near the introduction's close, the narrator depicts the world as a "shady wood" (l.14) in which grow thorns (l.15). He is elaborating on his earlier picture of the world as "forrests" (l.5) with "[i]ntangled thickets" (l.10), and offering a variant of the *selva oscura*/wood of error topos that pervades "A Dialogue." There is a significant difference, however, between the vision of the world expressed in the introduction to Beaumont's epic and that manifested in some of his more accomplished religious lyrics such as "A Dialogue," "Against Inordinate Loue of Creatures," and "An Expression of [the] Sibyll's Acrostichs." In the latter, images of thorns imply that the world is only dangerous and sterile; in the former, the speaker implies that because of the connection between thorns and Christ's Passion he has been able to derive the beautiful and rare from that which suggests the world's hostility, ugliness, and sterility – gathering "from the prickly Thorne / ... flowers, which yet no Muse hath worne" (ll.15–16; cf. ll.1–2).[10]

Not all those "flowers" are, however, by any means equal in attractiveness or in value. If anything, *The Crowne of Thornes* is more markedly uneven than any of Beaumont's shorter religious poems, reaching heights and depths not attained in them (which is hardly surprising, given the work's high ambition and voluminousness). There is neither the need nor the space in this chapter to examine the poem in all its unevenness; rather, its main concerns, its most striking principle of design, and its various style will be representatively illustrated from a study of passages in the opening Book. The passages to be focused upon are not brief but must be quoted at length, both because Beaumont creates his effects cumulatively and because the poem remains available only in manuscript.

In Book 1 the narrator prays to Christ, and reflects on his prayer, as follows:

> And thou deare Lord, whom cloth'd in loues bright fire
> My soule adores, and something would desire.
> To touch thy garments hemme forbid her not,
> She will not leaue without some blemish got.
> Forgiue thy suiters boldnesse I beseech;
> She courage takes from thy forerunner's speach.
> Who hath two coates (saith he) must giue the one,
> To his poore naked brother that hath none.
> Behold me void of cloaths; about me cast
> The worse of those two garments which thou hast.
> I am not so ambitious to require
> Thy seamelesse coat, an eminent attyre
> Thine vndeuided God-head to declare:
> Reserue that to thy-selfe, and let me share
> This purple ragg, thy sufferings to condole.
> This is my wedding robe, my richest stole,
> And thus shall I my lothed blacknesse hide,
> Like parched Negroes who with oker dy'de

Forget their hue, and are accounted faire.
This colour makes me Adam's happy heire,
In that bright state when he with wondrous birth,
Was pure created from the muddy earth.
Then am I Christ's true soldier, when I gaine
Some purple signe, to shew that I maintaine
His glorious realme, and in his bands enrol'd
A place in those victorious armies hold. (ll.474–499)

He then considers the torturing of Christ prior to the Crucifixion:

Now like a prince, who by the peoples choyce
Is rais'd to regall state, whom euery voice
Applauds, while he in kingly garments deckt,
Doth sitting in his throne the crowne expect,
Our Sauiour sits, when straight his hatefull foes
With platted thornes his sacred brows enclose;
And that they may more deeply pierce his braine,
With all their force this flowing wine-presse straine.
These fixed points, the more his head they wound,
The more they shew his kingdome's stedfast ground.
The strength that rests in their enraged armes
Seemes not enough for those desertlesse harmes;
But they strong instruments and engines take
To wrest the Crowne, and it more straight to make.
Hence flow the streames which neuer shall be dry,
Which still with Abel's blood for vengeance cry:
And like the teares which wronged widdowes spend
Fall on the cheeke, and thence to heauen ascend.
O bruised head, the horrour of whose paines,
Like death's cold finger, gripes my stopped veines.
O swelling eyes, whose strain'd and bloody teares
Enforce my eye-balls to forsake their spheares,
Because this starre is dim'd with bloody streames,
Who to the blind hath giuen lightsome beames.
If hot reflections which the sunne doth yield,
When it beats strongly on a brasen shield
Makes blind Democritus, who loathes to see
The good in paines, the bad in high degree,
And thus his mind from sensuall obiects brings
To contemplation of more noble things,
How can my ... eyes maintaine their sight

And not turne darke, drown'd with deuotious light,
That they this dismall obiect may auoide,
Were worthlesse spite high vertue hath annoy'd.
As Gorgon's head to senselesse stones hath chang'd
The greedy gazers, so my soule estrang'd
From liuely sense growes dull with woe's excesse,
When she perceiues how deadly stings oppresse
And compasse round, like snakes with poysonous griefe,
That glorious head, which of all heads is chiefe,
Which both in course of nature and of grace
Hath ouer vs his members highest place:
Whose noble vigour vitall spirit brings
To dyeing limbs, whence ioyfull motion springs. (ll.508–551)

In the conclusion to Book 1 the narrator observes:

So those, who are by Christ in pompe conuey'd
In scornefull rags (his chosen robes) aray'd,
Must on the Crosse, his conquering chariot ride,
And feele this garland which his browes haue tri'd.
Come forth, and shew thy pretious Crowne and stole,
True Mardochaeus faithfull Christian soule,
Who carriest contrition in thy name,
Put on th' attire which Christ for thee doth frame,
That at thy sight when he beholds thy choice,
The Church, God's glorious city, may reioyce. (ll.1131–1140)

The first of those quotations, the prayer followed by a
soliloquy, suggests clearly the Christ-centredness of Beaumont's epic. The narrator dwells on his need to have his sins
covered by Christ's blood if he is to be a true member of the
Church Militant and thence, as the allusion to "victorious
armies" (l.499) implies, of the Church Triumphant. Moreover,
he identifies eternal beatitude with the Spiritual Marriage, an
idea introduced at the beginning of his prayer (ll.474–475) and
crystallized in the conceit of the "wedding robe" (l.489). That
emphasis on Christ's centrality to human experience is heightened in the subsequent quotation. There the narrator depicts
Christ's Passion as the source of eternal life to fallen humanity
(ll.550–551) and as central to the divine pattern of history
(ll.516–517, ll.522–523, ll.547–551). He implies, too, the

necessity of sharing in the anguish of the Passion if one is to be indeed a member (cf. ll.549–551) of Christ's spiritual body, his Church (ll.532–541). The final quotation both confirms and in part extends the arguments of its predecessors. In that passage eternal beatitude is associated primarily with Christ, and his Passion is indicated to lie at the heart of history's divine schema (see especially ll.1136–1140; cf. l.489). Yet whereas the first quotation stresses the necessity of one's sins being covered by Christ's blood, and the second the necessity of one's sharing in the anguish of the Passion, the last quotation emphasizes that one must also enter upon the purgative way – share in the Passion by "rid[ing]" on the "conquering chariot" of the cross (l.1133) and by wearing the "pretious Crowne" of thorns (l.1135) as well as the "stole" of blood (ibid.) – if beatitude is to be won. As the reader goes on to discover, the elements which, in those quotations, suggest the Christocentrism of *The Crowne of Thornes* are precisely those that Beaumont diversely develops and amplifies throughout the poem as its main concerns: the centrality of the Passion to human life and to history (see Books 2–8, especially 4, 5, and 8); the need for one to be "crucified with Christ" (*Galatians* 2,20) and so to embark upon the first, at least, of the mystical ways (see, in particular, Books 2, 4, 5, 9, and 12); true adherence to the spiritual body of Christ and thus to the Church which is true (see especially Books 2–5, 7, 9–12).[11]

The most striking principle of design in Beaumont's epic, and his poem's stylistic range, can also be representatively illustrated from those passages in Book 1. The lines depicting Christ's torture prior to the Crucifixion fuse the high style and the meditation. That strategy, in conjunction with Beaumont's use of emblems such as the crown of thorns and the circle, recurs throughout *The Crowne of Thornes* to create set-pieces whose style can be unusually spectacular, even in a poem which pervasively focuses on the marvellous. The account of Christ's crowning with thorns opens with an ironic epic simile, proceeds with *incrementum* and *testamentum*, then continues with *exclamatio/apostrophe*, *exuscitatio*, and another epic simile in a larger pattern of *incrementum* which likewise closes in *testamentum*. Those figures are Janus-faced, for they structure the passage in both a rhetorical mode – the high style – and a specifically devotional one.[12] Beaumont's speaker indicates in lines 526–551 that his account of the crowning with thorns is a meditation; the meditative form realized by his rhetoric is distinctly Ignatian. The initial epic simile, for example, briefly sets the scene for the crowning with thorns and so acts as a concise composition of place (ll.508–512) for the subsequent depiction of the crowning itself. That is at once vividly imaged and analysed in a series of points, the speaker presenting an analysis conducted through an application of the senses (ll.512–525): the first instances of *incrementum* and of *testamentum* in the passage enact tactics from the middle section of an Ignatian meditation. Then follow what are, in effect, two colloquies – one with the tortured head of Christ, the other with the speaker's self as he considers his experience of meditation on the crowning (ll.526–551). The second instances in the passage of *incrementum* and of *testamentum* enact an Ignatian meditation's penultimate tactic. Beaumont's epic is not, of course, invariably in the high style, nor is that style always fused in his poem with the meditation; moreover, sometimes the meditation is combined in his work with another of the three styles, and it is not always distinctly Ignatian (though it never clearly resembles any other meditative form), no matter with what style it may be united.[13] For all that, Beaumont's fusion of the high style and the meditation in *The Crowne of Thornes* creates some of his poem's more memorable – in fact, more impressively baroque – moments.[14]

Something of that can be clearly seen when one relates the account of Christ's crowning with thorns to the other passages quoted above. As a meditation, the account of the crowning recreates Christ's physical torment, images its emotional as well as physical impact on Beaumont's narrator, and seeks to evoke the reader's sympathetic response to both the representation of Christ and the narrator's self-representation.[15] Hence the rhetoric of the passage tries to make the reader share in extreme physical sensations (see, for examples, ll.514–515 and ll.526–530), in heightened psychological states (ll.526–547), in intense emotions ranging from hatred for Christ's persecutors (ll.512–521) to compassion (ll.508–519, and so on), awe and love (especially in ll.543–551) for Christ himself. But the affectiveness of that rhetoric, insofar as it enacts the tactics of

Ignatian meditation, is realized with added force because Beaumont fashions it in the high style. As a result, the images of Christ in the passage are insistently hyperbolical and passionately dramatic (see especially ll.514–528). The narrator declaims his inner drama, vividly recreating legend or myth then transforming it through extravagant conceits and paradoxes (ll.526–547). The climactic image of Christ, furthermore, uses the crown of thorns as an emblem to imply the centrality of the Passion to the sacred plan of history (see ll.547–551; cf. ll.1131–1140, where that emblem is used to indicate the centrality of the Passion to the individual's search for spiritual union with Christ). The fusion of Ignatian meditative tactics with the grand manner in the passage makes it strikingly baroque: Beaumont's fashioning of the baroque there is, if undeniably uneven (the allusion to Democritus, for instance, seems rather awkward), also often visually startling and conceptually acute (as in the conceit of the "wine-presse" and in the epic simile of the "Gorgon's head"). The similarities and contrasts between that moment in his epic and the others (including the introduction) taken from its first Book are revealing.

The introduction to *The Crowne of Thornes* is, like the account of Christ's crowning, in the high style, yet only in some places is it also baroque in style: where the narrator announces the argument of his work (ll.1–4) and where he appeals for protection by Christ's "firy ... blood" (l.13). The passage is remarkable but clearly does not aspire to the marvellous, to the dazzling, with the frequency of the passage just examined. However the narrator's prayer that he may be washed in Christ's blood (ll.474–499) stylistically resembles the account of the crowning more than does the introduction. The narrator speaks, for the greater part, in the grand manner and seems to unfold what he says in a meditative form – an irregularly Ignatian one. As a result his prayer is both predominantly baroque in style and insistently emotive, rising to a spectacular climax in its elaboration on the baroque conceit of the two coats (ll.484–492). The passage from the conclusion to Book 1 (ll.1131–1140) mingles the high style with a series of paradoxical conceits and with the crown of thorns emblem to create an icon of spiritual triumph gained from following the purgative way (ll.1131–1134). The baroque icon thus pre-

sented is hardly as brilliant as the account of Christ's crowning
or as the climax to the narrator's meditative prayer, but it does
suggest how shrewdly Beaumont could write in a baroque
style to confront the reader with compelling images of his main
concerns. If, as a Catholic religious poet, Beaumont is now
remembered for having penned some elegant lyrics, he should
also be remembered for having been the only Catholic
religious poet in the English Renaissance to have significantly
attempted a sacred – and recurrently baroque – epic in his
native language, some moments of that work being memorable
and, arguably, better than the best of his shorter poems.

William Habington

It was suggested at the start of this chapter that, as a maker of
short religious poems, Habington is more even, and sometimes
more intellectually and stylistically astute, than Beaumont but
also narrower in thematic range. To begin illustrating that
argument one has only to turn to the initial poems of *Castara:
The Third Part* (1640), which contains nearly all Habington's
religious verse. The first poem has as its title a familiar quotation from psalm 51 ("*Domine labia mea aperies*"), indicating
that the poem's speaker may in some way be a Davidic figure.
Habington's speaker subsequently blends the poem's title into
the poem itself – and thereby consciously aligns his art with
that of David – when, after repudiating "wanton" art (l.5)
focused on feminine beauty (ll.1–15), he expresses a desire to
write of God:

> Open my lippes, great God! and then
>   Ile soare above
> The humble flight of carnall love.
> Vpward to thee Ile force my pen,
> And trace no path of vulgar men. (ll.16–20)[16]

However, the reader almost immediately discovers that the
speaker's broadly Davidic role does not involve the repudiation of "wanton" art alone, for the speaker goes on to reject as
well all the finite and mutable goods of the world, as is implied
by his rejection of courtiership (ll.26–28), domination of land

and people (ll.29–30), wealth (l.31) and "female beauty" (ll.32–35). In their place he espouses God, and hence goods either limitless and eternal or founded on the limitless and eternal (ll.35–50, cf. ll.21–25). The poem offers, then, an image of spiritual transformation in which a persona manifests himself as now being (what he was remains unclear) both a sacred poet and devout man in contempt of the world. The theme of spiritual transformation recurs in Habington's religious verse, and here his variation on the Davidic archetype indicates how inventively he can use it.[17] Yet no less important in the poem, and more pervasive throughout the third part of *Castara*, is his emphasis on *contemptus mundi* (ll.21–50). That is one of the two themes predominant in his religious verse; an instance of the other forcibly confronts the reader in "*Versa est in luctum cythara mea*," the following poem, which also reveals how accomplished a religious poet Habington can be.

"*Versa est in luctum cythara mea*. IOB" forms an image of spiritual transformation which complements and clarifies that in the preceding poem. Apparently the same persona speaks in each poem since the second, like the first, is spoken by a persona who announces both his repudiation of earthly love and wanton art (ll.1–20) and his espousal of a devout life and sacred art (ll.21–52). In the second, though, Habington presents the process of spiritual transformation differently by fashioning his persona in accord with the figure of Job, rather than with the Davidic archetype, as the poem's title and its incorporation into the poem itself (ll.39–40) imply. The persona of "*Versa est . . .*," moreover, explains his spiritual transformation in terms of *contemptus hominis* rather than of *contemptus mundi*, and unites to that motif the theme of (neostoic) retirement (ll.21–52). The two poems thus form complementary images of a single spiritual process – images which affirm each other's values and develop each other's analyses of experience in the fallen world.[18]

That mutual affirmation and development can be usefully instanced by an examination of the second poem's study in *contemptus hominis*, which is its centrepiece and displays some of Habington's most sophisticated religious writing. Bequeathing earthly love "[t]o the soft silken youths at Court" (l.14) with their "witty passions" (l.15), the persona remarks:

They'le smooth thee into rime,
Such as shall catch the wanton eare:
And win opinion with the time,
To make them a high sayle of honour beare.

And may a powerfull smile
Cherish their flatteries of wit!
While I my life of fame beguile
And under my owne vine uncourted sit.

For I have seene the Pine
Famed for its travels ore the Sea:
Broken with stormes and age decline,
And in some creeke unpittied rot away.

I have seene Cædars fall,
And in their roome a Mushrome grow:
I have seene Comets, threatning all,
Vanish themselves: I have seene Princes so.

Vaine triviall dust! weake man!
Where is that vertue of thy breath,
That others save or ruine can,
When thou thy selfe art cal'd t' account by death?

When I consider thee
The scorne of Time, and sport of fate:
How can I turne to jollitie
My ill-strung Harpe, and court the delicate? (ll. 17–40)

The lucid language and stanzaic form of those lines, suggestive of Jonson's influence, their paradoxes and elegant conceits in the manner of Donne, indicate at once Habington's stylistic affinities with his fellow cavaliers. The imaginativeness with which he uses that cavalier mode of writing to argue the instability, the insignificance, of man and hence the necessity of forsaking earthly love and public life is remarkable: there are the ironic, Donnean conceits of love being "smooth[ed] ... into rime" to allure "the wanton eare" (ll. 17–18), the graceful and variously allusive conceit of the persona's wish to sit "uncourted" beneath his "owne vine" (*transmutatio*, l. 24), the vivid, archetypal conceit of "the Pine" (ll. 25–28), the paradoxes of the "Cædars" (ll.29–30) and of the "Comets" (ll.31–32), which are almost optical illusions – the persona deftly heightening the second paradox with his terse reference to "Princes." The reader is confronted by a vigorous and protean study in *contemptus hominis* which functions in several ways: it provides, or is intended to, a main reason for the persona's spiritual transformation; it complements and amplifies the preceding poem's reason for that change – *contemptus mundi*; in doing the latter, it also clarifies the reader's view of Habington's persona, for it highlights his preoccupation with death; finally, it reveals – in verse which Habington could equal but not surpass elsewhere in his third part of *Castara* – that other theme which is predominant in his religious poems.[19]

"*Domine labia mea aperies. DAVID*" and "*Versa est in luctum cythara mea. IOB*" are, then, closely related renunciations of values and attitudes which are essential to the earlier parts of *Castara*, and in the two lyrics can be seen much that is of importance throughout Habington's religious verse. Yet in them cannot be seen either his imaging of sanctity or his mastery of a style carefully and specifically modelled on Donne's, each of which also contributes significantly to his achievement as a religious poet. Those aspects of his art are well exemplified in "*Qui quasi flos egreditur*. To the Right Honourable, the Lady *Cat. T*" and in "Elegie, 7" from *The Funerals of the Honourable, my best friend and Kinsman, GEORGE TALBOT, Esquire*, the former presenting an image of female holiness and being written in the style of the lyrics discussed above, the latter representing male holiness and being written after the strong-lined manner of Donne's satires, epistles, and elegies.

"*Qui quasi flos egreditur*" begins with a meditation on a rose, in which Habington's speaker offers a lady a reading from the book of nature on the theme of *contemptus hominis*:

> Faire Madam! You
> May see what's man in yond' bright rose. (ll.1–2)

> Poore silly flowre!
> Though in thy beauty thou presume,

And breath which doth the spring perfume;
Thou may'st be cropt this very houre. (ll.9–12)[20]

The book of nature is, of course, itself being read in the light of
The Book of Job – that is, in the light of the quotation from *Job*
14,2 which acts as part of the poem's title – and hence of divine
revelation: Habington's speaker uses the book of nature to
demonstrate the truth of, and to elaborate on, Job's comparison of man to a flower.[21] He puts before the lady an attractive
and uncompromising illustration of scriptural wisdom. The
celebration of the lady to which he proceeds is, however, rather
more striking than his meditation on the "bright rose."

After that meditation, the speaker remarks on humanity's
reluctance to confront its own decay, mortality, and ultimate
insignificance (ll.21–28); then he immediately suggests that
"the Lady *Cat. T*" is exempt not only from mankind's reluctance to confront its evanescence, but from moral (if not
physical) vulnerability or decline. He presents her as possess-
ing so great a holiness that she transcends those things:

    But Madam these
Are thoughts to cure sicke humane pride.
And med'cines are in vaine applyed,
To bodies far 'bove all disease.

    For you so live
As th' Angels in one perfect state;
Safe from the ruines of our fate,
By vertues great preservative.

    And though we see
Beautie enough to warme each heart;
Yet you by a chaste Chimicke Art,
Calcine fraile love to pietie. (ll.29–40)

The speaker describes the lady as being virtually angelic (ll.33–
34) and not subject to "the ruines of our fate" (l.35) – to the
moral weakness and inconstancy of fallen human nature (cf.
the play on "fall" in l.28) – which is to place her almost on a
level with the Virgin Mary. Such praise implies that he celebrates her as fulfilling the devout ideal of womanhood made

fashionable at court by Henrietta Maria and delineated in works such as Caussin's *The Holy Covrt*, the English translation of which was dedicated to the Queen.²² In *The Holy Covrt*, for example, the ideal courtly lady is indicated to be one who has "take[n] the way of holy & solide vertues, [and] enter[ed] into a life wholy Angelical ..."²³ The speaker's subsequent praise of the lady also implies that she fulfils the ideal of womanhood advocated by Henrietta Maria. He claims that she unites (transcendent) beauty with (perfect) chastity and refines earthly love directed toward her into sacred love (cf. *The Holy Covrt*, 2, p.256 and Davenant's "You that so wisely studious are," ll.15–28).²⁴ The image of female holiness that concludes Habington's poem indicates precisely the Catholic milieu from which his religious verse derives.

"Elegie, 7" commemorates Habington's dead "friend and Kinsman" George Talbot, and so might not at first be thought a religious poem (it is not, of course, from the third part of *Castara*). But the poem's speaker, in reflecting on Talbot's death, focuses on the world's pervasion by vice and on the regenerative effect that Talbot, as an embodiment of the virtues, could have had on fallen humanity: in honouring Talbot, the poem presents an image of male holiness that emphasizes the beauty and power of Christian virtue, and its necessity to mankind.

The poem opens with indirect homage to Donne, for its style clearly acknowledges the authority of his in the satires, verse epistles and elegies by brilliantly recreating it. Habington's strong lines, however, directly and no less brilliantly pay homage to Talbot as an incarnation of the Christian virtues:

> There is no peace in sinne. Æternall war
> Doth rage 'mong vices. But all vertues are
> Friends 'mong themselves, and choisest accents be
> Harsh Eccho's of their heavenly harmonie.
> While thou didst live we did that union finde
> In the so faire republick of thy mind,
> Where discord never swel'd. And as we dare
> Affirme those goodly structures, temples are
> Where well-tun'd quires strike zeale into the eare:
> The musique of thy soule made us say, there

God had his Altars; every breath a spice
And each religious act a sacrifice.
But death hath that demolisht. (ll.1–13)

It is as if in imitating the rhythms and diction of Donne's verse,
and the design of its conceits, Habington were also recreating
some of Donne's actual images: those of the "temple" (see l.8)
from "As due by many titles …" (though the image is a
familiarly biblical one) and of the "musique" of the soul (see
l.10) from "Hymne to God my God, in my sicknesse."[25]
Whatever the case, they are anticipated by the astute conceit of
the "republick" (l.6), that introduces the idea on which they
elaborate – the virtuous concord of Talbot's soul – and which
forms the basis of the poem's assertion that as an incarnation of
the Christian virtues Talbot could (God willing) have brought
the concord of his soul to fallen and morally disordered humanity, restoring it to a paradisal moral state: "But thy example (if
kinde heaven had daignd / Frailty that favour) had mankind
regaind / To his first purity" (ll.23–25).
     Habington's speaker makes the assertion in this way:

     [T]hou didst uncloyster'd live:
Teaching the soule by what preservative,
She may from sinnes contagion live secure,
Though all the ayre she suckt in, were impure.
In this darke mist of error with a cleare
Vnspotted light, thy vertue did appeare
T' obrayd corrupted man. How could the rage
Of untam'd lust have scorcht decrepit age;
Had it seene thy chast youth? Who could the wealth
Of time have spent in ryot, or his health
By surfeits forfeited; if he had seene
What temperance had in thy dyet beene?
What glorious foole had vaunted honours bought
By gold or practise, or by rapin brought
From his fore-fathers, had he understood
How *Talbot* valued not his owne great blood! (ll.27–42)

The speaker's praise of Talbot continues in the same, or in a
similar, vein for another fourteen lines, but his representation
of the man can be seen clearly enough in the quotation above.

A quasi-messianic role is said to have been possible for Talbot, and the speaker's description of that role offers a telling image of male holiness – telling not because it connects virtue in a man and the role of messiah, but because of what it suggests about Christian virtue. The image emphasizes virtue's beauty and the power of its beauty to transform the personality, to regenerate fallen humanity. In emphasizing that, though, the image reveals a radical problem: if through virtue lies mankind's road to "the paradise within" (see ll.23–25), yet only as exceptional a person as Talbot could draw mankind to the way of virtue (see ll.49–56). The poem's image of male holiness forcefully indicates virtue's beauty, power, and necessity to mankind, and at the same time how unfamiliar to, and how remote from, individual experience a truly virtuous life is.

Habington's skill in recreating Donne's strong lines can also notably be seen in one of his poems on retirement, which is another of the recurrent concerns in his religious verse. In "*Perdam Sapientiam Sapientum*" his speaker addresses "the Right Honorable the Lord *Windsor*" as follows:

> Forgive my envie to the World; while I
> Commend those sober thoughts perswade you fly
> The glorious troubles of the Court. For though
> the vale lyes open to each overflow,
> And in the humble shade we gather ill
> And aguish ayres: yet lightnings oftner kill
> Oth' naked heights of mountaines, whereon we
> May have more prospect, not securitie. (ll.1–8)

The poem's imitation of Donne has the same precision and confidence as does that in the elegy on Talbot, but here one recognizes as well a considered imitation of Horace (ll.4–8). Habington writes of retirement in the third part of *Castara* only once, if memorably, in the manner of Donne; his religious poems treating of retirement frequently express, however, an Horatian influence (for example, see "*Et alta a longè cognoscit. DAVID*"). That is unsurprising, as Habington imitates or alludes to Horace often throughout his religious verse and seems fond of fashioning his personae, to varying degrees, after Horace's version of the stoic wise man (see especially "*Quid gloriaris in malicia?* DAVID").[26] For all that, stoicism is not of course the final point of reference for Habington, either in the poems focused on retirement or in any others from the third part of *Castara*: their stoic elements are framed by, and subordinate to, Christian ideas and values; divine wisdom is shown as perfecting its human counterpart. In *"Quid gloriaris in malicia?* DAVID," for instance, the poem's title indicates scriptural wisdom, and that is subsequently illustrated with motifs from Horatian stoicism; the two are complementary, but which has primacy is clear. Just so, in *"Versa est in luctum cythara mea.* IOB" the sacred context of the speaker's stoic withdrawal into retirement (l.24) is implied by the poem's title. Not stoicism but neostoicism informs the accounts of retirement given in Habington's religious verse.

Habington is one of the more attractive writers from the predominantly Catholic literary circle centred on Henrietta Maria. The thematic range of his religious poems, as has been suggested above, could hardly be called broad, but within it lie intellectual shrewdness and variety; furthermore, his religious poems have greater deftness and acuity of style than have been usually acknowledged. In contemplating the littleness of mankind and the insignificance of the world, he became one of the few cavalier poets to write interestingly on sacred as well as on secular themes.

Minor Catholic poets from Heywood to Cary

Within the compass of this study there is no space for consideration of all the minor Catholic religious poets who wrote approximately between the early 1580s and the death of Crashaw – and even those who must be taken into account can be mentioned only briefly. Jasper Heywood, uncle of John Donne and a Jesuit priest, wrote at least seven poems printed in various editions of *The Paradise of Dainty Devices* (1576, 1578, 1585).[27] One is a plain-styled celebration of the Resurrection; two, which focus on repentance, seem to unite the plain style with something of Jesuit meditative practice (both appeared in 1585). *Odes. In Imitation of the Seaven Penitential Psalmes, With Sundry other Poemes and ditties tending to deuotion and pietie*, by Richard Verstegan (Rowland), was published in 1601.[28] Verstegan wrote in all three levels of style, with great metrical variety and some variety of stanza. His poems are Counter-Reformation in their attitudes and values, but are seldom stylistically so; notable among them is his imitative *Saint Peeters Comfort*, prompted apparently by Southwell's treatment of Saint Peter's penitence.

John Brereley, conventionally agreed to be the Jesuit priest Lawrence Anderton, produced *Virginalia. or Spiritvall Sonnets in prayse of the most Glorious Virgin Marie, vpon euerie seuerall Title of her Litanies of Loreto* (1632) and *Mirrovr of New Reformation . . .* (1634).[29] In the former are middle-styled and polemical celebrations of the Virgin which are supported by references to thirty-nine Fathers of the Church. Emphatically Counter-Reformation in doctrine, the sonnets seem also to bear the impress of Jesuit meditative technique (see perhaps especially the second poem in the sequence). The *Mirrovr* is a collection of satirical epigrams directed against the Reformers and their beliefs. As in *Virginalia*, Brereley adds footnotes to his poems – though here his footnotes are often many and sometimes long. He has a finely varied control of the plain style: through it he creates vigorous, coarse caricatures of Luther and Calvin (among others); he also creates acute characterizations that transcend caricature (as in "A Letter to a Minister" and "The Minister's Answer to the former letter"); he addresses Charles I with an adroit mixture of praise and counsel ("To the King's Most Excellent Maiesty my dread Soueraigne").

In 1633 there appeared Henry Hawkins's elaborate emblem book *Partheneia Sacra*, followed in 1634 by his *The Devovt Hart*, a translation of an emblem book by a fellow Jesuit named Luzvic.[30] The poems in the former explicate emblems celebrating the Virgin. Those in the latter are hymns that Hawkins inserted into his translation of Luzvic's work; they are placed directly after the emblem book's pictures and affectively interpret them. Emblematic and other poems constitute the sacred verse of Patrick Cary, seemingly written in 1650.[31] He writes in the plain style or in strong lines – often meditatively, sometimes dramatically, and pervasively on the theme of *contemptus mundi*. The influences of Donne, Herbert, and the

Counter-Reformation mingle in his verse. Among his more successful poems are "Whilst I beheld the necke o' th' Dove" (a meditation on the book of nature in light of *Romans* 1,20), "*Crucifixus pro Nobis*" (an insistently sensuous meditation on episodes from the life of Christ), and "*Nulla Fides*" (a dramatic meditation on the insignificance of "*Honour,* the *World,* & *Man*"). His is not unpleasant verse; with that of the other minor Catholic poets, however, it indirectly reminds one of how accomplished Crashaw's religious poems are, and to them discussion now turns.

CHAPTER FIVE

Richard Crashaw

Crashaw's epigram "*Felices! properâstis...*" contrasts the happiness of a life cut (apparently) short by martyrdom to the wretchedness of one that drags its length through the world. Drawing upon a number of familiar topoi, most notably the *navis animae* motif, the poem at one point says this of a lingering, mundane existence: "*Nos aevo, & senio, & latis permittimur undis. / Spargimur in casus, – porrigimur furijs.*"[1] The lines evaluate temporal life with a contempt not unusual, if not always so bitter, in Crashaw's religious verse when he scrutinizes the world. A better known instance of *contemptus mundi* in his poems occurs in "To the Same Party COVNCEL Concerning Her Choise" where "this lower sphear / Of froth & bubbles" (ll.8–9) is pictured as the realm of "[P]ainted shapes, / Peacocks & Apes, / Illustrious flyes, / Guilded dunghills, glorious LYES..." (ll.11–14). What, then, do Crashaw's religious poems identify as making human life truly valuable? The answer to that question can be seen in the poem just considered, for it goes on to counsel the lady whom it addresses as follows:

> 'Tis time you listen to a brauer loue,
>   Which from aboue
>   Calls you vp higher
>   And biddes you come
>   And choose your roome
> Among his own fair sonnes of fire . . . (ll.20–25)

The "brauer loue" here is Christ, and hence the lines identify sacred love as the truly valuable, and attractive, element of human life. As the magisterial opening of *A Hymn to the Name and Honor of the Admirable Sainte Teresa...* declares: "Loue, [that is, sacred love] thou art Absolute sole lord / Of LIFE & DEATH" (ll. 1–2).

Crashaw's religious verse is dominated by study of the love descending from God to man, of that reaching from man to God, and of those loves' intermingling. His poems' pervasive studying of sacred love is characterized by several concerns. He focuses often on illuminative and on unitive experience, more often than do any of the other Catholic poets (with the possible exception of Beaumont). He examines how sacred love transforms human perception and identity, how it perfects or transcends human reason; he presents it as transforming, extending, traditional modes of religious discourse. In so considering sacred love, then, his poems emphasize its intensity, generosity – and wit ("O wit of loue!"). Furthermore they almost constantly, and always memorably, manifest what Austin Warren finely described as Crashaw's "baroque sensibility."[2] One might add finally that his poems surpass in stylistic sophistication those of his Catholic predecessors and study virtually all the spiritual interests of their verse with a subtlety that they could seldom equal.

The Holy Name and the Good Shepherd

What has been suggested above of Crashaw's religious verse could be illustrated by reference to either his English or his Latin poems. Though in the following discussion mention will necessarily be made of the Latin poems, it is of course those in English which will be given most attention, especially those in *Carmen Deo Nostro* (the final collection of Crashaw's verse). In offering an account of the English poems one needs to begin with the poems which are directly centred on Christ: there Crashaw identifies the source and the end of sacred love; there he most thoroughly considers its nature. They indicate, moreover, that his English poems as a whole, for all their frequent and ardent celebrating of female saints, are undoubtedly Christocentric. Examining Crashaw's *To the Name above Every Name, the Name of Iesvs. A Hymn* and some of his poems on, or connected with, Christ as the Good Shepherd will suggest that his poems directly centred on Christ do indeed help to set in perspective those others wherein he studies sacred love. In addition, to examine the poems is to show that Crashaw could fashion interestingly contradictory (if nonetheless convergent) images of Christ, for the *Hymn* uses the Holy Name to represent Christ as the all-encompassing Word, the Logos – and so to emphasize his incomprehensible, as well as loving, divinity – whereas the Good Shepherd poems tend to picture Christ as the protector of and the provider for individual souls – stressing the immediacy of his humanity.

The *Hymn* to the name of Jesus images both celebration of that *"Name above Every Name"* (the poem's title alluding to *Philippians* 2,9) and invocation of its presence. The poem begins with Crashaw's visionary speaker praising and interpreting the Name, in doing which he represents it as the source, focus, and end of sacred love, the centre of the Church Triumphant. Later in the *Hymn*, the speaker pleads that the Name become present within the Church Militant and so grant to the faithful on earth a foretaste (see ll.154–158) of heavenly beatitude.[3] The speaker's invocation of the Name, and his subsequent account of its appearance in the world, resplendently affirm and develop his initial perception of it as sacred love's embodiment. To convey something of the richness and comprehensiveness with which Crashaw's poem thus studies sacred love, one must now look more closely at the work itself.

The *Hymn* opens with topoi of humility (see especially ll.1–2, l.6), Crashaw's speaker beginning to celebrate the Name, but at the same time acknowledging his innate unworthiness, and inability, to do so. Amidst his hesitancy, however, he tells much of the Name, for in starting to praise it he indicates what he sees as its significances. The speaker interprets the Name as signifying the spiritual life and fulfilment of humanity (because of Christ's self-sacrificial love); he implies, moreover, that it signifies the focal point of true human love. He sings of the Holy Name as "The Name of our New PEACE; our Good: / Our Blisse: & Supernaturall Blood: / The Name of All our Liues & Loues" (ll.3–5). In so interpreting the Name, Crashaw's speaker emphasizes that Christ's selfless love encompasses, as well as completes, human existence ("our New PEACE" alluding to God's redemptive scheme to history). He also stresses that Christ is true human love's ultimate desire ("Our Blisse"; "The Name of All our ... Loues"). That initial,

compressed explication of the Holy Name is then elaborated
into a luminous vision of unitive experience when the speaker
climactically prays for aid from, and describes the members of,
the Church Triumphant:

> Hearken, And Help, ye holy Doues!
> The high-born Brood of Day; you bright
> Candidates of blissefull Light,
> The HEIRS Elect of Loue; whose Names belong
> Vnto The euerlasting life of Song;
> All ye wise SOVLES, who in the wealthy Brest
> Of This vnbounded NAME build your warm Nest. (ll.6–12)

The passage images the beatitude of the Church Triumphant,
and represents it as the immaculate, incandescent (ll.7–8) existence of the Many in the One, of "Names" (l.9) in the
"vnbounded NAME" (l.12) of the Word made flesh; that
blessedness is indicated to be sacred human love's fulfilment in
the ineffable (at least, here – for the name of Jesus remains
unuttered throughout the *Hymn* – cf. l.2), all-encompassing
(l.12) Holy Name, whose primal love (ll.7–9) has gathered
those who are now the "holy Doues" (l.6) – wise in their love
of the Name (l.11) – into "The euerlasting life of Song" (l.10).
In thus closing the introduction to the *Hymn*, the passage
amplifies and extends the interpretation of the Name implied
in the poem's opening lines, thereby concluding their analysis
of sacred love. Many ideas and images in that analysis pervade
Crashaw's religious verse. As can be seen recurrently in his
poems, but most notably in those to or about women, he
implies that Christ, having physically manifested God's love in
the world and having redemptively shaped history, embodies
primal love that encompasses all human experience; just so,
Crashaw again and again depicts heavenly beatitude, or anticipatory sensation of it, as spiritual union with Christ, the
ecstasy of that oneness often being suggested through images
of incandescence or of musical harmony. He centres his studies
of love, that is to say, on Christ as the embodiment of total life,
at once the divine source of sacred love (insofar as he directly
expresses God's saving love for mankind), the focus of sacred
human love, and its final goal.

The Christocentrism of Crashaw's religious verse is also indicated in the immediately following sections of the *Hymn* (ll.13–114), wherein the speaker proceeds from contemplation of the Holy Name to reflection on himself and then to evocation of universal harmonies. There the speaker in effect explains the hesitancy that he revealed in the poem's introduction, for he asks whether the "fair WORD" (l.14), "SOVL" (l.13), could be applied to his spirit in the poverty of its self-centredness (ll.19–23), implicitly contrasting his spiritual state with the rich Christ-centredness of the blessed "Names" – see ll.9–12), and he wonders how as "empty" (l.21) a creature as himself, to whom the term for spiritual identity may not have applicability, can become sufficient to celebration (and invocation) of the Name which signifies Being and embraces all things. His need of spiritual sufficiency impels him subsequently to summon the musical harmonies of nature, art, and heaven to join with him in concordant celebration of the Name to which all true love is directed:

> Come, nere to part,
> NATVRE & ART!
> Come; & come strong,
> To the conspiracy of our Spatious song.
>   Bring All the Powres of Praise
> Your Prouinces of well-vnited WORLDS can raise;
> Bring All your LVTES & HARPS of HEAVN & EARTH;
> What e're cooperates to The common mirthe
>   Vessells of vocall Ioyes,
> Or You, more noble Architects of Intellectuall Noise,
> Cymballs of Heau'n, or Humane sphears,
> Solliciters of SOVLES or EARES;
>   And when you'are come, with All
> That you can bring or we can call;
>   O may you fix
>   For euer here, & mix
>   Your selues into the long
> And euerlasting series of a deathlesse SONG;
> Mix All your many WORLDS, Aboue,
> And loose them into ONE of Loue. (ll.68–87)

In seeking sufficiency to praise the "Rich WORD" (l.95), that is, the Name of the incarnate Logos, he aptly evokes a universal symphony, *concordia discors*. But his doing that is not what justifies him as the poet of the Name which is at once his theme and his muse. Rather, he finds himself justified in his role because the "WORD" generates and subsumes all words that are in its service:

> Powres of my Soul, be Proud!
>   And speake lowd
> To all the dear-bought Nations This Redeeming Name,
> And in the wealth of one Rich WORD proclaim
> New Similes to Nature. (ll.92–96)

Moreover, he knows that the "WORD" lovingly condescends to accept the words directed to it in love by even the lowliest creature:

> Our Murmurs haue their Musick too,
> Ye mighty ORBES, as well as you,
>   Nor yeilds the Noblest nest
> Of warbling SERAPHIM to the eares of Loue,
> A choicer Lesson then the ioyfull BREST
>   Of a poor panting Turtle-Doue.
> And we, low Wormes haue leaue to doe
> The Same bright Busynes (ye Third HEAVENS) with you.
> (ll.103–110)

The speaker's quest for, and finding of, justification of his poetic role suggests that fallen humanity and its words can act in the divine service because both are empowered and made acceptable by the Word. Throughout Crashaw's religious poems his speakers insistently allude to Christ's making sufficient those who want to serve him but are weak, or unworthy as well as weak (representative instances, and ones interestingly comparable to the instance in this poem, occurring in the hymn to St Teresa, ll.1–80, and *The Weeper*, *passim*); they stress, furthermore, that Christ is the ultimate source of and the authority behind his servants' words (whether, for example, those words are in St Teresa's *Life* or in "*a little Prayer-book*"). It is indeed on the Word, not on the mediating figures and words of saints or of anyone else, that Crashaw's personae and their words are centred.

The speaker of the *Hymn*, having discerned his sufficiency to put words in the service of the Word, prays that the Holy Name descend from the Church Triumphant and manifest itself within the members of the Church Militant. In praying for (ll.115–150) and in witnessing (ll.151–196) the descent of the Name, he resplendently affirms and develops his initial perception of it as the source, focus, and goal of sacred love. When the speaker invokes the Name he requests, in effect, a pacific Second Coming:

> Come, louely NAME! Appeare from forth the Bright
>   Regions of peacefull Light
> Look from thine own Illustrious Home,
> Fair KING of NAMES, & come.
> Leaue All thy natiue Glories in their Gorgeous Nest,
> And giue thy Self a while The gracious Guest
> Of humble Soules, that seek to find
>   The hidden Sweets
>   Which man's heart meets
> When Thou art Master of the Mind.
> Come, louely Name; life of our hope!
> Lo we hold our HEARTS wide ope! (ll.115–126)

Asking that the Holy Name express again the accommodating love revealed in the Incarnation (see ll.115–121, with their allusion to humility), the speaker elaborates upon his earlier perception of the Name as the divine source of sacred love. His prayer emphasizes too (most obviously in ll.121–126) that the Name is the focus of sacred human love, but more interesting seems to be his inversion – to stress that the Holy Name is sacred human love's goal – of the image of beatitude with which his song began (ll.6–12). Now he asks that the One dwell in the Many, the Name in its servants (the reverse being depicted in ll.11–12), and allow momentarily (l.120) the Church Militant to know that unitive experience which is the blessedness of the Church Triumphant. Sensuously vehement in its incandescence and its luxuriance, the speaker's invocation confronts the reader with a compelling representation of the Holy Name as the Alpha and Omega of sacred love.

If the speaker's invocation of the Name resplendently amplifies his initial interpretation of it, his witnessing of its descent
does so with even greater brilliance. When the Name appears,
he cries:

> Lo, where Aloft it comes! It comes, Among
> The Conduct of Adoring SPIRITS, that throng
> Like diligent Bees, And swarm about it.
>   O they are wise;
> And know what SWEETES are suck't from out it.
>   It is the Hiue,
>   By which they thriue,
> Where All their Hoard of Hony lyes. (ll.151–158)

The richly sensuous and astute image of the hive, an *audacia*
which accords with Gracián's idea of the first species of conceit, suggests the Name to be the soul's nourishment, delight,
and home (cf. ll.11–12): the total life of the soul.[4] Having
identified the Name as total life, the speaker then pictures it as
total love – again in luxuriantly sensuous imagery: "Lo where
it comes, vpon The snowy DOVE's / Soft Back; And brings a
Bosom big with Loues" (ll.159–160). Affirming and developing his earlier association of the Name with spiritual illumination, the speaker here declares, "WELCOME to our dark
world, Thou / Womb of Day!" and prays, "Vnfold thy fair
Conceptions" (ll.161–163). The Name of the incarnate Logos
is the radiant origin of spiritual light.[5] As the speaker subsequently implies, the Name is every Good: "O thou compacted
/ Body of Blessings: spirit of Soules extracted!" (ll.165–166).
Hence his initial depiction of beatitude as union with the Name
is also amplified, in fact receiving amplification upon amplification. Praying that the Church Militant may now know
something of the blessedness experienced by its triumphant
counterpart, he asks: "O dissipate thy spicy Powres / (Clowd
of condensed sweets) & break vpon vs / In balmy showrs; / O
fill our senses . . ." (ll.167–170). He goes on to celebrate union
with the Name not merely in such intensely sensuous terms
but by overgoing, and so indirectly repudiating as inadequate,
the ecstatically sensuous language of the *Song of Solomon*,
traditionally taken to be an allegory of the Spiritual Marriage:

SWEET NAME, in Thy each Syllable
A Thousand Blest ARABIAS dwell;
A Thousand Hills of Frankincense;
Mountains of myrrh, & Beds of spices,
And ten Thousand PARADISES
The soul that tasts thee takes from thence. (ll.183–188)

Only by casting his words beyond even the language of Scripture does the speaker seem to feel that he can indicate what it is
to have the all-encompassing Name in one's heart, and thus
paradoxically if truly to hold paradise within the self. Crashaw's other religious poems tell with similar vehemence of
union with Christ, and often they too show that sacred love
transforms not only the self and its perceptions (as in this poem
can be variously seen, for example, in ll.169–224 – especially in
ll.197–224, which startlingly illustrate the metamorphic "witt
of loue") but the inherited language of sacred discourse. Aptly
enough, the *Hymn* ends with the speaker wishing that those
who in latter times know oneness with the Holy Name would
imitate Christ's self-sacrificial love with the heroic zeal and
loyalty of the early Martyrs, who themselves were "All full of
[the Name]" (l.198) – and with his warning that to turn from
"Loue's mild Dictate" (l.236) and deny the Holy Name is
ultimately to lose oneself (ll.236–239).

The *Hymn* to the Holy Name, a major work from Crashaw's mature years as a writer, offers a comprehensive and
Christ-centred analysis of sacred love, one whose ideas are
basic (as has been suggested above and will be subsequently
argued in detail) to the thinking on sacred love throughout his
poems, whether written after the *Hymn* or before it. Even so,
whilst the analysis offered in the *Hymn* may be comprehensive, it does not quite completely express Crashaw's main ideas
on sacred love. To see his other essential ideas on that subject
one has to look at his poems connected with the Good Shepherd topos.

Crashaw's paraphrase of the twenty-third psalm, in contrast
to the *Hymn*, is an early and minor work; nonetheless, it does
add significantly to the view of sacred love implicit in that
poem.[6] "Psalme 23" forms a celebratory image of illuminative
experience (see, for example, ll.1–20), and at the heart of that

experience the persona locates Holy Communion (ll.49–54). The result of his doing so seems clear enough, for Crashaw thereby transforms the biblical original into the pastoral of a (representative) soul whose existence is centred upon the sacrificial love of Christ: the "pastures" (l.5) of the original become symbols of the flourishing spirituality nourished by the Eucharist (see ll.49–56, ll.62–70). The view of sacred love suggested by the poem is, then, virtually the same – in microcosm – as that offered by the *Hymn*, except for the addition of two concepts by Crashaw's linking of Communion with the Good Shepherd topos or, more properly, its Old Testament versiõn. Before emphasizing the importance of the Eucharist within illumination, Crashaw's persona says of God: "When my simple weaknesse strayes, / (Tangled in forbidden wayes) / Hee (my Shepheard) is my Guide . . ." (ll.21–23). He later says:

> Still my Shepheard, still my God
> Thou art with me, Still my rod,
> And thy staffe, whose influence
> Gives direction, gives defence.
> At the whisper of thy Word
> Crown'd abundance spreads my Bord:
> While I feast, my foes doe feed
> Their rank malice not their need,
> So that with the self-same bread
> They are starv'd, and I am fed.
> How my head in ointment swims!
> How my cup orelooks her Brims! (ll.45–56)

Through their mingling of Old Testament with New Testament symbols, the lines stress the central importance of Christ's sacrificial love both to human existence in general and in particular to the experience of illumination; in doing so, however, they also stress the immediacy of God the Father (as Shepherd, cf. ll.21–23) and the Son (by means of his spiritual presence at Communion, see ll.49–50) to individual human life, and that God the Shepherd is the protector of, as well as the provider for (in the person of Christ), the individual soul. "Psalme 23," in celebrating illumination rather than union, necessarily argues – as the *Hymn* cannot – the pervasively direct association of the soul with God in sacred love.

In his paraphrase of psalm 23 Crashaw of course identifies the Father as the Good Shepherd but nonetheless places the Son at the poem's centre: it is through the Son that the Father, as Shepherd, is shown to feed his flock. Crashaw more forcefully images God as the immediate protector of and provider for the individual soul, however, when he depicts the Son himself as the Good Shepherd. Christ appears in that guise in several of Crashaw's poems (for example, see "*Lavda Sion Salvatorem*. The Hymn for the BL. Sacrament," sts XIII–XIV; cf. "On the miracle of multiplyed loaves"), yet it could reasonably be suggested that the most forceful and the ultimate instance in which Crashaw presents Christ as the Good Shepherd can be seen in his paraphrase of "*Dies Irae*": "The Hymn of the Chvrch, in Meditation of the Day of Ivdgment." That poem has been criticized because, as the claim runs, Crashaw brings into it both more concern for the individual soul than is apparent in the original and a tone of intimacy that the original lacks.[7] Neither part of the criticism could be denied, but one could reply that the things objected to are, in fact, basic to the poem's success, for "The Hymn of the Chvrch ..." is a subtle and ambitious paraphrase unfolding an eschatological vision in which sacred love is seen to transform the persona's perception of Christ, and hence "*Dies Irae*" and the biblical texts from which it comes.

As has been often remarked, though never closely considered, "The Hymn of the Chvrch ..." juxtaposes two images of the returned Christ. The first is an icon of Christ the Judge, an image which Crashaw makes far more forceful than that from which it derives in "*Dies Irae*." Following the original, and thus the Bible, he describes the Day of Judgment in terms of a trumpet blast, fire, a book, and the rising of the dead (sts 1–5). He gives those motifs an imaginative scope and vividness that they do not always have in their Latin source (compare, however, 3,1–2 of "*Dies Irae*" with 3,1–2 of the paraphrase). Yet it is not only their amplification that makes them affective, for Crashaw frequently represents the experience of beatitude in terms of musical harmony, of burning love, and thus here, in heightening the apocalyptic motifs of trumpet blast and corrosive fire he also strikingly (if necessarily) inverts motifs that elsewhere in his works suggest heavenly bliss. Through ampli-

fying the conventional detail of his original, Crashaw fore-
grounds his icon of Christ the Judge with a distinctness and, in
the main, an emotional emphasis greater than those given its
counterpart in "*Dies Irae*." Moreover, his icon of Christ is in
itself far more powerfully affective than that in the Latin hymn.
In fashioning the icon Crashaw uses a visual effect not present
in his original but drawn from Scripture (see *Revelation* 1,14
and 19,12): the "sharp Ray" (1,3), the "angry light" of Christ's
"eyes" (2,3). Christ the Judge appears as terrible, because
Crashaw portrays him as the Divine Intellect (the Logos)
penetrating and purging all things with the unendurable light
of his omniscient gaze (1,3–4 and 5,3–4).[8] Crashaw's presentation of Christ in judgment is, then, a remarkable recreation of
that in "*Dies Irae*."

The juxtaposed icon of Christ as Good Shepherd counters
the image of him as judge by indicating him to be the soul's
loving, attentive guardian, the Shepherd who will look to his
flock even at the end of all things when he is also fulfilling
another role and scrupulously weighing souls' good deeds
against their bad. Crashaw's persona prays to Christ:

> Dear, remember in that Day
> Who was the cause thou cams't this way.
> Thy sheep was stray'd; And thou wouldst be
> Euen lost thy self in seeking me. (8)

He adds:

> Though both my Prayres & teares combine,
> Both worthlesse are; For they are mine.
> But thou thy bounteous self still be;
> And show thou art, by saving me.

> O when thy last Frown shall proclaim
> The flocks of goates to folds of flame,
> And all thy lost sheep found shall be,
> Let come ye blessed then call me. (14–15)

Of importance here, however, are not only that the second
icon of Christ counters its predecessor, and that it does so by
implying a Christocentric view of sacred love, but also the way

in which the occurrence of that Good Shepherd icon has been managed in the poem, for Crashaw's strategy in making it appear tells one as much about the nature of sacred love in his verse as does its symbolic detail.

Crashaw's fashioning of two different images of Christ in his poem is an elaboration on a strategy of the original hymn. The speaker of *"Dies Irae"* prays to Christ the Judge: *"Rex tremendae maiestatis, / Qui salvandos salvas gratis, / Salva me fons pietatis"* (8). Then, using that latter trope as the basis for addressing Christ as a more accessibly human figure, he pleads: *"Recordare, Iesu pie / Quod sum causa tuae viae: / Ne me perdas illa die"* (9). Yet (and the ninth stanza of *"Dies Irae"* illustrates this point as well) Crashaw additionally derives from the Latin original his idea of giving "The Hymn of the Chvrch . . ." a tone of intimacy and a concern for the individual soul, an anxiety for the self – and it is through them that he introduces the Good Shepherd icon into his poem.[9] Crashaw structures his poem as a meditation offering from the start a dramatically individual response to the overwhelming phenomenon of the Apocalypse. His persona begins, "Hears't thou, my soul, what serious things / Both the Psalm and sybyll sings" (1,1–2), a note of urgent self-communion which makes the start of Crashaw's hymn different at once from that of *"Dies Irae."* After presenting the icon of Christ the Judge, his persona reflects:

> Ah then, poor soul, what wilt thou say?
> And to what Patron chuse to pray?
> When starres themselues shall stagger; and
> The most firm foot no more then stand. (6)

The persona's self-concern, then, implicitly pervades the hymn's initial image of Christ, and also explicitly frames it in his communings with his own soul. In the latter part of the hymn, however, whilst his self-concern remains pervasive and whilst intimacy of tone is still an intrinsic quality to his speech, both have revealingly altered.

Having asked his soul as to "what Patron" it will "chuse to pray" (6,2) when it is on the verge of meeting with judgment,

the persona subsequently addresses the very figure who will be
the apocalyptic judge and says:

> But thou giu'st leaue (dread Lord) that we
> Take shelter from thy self, in thee;
> And with the wings of thine own doue
> Fly to thy scepter of soft loue. (7)

The lines suggest that the persona, who has been anxiously
anticipating his need for an ultimate defender (see, in the sixth
stanza, his play on the biblical topos of "standing"), now
remembers with sudden relief the fact that his "dread Lord"
(l.1) is simultaneously his Redeemer (ll.1–4, especially l.4). To
put the point another way, the persona's anxious self-communing on the Apocalypse confronts him with the recollection
of Christ as sacred love's divine origin, and hence with the
paradox that Christ the Judge is simultaneously his refuge
from judgment: his self-concern and self-communion evoke
his remembrance of Christ's redemptive love, that remembrance and the sacred love in turn evoked by it (7,3ff.) then
transform his perception of Christ, enabling him to see Christ
the Judge as also, at the same time, the Good Shepherd (sts 8–
16), and in the whole process his self-concern and self-communion are themselves changed, for the first becomes a mingling
of fear with hope, and the second is transformed into intimate
colloquy with the embodiment of that hope.[10] But Crashaw's
hymn indicates that the metamorphic power of sacred love
does not effect only those transformations, for in manifesting
them the text necessarily expresses others. By presenting the
argument that, on the Day of Wrath, Christ the Judge will yet
be the Good Shepherd, the hymn forms a radical rewriting of
its original, a canonical text of the early Church. It therefore
implicitly becomes a rewriting of a greater canonical text: the
biblical account of the Apocalypse (on which of course it
directly draws in stanzas 1, 2, and 5). Through astute direction
of his persona's anxious self-communing, Crashaw fashions
his hymn as a spectacularly comprehensive affirmation of
sacred love's metamorphic power, and as affirmation indeed of
the idea that "Loue [is the] Absolute sole lord / Of LIFE &
DEATH."

The two hymns and the paraphrase of psalm 23 suggest a Christ-centred vision of sacred love that is variously restated or alluded to throughout Crashaw's religious verse. Before different forms of, or references to, that vision are considered, however, something should be said of what the three poems reveal also about the spirituality of Crashaw's writing – the more so because the paraphrase is an early and minor work, whereas the hymns are later works and undeniably major ones. Moreover, the paraphrase pre-dates (apparently by quite some time) Crashaw's conversion, whilst the hymns seem almost certainly to have been written after he became a Catholic.[11]

The paraphrase and the hymn on the Holy Name image spiritual states, of illumination and of union, that are depicted frequently in Crashaw's religious verse; some of his most famous poems celebrate the states themselves and the spirituality able to achieve them. The natures of those states, as represented here and generally by Crashaw, can perhaps best and most concisely be indicated by quotations from authors for whom he had from quite early on, or came to have, a special fondness. The paraphrase of psalm 23 images the experience of illumination.[12] St Teresa, in her autobiography, describes an aspect of illumination as follows: "This quiet and recollected-ness in the soul makes itself felt largely through the satisfaction and peace which it brings to it, together with a very great joy and repose of the faculties and a most sweet delight."[13] Not all that she says immediately before or after those words could be applied to Crashaw's imaging of illumination in his para-phrase; nonetheless, her words seem well to express the spiri-tual temper of his poem, and thus to imply that Crashaw's religious verse, even when not aspiring to depict the heights of mystical experience, can yet have an affinity with her spiritu-ality (although *here* that affinity may be accidental).[14] By contrast to his version of psalm 23, Crashaw's hymn on the Holy Name images unitive as well as illuminative experience. The nature of the latter, as it appears there and in other of his poems, can be indicated by two quotations from St Francis de Sales.[15] In his *Introduction to the Devout Life* the saint writes:

[T]hose who love God can never stop thinking about him, longing for him, aspiring to him, and speaking about him. If it were possible, they would engrave the holy, sacred name of Jesus on the breasts of all mankind. All things call them to this and there is no creature that does not proclaim the praises of their Beloved. As St. Augustine, following St. Anthony, says, all things in this world speak to them in a silent but intelligible language in behalf of their love. All things arouse them to good thoughts, and they in turn give birth to many flights and aspirations to God.[16]

In a letter to the Baronne de Chantal he writes:

I am so hard pressed that the only thing I have time to write to you is the great word of our salvation: JESUS. O, my daughter, if we could only for once really say this sacred name from our heart! What sweet balm would spread to all the powers of our spirit! How happy we should be, my daughter, to have only Jesus in our understanding, Jesus in our memory, Jesus in our will, Jesus in our imagination! Jesus would be everywhere in us, and we should be all in him. Let us try this, my very dear daughter; let us say this holy name often as best we can. And even if at present we can only say it haltingly, in the end we shall be able to say it as we should. But how are we to say this sacred name well? For you ask me to speak plainly to you. Alas, my daughter, I do not know; all I know is if we are to say it well our tongue must be on fire, that is, we must be saying it moved only by divine love which alone is capable of expressing Jesus in our lives and of imprinting him in the depths of our heart. But courage, my daughter, surely we will love God, for he loves us. Be happy about this and do not let your soul be troubled by anything whatever.

 I am, my dear daughter, I am in this same Jesus, most absolutely yours ...[17]

Whilst the paraphrase suggests, then, illuminative tranquility, the hymn on the Holy Name suggests a fervent illumination looking toward unitive ecstasy – those seeming to be the most recurrently imaged aspects of that level of mystical experience in Crashaw's verse.

 Reference to the same Counter-Reformation saints helps to elucidate the nature of unitive experience as it is depicted in the hymn and elsewhere by Crashaw. In the letter from St Francis de Sales which was just cited, the saint describes unitive experience in these passionate terms: "O, my daughter, if we could only for once really say this sacred name from our heart! What sweet balm would spread to all the powers of our spirit! How happy we should be, my daughter, to have only Jesus in our understanding, Jesus in our memory, Jesus in our will, Jesus in our imagination! Jesus would be everywhere in us, and we should be all in him." St Francis' ardent, exclamatory and, at one point, richly sensuous description of utter unity with Christ concisely (if not of course completely) characterizes the desire for unitive experience that pervades the climax of the hymn (ll.159–196; cf. ll.120–126). But another form or phase of unitive experience is pictured in the conclusion to the hymn (ll.197–239), and its nature is indicated by St Teresa's account of "Divine union": "The soul that has experienced ... union ... is left so full of courage that it would be greatly comforted if at that moment, for God's sake, it could be hacked to pieces. It is then that it makes heroic resolutions and promises, that its desires become full of vigour ..."[18] Using terms similar to Crashaw's yet more comprehensive than his (for his are historically specific), St Teresa makes explicit what he chooses rather to imply: that union is a source of transcendently heroic virtue.[19] As the hymn represents unitive experience, so Crashaw's other poems depict it.[20]

Whilst those poems reveal much about the spiritual states predominantly imaged by Crashaw, they – and the *Hymn of the Chvrch* – also imply that the spiritualities of his personae who undergo mystical experience, or who, at the least, are shown as devout and questing for beatitude, are not necessarily unproblematic. Furthermore, they imply that forming a clear view of the degrees to which Crashaw's poems deliberately suggest flaws or difficulties in the spiritualities of his personae can itself be far from easy. In the paraphrase of psalm 23 (to start with that early work) his persona says to God the Father, at the poem's climax:

> At the whisper of thy Word
> Crown'd abundance spreads my Bord:
> While I feast, my foes doe feed
> Their rank malice not their need,
> So that with the self-same bread
> They are starv'd, and I am fed.
> How my head in ointment swims!
> How my cup orelooks her Brims! (ll.49–56)

Echoes of the biblical original are distinct here (notably in ll.50–51 and ll.55–56) and, as regards Communion, the passage seems theologically orthodox. The problem is, though, that the persona's words can be read with equal plausibility as expressing assured faith, illuminative calm that verges on ecstasy, or as manifesting a sense of triumph, of dismissive complacency. The original rightly celebrates, in the contexts of Davidic story and of Old Testament values generally, triumph over enemies; and such a note can be heard repeatedly, on the basis of such precedents and values, in Reformation and Counter-Reformation controversial literature.[21] For all that, the climactic lines of Crashaw's paraphrase concern taking Communion: being in charity with one's (erstwhile) enemies was, when Crashaw wrote – as it is now – a doctrinal prerequisite for participation in Communion, and Crashaw's persona can quite reasonably be perceived as uncharitable in his description of his enemies' lack of charity, of the "rank malice" (l.52) which vitiates their participation in Communion and leaves them "starv'd" while he is "fed" (l.54).[22] There seems to be nothing in the paraphrase that prepares the reader for the ambiguous spirituality at its climax, nor does anything in or after the climactic lines themselves seem to signal that the persona is being deliberately revealed as a problematic figure. As a result, if the paraphrase does not raise doubts about the nature of illumination, it certainly raises doubts about Crashaw's imaging of that state.

The hymn on the Holy Name also has a persona whose mystical experience is, to an extent, curiously problematic; as is the case with the paraphrase, one cannot *know* whether or not Crashaw deliberately portrayed his persona's mystical experience so that it would reveal Christian paradoxes of unusual kinds. The title of Crashaw's poem openly announces it to be a hymn in honour of *the Name of* Iesvs. The poem's author proclaims, then, that *Name above Every Name* which the poem's persona does not utter.[23] At the outset, the persona declares, "I sing the Name which None can say / But touch't with An interiour Ray..." (ll.1–2), and thereafter he alludes to the Holy Name yet never speaks it. Having made that initial declaration he goes on (as has been discussed in detail above) to seek virtually universal aid, that he might overcome his unworthiness to celebrate the Name and subsequently both to celebrate the Name and to request its presence on earth – that request being answered. In other words, the persona who at first sees himself as unworthy even to say the Name later comes to recognize that he may not only celebrate it – and, in fact, "speake lowd / To All the dear-bought Nations This Redeeming Name" (ll.93–94) – but invoke its descent from heaven, though of course he still does not say the Name. The first paradox, that of the author's proclaiming the Name which his devout and spiritually enabled (see ll.44–153) persona does not utter, could perhaps be explained as the expression of a distinction between writing and speech: the author feels able to pen what his persona, apparently from humility, cannot allow himself actually to say, speaking the Name being given by Crashaw implicit pre-eminence over writing it. If that explanation were correct, such a distinction would itself nonetheless involve theological difficulties, and if one were to propose that the incongruity rather expresses a contrast between unconscious authorial self-assertion and the persona's humility, then the paradox would merely take on another aspect. In either case, moreover, the persona's humble reticence would remain problematic when related to his clear recognition of his spiritual enablement. That second paradox is the more important of the two. Crashaw's persona is obviously not unable to speak the Holy Name (compare ll.1–2 with ll.93–94, and l.118 with 1 *Corinthians* 12,3); his revelation of spiritual enablement (ll.93–94 are especially relevant here) makes his devout refusal to speak the Name seem a graceful, if not quite intelligible, act of adoration. The persona's reticence should possibly be seen as suggesting that to become a servant of the Name is to devote oneself to that which is holy beyond human expression – which would make his reticence appear no less problematic. It may be that one should see the persona's refusal to say the Name as an act of adoration at once decorous and beyond questions of logical consistency. Whatever conclusions are drawn about its function in the hymn, the persona's humble avoidance of speaking the Holy Name implies that the representation of his spirituality by Crashaw is not simply harmonious.

Unlike the other two poems, "The Hymn of the Chvrch"

has a persona whose paradoxicality of spirit is, beyond doubt, deliberately fashioned by Crashaw and designed to be representative rather than merely specific (for Crashaw elaborates upon the image of a communal spirituality in the liturgical source of his poem). His persona knows both fear and hope: fear cannot overcome his hope, yet neither can his hope cease to be troubled. Crashaw creates his persona, that is to say, as an affective image of spiritual self-division, but of a self-division in which another element – faith – finally predominates (that being the case also in "*Dies Irae*") and makes the persona's paradoxical spirituality fruitful:

> O hear a suppliant heart; all crush't
> And crumbled into contrite dust.
> My hope, my fear! my Iudge, my Freind!
> Take charge of me, & of my END. (st. 17)

Unable, of course, to resolve the contradictoriness that he experiences (as the *chiasmus* of 17,3 suggests), the persona brings at the last his hope and fear openly before Christ, acknowledging that they are in fact hope in and fear of Christ – and as he does so he resigns himself utterly to Christ's will, in faith which rises above (without escaping from) his spiritual conflict.[24]

In Crashaw's poems on Christ, as the two hymns and the paraphrase imply, can be seen a comprehensive vision of sacred love and varieties of illuminative, as well as of unitive, experience. It has been suggested above that what those poems reveal of sacred love and of mystical experience is elemental to Crashaw's other religious verse. To confirm that, one need turn only to his poems on (usually triumphant) female spirituality: there one sees his ideas on sacred love and on the mystical ways informing, or indicated by, works which are among his best and best known.

Poems on the Virgin

Most of the attention given to Crashaw's poems on female spirituality has been focused on those about St Teresa or St Mary Magdalen. His poems about the Virgin have not been ignored, but they seem to have been regarded as inferior to, or at the least, as less challenging than the Teresa poems and *The Weeper*. Individually the poems on the Virgin are probably not the equals of *A Hymn to ... Sainte Teresa* or *The Weeper*; however, "In the Gloriovs Assvmption of Ovr Blessed Lady. The Hymn" is certainly one of Crashaw's major works and, moreover, the poems on Christ's mother are important within the Crashaw canon because of their diversity: they interpret with ingenious variety the Virgin's relation to the Godhead, and so her receiving and manifesting of sacred love.

A useful place to begin suggesting how astutely Crashaw can image the Virgin is "Luke 2. *Quaerit Jesum suum Maria.*" The source of the poem is of course St Luke's brief account of the Christ child's separation from his parents after the Holy Family had celebrated the Passover in Jerusalem. The gospel story from which Crashaw develops his poem has to do with the Christ child's revelation of himself as Logos and Son of God, with his parents' anxiety at his separation from them, and with their incomprehension of his self-revelation (*Luke* 2,41–51). Here Crashaw omits reference to St Joseph and concentrates on the relationship between mother and child, the result being a study of the Virgin as mother of God which simultaneously and indirectly is a study of Christ.

Throughout the poem, Mary laments the immensity of her loss; in doing so she describes herself and, necessarily, Christ. To consider first Crashaw's representation of what the Christ child means (in general terms) to the Virgin – and, by implication, to mankind – makes it easier for one to appreciate Crashaw's representation of the grieving Virgin herself. All that Mary says of her son accords with what other personae suggest of him in the poems which Crashaw directly focuses on Christ; for example, she calls the Christ child her "soules sweet rest" (l.6), and the focus of her "joy" (l.3, ll.8–11, and *passim*). A more important instance than those, however, occurs when she says:

Oft haue I wrapt thy slumbers in soft aires,
    And stroak't thy cares.
Oft hath this hand those silken casements kept,

While their sunnes slept.
Oft haue my hungry kisses made thine eyes
Too early rise.

Dawne then to me, thou morne of mine owne day,
And lett heauen stay. (ll.31–36, ll.45–46).

There the Virgin climactically reveals why the Christ child's loss causes her so much grief (cf. ll.9–18). He is, she effectually suggests, at once her son and the sun of her life (her words remind the reader of Christ's being the Sun of Righteousness): her description of the Christ child indicates him to be the centre of her life and the power that sustains as well as illuminates it (see ll.17–18, and l.48 – where she calls him her "bosome God"). Her description of her son/sun affirms the idea, evident in the poems on Christ which were discussed above, that he is total life (cf. ll.41–42).

To have looked initially at the poem's images of Christ reveals how comprehensive the Virgin's sense of loss is, and thereupon one can more readily perceive what that sense of loss reveals of the Virgin herself. Those lines in which the Virgin implies that Christ is the focal point of her universe suggest that, in losing her son/sun, she has not only lost her "joy" (l.3, l.8, and *passim*) but has herself become displaced: the sustaining principle of order in her life has gone; she has lost her telos (cf. "My soules sweet rest," "My bosome God"). Hence in expressing her loss the poem pervasively expresses her confusion. More important, though, those lines cited above also suggest the Virgin's incomprehension of the Christ child, and that too pervades the poem's telling of her loss. In the Lucan narrative, Mary and Joseph fail to understand the boy Jesus' explanation of his disappearance ("How is it that you sought me? Did you not know that I must be in my Father's house?").[25] In "Luke 2. *Quaerit Jesum* ..." Crashaw indicates instead Mary's incomprehension of who and what her son actually is. She knows him to be her delight, the vital centre of her being, and her God – knowledge gained experientially or from divine revelation; however, she seems to have no real idea of why her son cannot be entirely hers, of his role on earth (which his separation from her, to teach in the Temple, foretells):

> Oh, would'st thou heere still fixe thy faire abode,
>> My bosome God:
> What hinders, but my bosome still might be
>> Thy heauen to thee? (ll.47–50)

Thus whilst the loss of her son evokes intense grief, it also evokes loss of self, confusion – and reveals the necessary failure of her reason to understand Christ.

That failure is amplified by the poem's approximation to the form of a deliberative oration. The opening couplets act as an introduction or *exordium* (ll.1–4), and then the poem continues as if with *narratio* (ll.5–14), *aversio/obsecratio* (ll.15–18), *confutatio* (ll.19–24), *confirmatio* (ll.25–44), *obsecratio/conclusio* (ll.45–50). Whether or not that deliberative pattern was consciously imposed by Crashaw, the point is that his poem unfolds as a carefully organized argument and, in doing so, does not lead to resolution of the Virgin's incomprehension (see ll.46–50), but rather, by the very fact of its lucid, reasonable, powerless unfolding, emphasizes the Virgin's inability to understand her son through reason (Mary will find him when he is manifesting himself in the Temple as Logos). Highlighting individual rationality's limitations in dealing with Christ, the poem suggests indirectly the failure of all human reason to understand him. Yet the poem's stress on Mary's incomprehension has a function more direct than that: it emphasizes her capacity to love. It seems that in amplifying Mary's incomprehension, Crashaw's poem also amplifies the importance of her total, loving devotion to Christ. Reason being depreciated, love is given distinct primacy in her relationship with her son, and thus Crashaw represents her as typifying the soul truly focused on Christ – the soul utterly and lovingly centred on him as its God, whose ability to apprehend him rationally matters far less than its capacity for devotion to him – and as the type of maternal love.

If "Luke 2. *Quaerit Jesum suum Maria*" celebrates the Virgin by imaging her as a figure in whom sacred love far

transcends human reason, *Sancta Maria Dolorvm* honours her
in a complementary way. Whereas the former poem cunningly
plays reason against sacred love, the latter implies that the
Virgin's love for her son transcends notions of ideal secular
love. In the third stanza of *Sancta Maria Dolorvm*, Crashaw's
persona says wittily:

> O costly intercourse
> Of deaths, & worse,
> Diuided loues. While son & mother
> Discourse alternate wounds to one another;
> Quick deaths that grow
> And gather, as they come & goe:
> His Nailes write swords in her, which soon her heart
> Payes back, with more then their own smart;
> Her SWORDS, still growing with his pain,
> Turn SPEARES, & straight come home again.

There, as in the poem looked at a moment ago, the Virgin is
pictured grieving for her son – but the differences between the
images of her are immense. In "Luke 2. *Quaerit Jesum* ..." she
appears as the imperfectly comprehending mother of the
Christ child, grief-stricken by (temporary) loss of him; in this
poem, she is shown grieving as her son dies on the cross, and
paradoxically to be at one with him throughout the time she is
losing him. The second of those images is certainly the more
sophisticated (which is not to say that the first is unsophisticated), and that can be seen immediately in the lines quoted
above. There Crashaw's persona suggests the unity of mother
and son by allusion to prophecies about them – Simeon's of the
Virgin (*Luke* 2,35) and Christ's of himself (as in *Luke* 9,22) –
which the Crucifixion both fulfils and reveals to have been
interwoven, but he uses Simeon's symbol of the sword (l.9) and
the accoutrements of the Crucifixion (l.7, l.10) to imply that,
during the Crucifixion, the Virgin and Christ are connected
not merely by the simultaneous fulfilment of prophecies.[26] In
declaring, "[S]on & mother / Discourse alternate wounds to
one another" (ll.3–4), then using the scriptural "Nailes" (l.7),
"SWORDS" (l.9), and "SPEARES" (l.10) to describe that process, Crashaw's persona implies that the Virgin and Christ,

though being separated by death, so love each other that they interchange pain and grief – and become virtually one in suffering. The concept that ideal secular love is the sharing of existences, but the achievement of emotional and intellectual oneness rather than of physical oneness, was often and variously formulated in the Renaissance.[27] Crashaw's persona indicates in this poem, however, that the Virgin's love for Christ transcends that secular ideal. True, she and her son appear to be emotionally and almost physically at one during the Crucifixion, but it is that context of their oneness which of course makes all the difference. The Virgin is pictured as being, in effect, "crucified with Christ": Crashaw's meditative persona images her as enacting *Galatians* 2,20 (if not precisely in the Pauline sense) and so as going beyond the secular ideal of achieving unity in love, self-sacrificially achieving unity in sacred love with God himself. She sees "her life [that is, Christ] dy," and retains "only so much Breath / As serues to keep aliue her death" (4,8–10); she loses herself in him and becomes an archetype of Christocentric existence that Crashaw's persona wishes he could imitate (sts 5–11).

Far different from the icons of the grieving Virgin is the triumphant image of her in the haunting "In the Gloriovs Assvmption of Ovr Blessed Lady. The Hymn." That poem does not picture her as focused on Christ but as the spouse, the "syluer mate" (l.8), focused upon by the Holy Spirit, who now summons her to heaven. She is imaged as the "doue" (l.14) of the Holy Dove, called by him to her virtual apotheosis (cf. "O Mother turtle-doue!" in *Sancta Maria Dolorvm*, 5,1). In so depicting her, Crashaw's speaker presents her in accord with conventional exegesis of episodes in *The Song of Solomon*. The speaker imagines that he hears:

> Rise vp, my fair, my spottlesse one!
> The winter's past, the rain is gone.
>   The spring is come, the flowrs appear
> No sweets, but thou, are wanting here.
>   Come away, my loue!
>   Come away, my doue! cast off delay,
> The court of heau'n is come
> To wait vpon thee home; Come come away! (ll.9–16)

As those lines clearly imply, Crashaw interprets the Assumption as a celebration of Mary's unique role in the redemptive pattern of history (cf. l.41). Yet his poem may have something further to suggest. Near its end Crashaw's speaker says to the Virgin, "LIVE, rosy princesse, LIVE" (l.60). The words remind one of *"The Authors Motto"* in *Steps to the Temple*, "Live Jesus, Live, and let it bee / My life to dye, for love of thee," and that likeness seems to indicate a similarity – if by no means an equality – of importance to Crashaw between the Virgin and Christ.

To have examined Crashaw's poems on Christ and on the Virgin is to have studied a fair range of his religious verse, and so it would seem reasonable now to consider what those poems tell of his style. Most discussion of Crashaw's style in his religious verse has been concerned primarily with his links to the devotional literary traditions of the Counter-Reformation. That issue certainly has to be looked at here; however, a couple of remarks need to be made beforehand.

First, Crashaw's literary relations with the Counter-Reformation are diverse and cannot be restrictively described. Finally, since the Counter-Reformation does not provide the only stylistic models for his religious verse, the use that he makes of others – such as the medieval religious lyric and Herbert's poems – has to be considered too.

Perhaps the best way to begin is by considering Crashaw's youthful paraphrase of psalm 23 and then his later *"Charitas Nimia."* "Psalme 23" clearly indicates major continuities of style in Crashaw's sacred verse. There he interplays a Christian plainness – and the influence of his father – with some catachrestic, sensuous conceits (see, for example, ll.13–15) and moments of ecstatic exclamation (l.1, ll.55–56). Thus the poem suggests that (presumably) long before he became a Catholic, Crashaw had a marked interest in elements of style which were, as he could hardly not have known, prominent in Counter-Reformation writings.[28] The elaborate, vividly sensuous conceits and tendency to fervent exclamation which pervade his subsequent work can be seen initially in the paraphrase, whose plain style he would thereafter all but forsake and central tenets of whose eucharistic theology he would come to abandon. To glance at "Psalme 23," in other words, is to see at once that Crashaw's English religious verse had from the start affinities with Counter-Reformation artistry, and hence that its strengthening as well as broadening of those affinities expressed not only his movement toward Catholicism but the development in him of long-established aesthetic interests.

Turning from the paraphrase to "*Charitas Nimia*" affirms and complements what has just been argued. From the poem's very opening one hears the echo of a familiar voice:

> Lord, what is man? why should he coste thee
> So dear? what had his ruin lost thee?
> Lord what is man? that thou hast ouerbought
> So much a thing of nought?
>
> Loue is too kind, I see; & can
> Make but a simple merchant man.
> 'Twas for such sorry merchandise
> Bold Painters haue putt out his Eyes. (ll. 1–8)

The rhythms, imagery, and tone of the poem (especially in ll. 5–6) unmistakably bear the impress of Herbert; Crashaw carefully recreates his predecessor's mingling of Christian plainness with strong lines (in which dramatically plain speech is often, in any case, an element). Crashaw greatly admired Herbert's verse, the style of this poem and the title *Steps to the Temple* respectively expressing the specificity and the scope of his admiration.[29] Nonetheless, if Herbert's verse offered Crashaw models of style that he clearly found attractive throughout his literary career – as the publication date of "*Charitas Nimia*" suggests – those models seem to have strongly influenced almost none of his important poems; they were, moreover, increasingly supplanted in his favour by Counter-Reformation models of style, with which, in his early days as a poet, they had arguably held at least equal value.[30] To consider "*Charitas Nimia*" after "Psalme 23" is to be reminded that the limited influence of Herbert's poems on Crashaw's highlights simultaneously the closer relations between Crashaw's poems and Counter-Reformation writings, and the distance that Crashaw moved from contemporary Anglican poetic modes.

The flamboyance, the occasional strangeness, of those poems which express Crashaw's interest in Counter-Reformation artistry have frequently been noted, much attention having been given necessarily to his fashioning of conceits. The devout aspect of the baroque in Crashaw's verse, then, has indeed been studied, often innovatively and learnedly; even so, the variety and subtlety of his religious poems' baroque strategies – used to represent, for the most part, the diversity and the nuances of spiritual illumination or union, and of sacred love's transforming power – invite further discussion. Yet once more, "Psalme 23" seems the place to begin. In describing and celebrating the experience of illumination, Crashaw's speaker says:

> At my feet the blubb'ring Mountaine
> Weeping, melts into a Fountaine,
> Whose soft silver-sweating streames
> Make high Noone forget his beames.... (ll.13–16)

There, as sometimes elsewhere in the poem, the speaker images illumination in terms not merely pastoral, but luxuriantly pastoral.He does not, however, suggest only in doing so that sacred love (cf. ll.3–4) has radically transformed the conditions of his soul's existence. He traces an elaborately sensuous process of transformation (the mountain's metamorphosis into a fountain) to suggest sacred love's radical transformation of his illumined soul's perceptions. In accord with the poetic theory and practice of the Counter-Reformation, Crashaw fashions vividly physical and extreme conceits (*conformatio* and *audacia*) to make transcendent spiritual experience sensuously apprehensible – and to convey the wonder of it. It may be that the stylistic affinities of "Psalme 23" with Counter-Reformation poetry and poetics reflect the sensibility of the young Crashaw rather than his imitation of Counter-Reformation texts, but the affinities are there, and they foreshadow the sophistication with which, as well as basic functions for which, baroque strategies (that were certainly used quite deliberately) appear in his later poems.

Crashaw's more sophisticated and more ambitious use of those strategies can be seen in his hymn on the name of Jesus, in which can also be seen the resplendence of his baroque style at its most impressive. The poem does not, of course, reveal the full range of his achievement in the baroque; it does, however, show the greater sophistication, higher ambition, and resplendence with which he could use that style in connection with a central concern of his religious verse – spiritual union. When perceiving the descent of the Holy Name to the world, Crashaw's persona cries:

> Lo, where Aloft it comes! It comes, Among
> The Conduct of Adoring SPIRITS, that throng
> Like diligent Bees, And swarm about it.
> O they are wise;
> And know what SWEETES are suck't from out it.
> It is the Hiue,
> By which they thriue,
> Where All their Hoard of Hony lyes. (ll.151–158)

The lines celebrate the Name by identifying union with it as heaven's bliss. Their main strategy is the conceit, and their conceits function much as do those in lines 13–16 of "Psalme 23": they seek to make transcendent spiritual experience intelligible in sensuously affective terms (see especially l.155), and to communicate the marvellousness of it. In other words, although the conceits here are used to a more ambitious end than the ones considered above from "Psalme 23," they seem nonetheless to function similarly and thus to have no greater sophistication than the conceits of the earlier work. The only significant difference between them appears to be that whereas the mountain/fountain conceits of the paraphrase image sacred love's transforming of individual perception, the bees/hive conceits from the hymn act primarily as an Augustinian accommodation of the divine to the human (that is, of divine truth to the human mind). Yet if lines 151–158 of the hymn suggest continuities between the baroque strategies of that poem and those of the earlier paraphrase, a subsequent passage tends rather to emphasize discontinuities.

Describing what the earthbound soul will experience in union with the Name, Crashaw's speaker rhapsodizes:

SWEET NAME, in Thy each Syllable
A Thousand Blest ARABIAS dwell;
A Thousand Hills of Frankincense;
Mountains of myrrh, & Beds of spices,
And ten Thousand PARADISES
The soul that tasts thee takes from thence.
How many vnknown WORLDS there are
Of Comforts, which Thou hast in keeping! (ll.183–190)

Like the preceding passage, this one is dominated by sensuously affective conceits that seek to communicate the wonder of spiritual union. The main stylistic difference between the two would seem to be that here Crashaw fashions his conceits both to mediate the divine to the human – to impress something of the transcendent upon the human – and to intimate the tremendous strain placed on language in that role. In attempting to suggest experience of the infinite, of the Name of the Word, in human words, Crashaw's speaker gestures rather than depicts. His conceits imply the visual, yet defy visualization. Moreover, they indicate union with the Name to be the satiety of pleasure and complete felicity, yet call attention by their labouring extravagance to the fact that they can do no better than to indicate such ecstasy. Their extraordinary multiplication of the historically unique ("A Thousand Blest ARABIAS"; "ten Thousand PARADISES"), their use of the plurality of worlds motif (ll.189–190), and their multiplication of images from *The Song of Solomon* ("A Thousand Hills of Frankincense; / Mountains of myrrh, & Beds of spices") reveal Crashaw's speaker as striving necessarily to overgo the limits of language – the language of ordinary signification and also that of Scripture. (As is apparent, Crashaw's speaker expresses himself in hyperboles; Puttenham calls hyperbole the "Ouer reacher.") Those extravagant and luxuriant conceits reveal, that is to say, the inexpressibility topos as implicit in the speaker's attempt at representing unitive ecstasy. Implicitly connecting affective conceits with that topos is a strategy recurrent in Crashaw's developed baroque style, which means (among other things) that his Counter-Reformation artistry sometimes both represents the divine and indirectly acknowledges its own, as well as all human words', unavoidable failure to do so adequately.

The baroque strategies in that moment of the hymn on the Holy Name certainly aspire higher, are more resplendent, and are more subtle than those in "Psalme 23" or in lines 151–158 of the hymn itself. One could continue to examine the linking of the inexpressibility topos to the conceit in Crashaw's religious verse, for example in the hymn to St Teresa (ll.105–121), the ode on a prayer book (ll.76–86), the hymn in the Assumption (ll.64–69), and *The Weeper* (sts 6–14. Cf. "*Lavda Sion Salvatorem*," st. 1, and "The Hymn of Sainte Thomas ...," *passim*). More significant at this point, however, might be to consider how the strategies studied so far, and yet others, are used by Crashaw in relation to larger units of design – of which he draws on a range familiar in seventeenth-century religious verse.

The poems on Christ and on the Virgin that have been discussed above illustrate a variety of forms: most are hymns; some are both hymns and meditations; one is a biblical paraphrase; another is a complaint. Many reflect Crashaw's interest in the epigram. None, for all the applicability of those terms, can be contained in a simple generic description (nor, of course, do the poems instance quite all the forms employed in Crashaw's religious verse). Something of how Crashaw uses the conceit and the inexpressibility topos in relation to the meditation and the hymn has already been considered with regard to the hymn on the Holy Name. Relations between the conceit, the meditation, and revision of a canonical hymn have been looked at in discussion of "The Hymn of the Chvrch ..."; Crashaw's paraphrase of "Psalme 23" has been studied in much the same way. His astute interplay of the conceit, the inexpressibility topos, the hymn, and the meditation will be focused on later and anew in the contexts of the hymn to St Teresa and *The Weeper*. Here, though, one can further illustrate the rich diversity of Crashaw's baroque strategies and, in doing so, consider particularly how he seeks to use musicality in relation to a larger form, by returning to "Luke 2. *Quaerit Jesum*....."

One of that poem's most attractive strategies is the conceit. Sometimes delicately sensuous, sometimes passionately so, its conceits are always elegant. For example, consider:

Oft hath this hand those silken casements kept,
    While their sunnes slept. (ll.33–34)

Oft from this breast to thine my loue=tost heart
    Hath leapt, to part. (ll.39–40)

Dawne then to me, thou morne of mine owne day.... (l.45)

Perhaps the most interesting feature of those lines, however, is that they illustrate the subtlety with which Crashaw can connect the conceit and the emblem, connection of the two being a more recurrent strategy in his religious verse than the linking of the conceit to the inexpressibility topos. At some points in his religious verse Crashaw displays emblems directly, manifesting them in single or throughout several conceits (see, for an instance of the latter, *Sancta Maria Dolorvm*, XI,1–4 – as that passage also shows, he may add individual touches to such conventional images); at others, he rather alludes to emblems through one or more conceits. Here, through the conceit of the "sunnes" (l.34) and that of the "morne" (l.45), he does not directly present but cunningly alludes to the emblem of Christ as the Sun of Righteousness (cf. ll.35–36). His cunning lies partly in the fact that the figure of the grieving Virgin who utters those conceits, emphasizing her son's vital centrality to her existence, does not of course know that she is thereby obliquely identifying her son in profound, scriptural terms. Yet Crashaw's connection of the conceit and the emblem is more sophisticated than that. The conceit of the "sunnes" comes from the Petrarchan tradition; the "morne" conceit, too, has Petrarchan associations. Through images related to secular love verse, Crashaw at once communicates the sacred love of the Virgin for the Christ child and evokes a great emblem representing the majesty of Christ.

Although Crashaw's linking of the affective conceit and the emblem is one of the more important baroque strategies in his religious verse, and although he uses it at the climax of "Luke 2.

Quaerit Jesum ...," it apparently occurs only once, and is an indirect presence, in the poem. A strategy (other than that of the conceit itself) which both openly pervades the lyric and which Crashaw develops astutely from the start as an element of the lyric's design is the creation of musical effects. The suggestion was made earlier that "Luke 2. *Quaerit Jesum* ..." approximates to the form of a deliberative oration, and that it does so not to reveal the Virgin's lament for her son as coherently reasoned but to emphasize instead the failure of her reason to understand the Christ child. Against the unfolding failure of reason in the poem, Crashaw plays an elaborately patterned musicality, using the affective power of music to amplify the Virgin's expression of grief and to arouse the reader's sympathy with – to make the reader share in – her extreme emotion: to contribute, that is to say, to the poem's implicit privileging of sacred love over human rationality. The following lines well illustrate the poem's intricate harmony of repetitions and contrasts, its finely controlled modulation of cadence and of tone:

> And is he gone, whom these armes held but now?
>   Their hope, their vow?
> Did ever greife, & joy in one poore heart
>   Soe soone change part?
> Hee's gone. the fair'st flower, that e're bosome drest,
>   My soules sweet rest.
> My wombes chast pride is gone, my heau'en=borne boy;
>   And where is joy?
> Hee's gone. & his lou'd steppes to wait upon,
>   My joy is gone.
> My joyes, & hee are gone; my greife, & I
>   Alone must ly.
> Hee's gone. not leaving with me, till he come,
>   One smile at home.
> Oh come then. bring thy mother her lost joy:
>   Oh come, sweet boy.
> Make hast, & come, or e're my greife, & I
>   Make hast, & dy. (ll. 1–18)

Through the elaborate musicality of his verse, Crashaw in effect makes the Virgin's lament an aria at the same time as, by

other means, he virtually (and perhaps consciously) makes it a
deliberative oration. There indeed one sees what Pontanus
could have called "*compositissima oratio.*"

To consider even briefly the style of Crashaw's religious
verse is to recognize the subtlety, resplendence, frequent ambi-
tiousness, and diversity of his Counter-Reformation artistry,
and thus how well his artistry realizes many of the ideals of
style proposed by Pontanus and by Gracián.[31] If his style at
times reflects his admiration for Herbert, or suggests his interest in medieval religious poetry, Herbert's influence on his
important poems seems rare, and it is apparent that he tended
not only to imitate but to recreate those aspects or instances of
medieval religious verse that drew his pen to paper (as "Luke 2.
Quaerit Jesum ...," "The Hymn of the Chvrch ...," "The
Hymn of Sainte Thomas ...," and *Sancta Maria Dolorvm*
notably attest). What one recognizes, in other words, when
considering Crashaw's style in his religious verse is a mastery
of the baroque in its devout guise unequalled in England by
any other poet during the first half of the seventeenth century.

The hymn to St Teresa and The Weeper

Having examined the spirituality and the style of Crashaw's
poems on Christ and/or on the Virgin leads one to his other
poems on holy figures filled with sacred love, the outstanding
instances of which are the hymn to St Teresa and *The Weeper*.
Those poems are among Crashaw's finest and best known.
In them he studies more thoroughly than he does elsewhere in
his religious verse the effects of sacred love on the (merely)
human personality, and it is in them that some of his most
brilliant writing in the baroque appears. His often incandescent rhetoric seeks to image St Teresa and St Mary
Magdalen as exemplifying (on a lower level, of course, than
that of the Virgin, and Christ is necessarily a quite different
case) the human personality alight with sacred love and transformed by its almost unimaginable power. To read the poems
is to witness, as arguably nowhere else in Crashaw's works, his
wit of love.

Whilst each of Crashaw's three poems concerned with St
Teresa notably honours that saint, the greatest of them is

clearly *A Hymn to the Name and Honor of the Admirable Sainte Teresa* ..., a more complex and daring work than its companion pieces, and one which all but comprehends their achievements. As an essay in hagiography the hymn at once recounts, interprets, and celebrates St Teresa's life, yet the interest of the poem does not only lie in how Crashaw, wishing to glorify a favourite saint, edits and rewrites her autobiography. Interesting too, and more important (as was foreshadowed above), is how Crashaw, in retelling the saint's life, honours her by using it both to prove the centrality of sacred love to, and to study sacred love's mighty transformation of, the human personality.

Crashaw retells the life of St Teresa to fulfil those ends by presenting it in a hymn which has a deliberative design; that is to say, whereas in "Luke 2. *Quaerit Jesum* ..." he can reasonably be perceived as bringing together the lyric and a stylized argumentation, an aria and a version of the deliberative form, here he seems distinctly to unite the religious song of praise with, in the first place, a variant of the deliberative form (the most notable change to the form being that here, as in the Virgin's lament, *confutatio* precedes *confirmatio*). The poem begins with the resounding "Loue, thou art Absolute sole lord / Of LIFE & DEATH" (ll.1–2), *testamentum* acting as *propositio* by way of *exordium*, then "[t]o proue the word" (l.2) proceeds to *confutatio* (ll.2–14, containing some narrative elements), wherein evidence is sought not from the ranks of "Ripe Men of Martyrdom" (l.5) but from – initially – the example of the infant Teresa. Thereupon the poem proceeds to *confirmatio/narratio* (ll.15–180), offering three icons of the saint, and finishes with *acclamatio/conclusio* (ll.181–182). Constantly heightening the persuasiveness of the poem's deliberative form is an affective rhetoric which can be pathetic, wryly comic, forcefully sensuous, and dazzlingly resplendent.

If the proposition that opens the hymn is undeniably arresting, its exact meaning does not become clear until Crashaw's speaker says how he will not, and will, set about proving it:

Wee'l now appeal to none of all
Those thy old Souldiers, Great & tall,
Ripe Men of Martyrdom, that could reach down

With strong armes, their triumphant crown;
Such as could with lusty breath
Speak lowd into the face of death
Their Great LORD's glorious name, to none
Of those whose spatious Bosomes spread a throne
For LOVE at larg to fill: spare blood & sweat;
And see him take a priuate seat,
Making his mansion in the mild
And milky soul of a soft child. (ll.3–14)

The shrewd confutation uttered in those lines is no simple denial of one tactic of argumentation in favour of another. To begin with, there Crashaw's speaker reveals that the "Loue" which he has declared to be sovereign over "LIFE & DEATH" is in fact love for and – as his words also though less directly imply – by Christ (see ll.7–11). In having his speaker associate love, as the dominant principle of human experience, with Christ alone, Crashaw indicates the ultimate Christocentrism of human experience. Thus he indicates as well that if the hymn primarily glorifies St Teresa it ultimately glorifies Christ, since (as his speaker suggests toward the end of the confutation and pervasively thereafter) what made her so praiseworthy was her exemplary love for Christ, her virtually lifelong desire for spiritual union with him (the Spiritual Marriage), and his marvellous reciprocation of her love.

The confutation, then, although certainly a denial of one rhetorical tactic in favour of another, is more than just that, since it functions to orient the reader, at once defining the "Loue" of which the hymn treats and suggesting the true, the final focus of human existence in and beyond the world. But the actual rhetorical tactics in the confutation are not themselves insignificant. Crashaw's speaker may reject an appeal to any of the "old Souldiers" (l.4) of love as a way of proving his proposition, yet in doing so he implies what the highest form of male heroic virtue is in the Church Militant: victory over the world and death through complete self-negation for love of Christ. Moreover, in choosing to use St Teresa's infancy as his evidence, rather than to instance the adulthood of any of the Church's male heroes, the speaker also goes beyond the idea that love for Christ inspires the highest form of male heroism in the Church Militant, for he introduces the notion of love for Christ as able to inspire supreme heroic virtue in anyone, virtually regardless of his or her age, physical strength, and gender (see especially ll.11–14). With the choice of a female saint's infant heroism as his evidence, the speaker goes on to argue that sacred love has dominion over all human experience.

The speaker's argument does not, however, rely only on the story of the infant Teresa's quest for union with Christ through martyrdom.[32] He evinces that story as the first, but not sole proof of his proposition. In fact, to confirm it he narrates rather more of the saint's life, offering three icons of her: the one of her as infant heroine in search of spiritual union through physical martyrdom, one of her finding in adulthood intimations of spiritual union through spiritual martyrdom, and a last of her entering heaven and receiving eternal beatitude. Nor is love-inspired heroic virtue the only quality which he considers and celebrates in her doubly exemplary life.

The first icon, in picturing the heroic virtue inspired in the young Teresa by sacred love, implies that sacred love does indeed rule "LIFE & DEATH" as "Absolute sole lord." It shows that before she has long known temporal life (and even before she understands the connection between sacred love and martyrdom) love for Christ impels her to seek a death which will bring her to eternal life in him, to spiritual union with him: sacred love is indicated to have a sovereignty over life and death that is unique in its completeness. Crashaw's speaker describes the infant Teresa as follows:

> Scarse has she learn't to lisp the name
> Of Martyr.... (ll.15–16)

> Scarse has she Blood enough to make
> A guilty sword blush for her sake;
> Yet has she 'a HEART dares hope to proue
> How much lesse strong is DEATH then LOVE. (ll.25–28)

> LOVE touch't her HEART, & lo it beates
> High, & burnes with such braue heates;
> Such thirsts to dy, as dares drink vp,
> A thousand cold deaths in one cup.
> Good reason. For she breathes All fire.

Her weake brest heaues with strong desire
Of what she may with fruitles wishes
Seek for amongst her MOTHER's kisses. (ll.35–42; cf. ll.65–66)

  She'l to the Moores; And trade with them,
For this vnualued Diadem [of martyrdom].
She'l offer them her dearest Breath,
With CHRIST's Name in't, in change for death.
She'l bargain with them; & will giue
Them GOD; teach them how to liue
In him: or, if they this deny,
For him she'l teach them how to DY.
So shall she leaue amongst them sown
Her LORD's Blood; or at lest her own. (ll.47–56)

As those lines suggest, furthermore, the description of the infant heroine is heightened in its persuasiveness by the speaker's shrewd and affective use of contrasts. To emphasize the unique power of sacred love he amplifies the paradoxical nature of his evidence, gesturing toward the simultaneous presence in Teresa of sublime heroic resolve and pathetic, childish vulnerability (ll.25–28), of the most intense as well as extraordinary passion and childish innocence (ll.35–42), of naivete and astuteness (ll.47–56). A less obvious, but no less interesting, aspect of the icon is its implication that when sacred love inspires heroic virtue in Teresa it also confers wisdom on her. Stressing her necessary ignorance of theology, the speaker observes, "Scarse has she learn't to lisp the name / Of Martyr" (ll.15–16), and goes on to elaborate (ll.17–22). However, he then makes this point: "Yet though she cannot tell you why, / She can LOVE, & she can DY" (ll.23–24). Sacred love takes the child's barely educated mind beyond reason (l.23; cf. l.39), beyond prudence (*prudentia*), and gives it wisdom (*sapientia* – see l.24, ll.16–18, l.32, ll.47–56, ll.65–66).

The first icon's shrewdly affective presentation of Teresa as a love-impelled child would by itself well argue the speaker's case for sacred love's sovereignty over human experience. Nonetheless, he proceeds to affirm his case with an icon of her finding, in adulthood, something of spiritual union through spiritual martyrdom. The second icon of Teresa is introduced

by the speaker's sympathetic, but also wryly amused, address
to his image of the saintly child:

> SWEET, not so fast! lo thy fair Spouse
> Whom thou seekst with so swift vowes,
> Calls thee back, & bidds thee come
> T'embrace a milder MARTYRDOM. (ll.65–68)

According to the speaker, then, Teresa's childhood quest for
physical martyrdom merely prefigured her adult role (assigned
her by the Bridegroom whom she had been seeking) as a
martyr of the soul rather than of the flesh (see l.65 and l.76). In
the remainder of the introduction the speaker describes her
mystical death, her death in the soul, as being a form of
spiritual oneness with Christ (ll.79–87) and as making her a
counterpart to St Sebastian (ll.91–96).

Thereafter follows the memorable icon of St Teresa's passion. (In the second icon, as from l.74 of the introduction to its
end, the speaker's narration is, of course, in the future tense
since there, as before, he is announcing to his dramatic representation of the infant Teresa what her future holds – and so
offering the reader an analysis of the saint's history. In fact,
from l.65 of his work to its end Crashaw unites a *suasoria* with
the larger rhetorical pattern of the hymn to confirm its deliberative function, his speaker's feigned counselling of the infant
Teresa being intended at once to celebrate the canonized Teresa and for persuasion of the reader.)

> O how oft shalt thou complain
> Of a sweet & subtle PAIN.
> Of intolerable IOYES;
> Of a DEATH, in which who dyes
> Loues his death, and dyes again.
> And would for euer so be slain.
> And liues, & dyes; and knowes not why
> To liue, But that he thus may neuer leaue to DY.
>   How kindly will thy gentle HEART
> Kisse the sweetly-killing DART!
> And close in his embraces keep
> Those delicious Wounds, that weep
> Balsom to heal themselues with. (ll.97–109)

Through the intensely sensuous, paradoxical conceits which pervade the icon, and which are drawn at once from familiar passages in Teresa's autobiography and from Petrarchan love verse, the speaker implies that the saint's maturity was a complex restatement of sacred love's power: she is depicted, in her womanhood set apart for Christ (see ll.167–177), undergoing spiritual deaths wherein she receives partial foreknowledge of the ecstasy of the Spiritual Marriage (see l.106, ll.79–87, and the twenty-ninth chapter of her autobiography); the speaker images sacred love's mystical interplay within the adult Teresa of death in life and life in death.[33] Yet if the second icon thereby presents more elaborate evidence of the speaker's initial proposition than does the first, it does so in other ways as well. The first icon indicates sacred love's conferring of wisdom on Teresa in her mere infancy; here she is represented as once again being led by sacred love beyond rationality (see especially ll.100–104), to moments of experience that intimate spiritual union – the (necessarily limited) fulfilment of the wisdom given her when she was just "six yeares" old (l.29). Finally, whilst sacred love is shown in the first icon to have transformed the infant Teresa into a heroine in quest of physical martyrdom, here it is shown as transforming the adult Teresa into a figure repeatedly and blissfully passionate, filled both with deathly suffering and with ecstatic desire: into, as the introduction suggests, a St Sebastian of the spirit (cf. ll.91–96).

The second icon of the saint ends with an image of her bodily death, which is pictured as a physical transformation caused by the transformation of her soul. The speaker observes (continuing of course to narrate in the future tense):

> Thus
> When These thy DEATHS, so numerous,
> Shall all at last dy into one,
> And melt thy Soul's sweet mansion;
> Like a soft lump of incense, hasted
> By too hott a fire, & wasted
> Into perfuming clouds, so fast
> Shalt thou exhale to Heaun at last
> In a resolving SIGH.... (ll.109–117)

Then, by way of the inexpressibility topos (ll.118–121), the speaker turns from retelling Teresa's life, from rewriting her autobiography, to imagining her experience of eternal life, to completing her biography and so offering comprehensive proof of sacred love's unique lordship over life and death.

The third icon of Teresa images her apotheosis – her entry into heaven and inheritance of eternal beatitude. It is not hard to see why Crashaw has his speaker add this picture of the saint to the others, for the icon forms the poem's climactic evidence of love's sovereignty. The icon presents Teresa as elevated, because of her fervent love for Christ, beyond spiritual and physical death to eternal life in Christ, to consummation of the Spiritual Marriage. That is to say, the icon pictures Teresa's love-filled temporal life, and love-caused deaths, as having led her to immutable and perfect experience of sacred love.[34] The blessedness of heaven is shown to be sacred love alone, and sacred love alone is shown to have led Teresa to that blessedness. In the celebratory words of the speaker to the saint:

> O what delight, when reueal'd LIFE shall stand
> And teach thy lipps heau'n with his hand;
> On which thou now maist to thy wishes
> Heap vp thy consecrated kisses. (ll.129–132)

> Thou with the LAMB, thy lord, shalt goe;
> And whereso'ere he setts his white
> Stepps, walk with HIM.... (ll.178–180)

The image of Teresa's apotheosis depicts sacred love's ultimate transformation of her, and its fulfilment of the wisdom that it gave her when she was an infant.

Having fashioned that triumphant image of Teresa, the speaker concludes his argument with an indirect exhortation that the reader become as she in self-sacrificial and Christ-centred love. At the end of his deliberative song of praise the speaker finally honours Teresa by emphasizing the doubly exemplary nature of her life: "[W]ho in death would liue to see [the "wayes of light"], / Must learn in life to dy like [the saint]" (ll.181–182).

There is a moment in Crashaw's hymn where his speaker alludes to the "witt" (l.156) with which sacred love informed St

Teresa's "rare WORKES" (l.155); "loue is eloquence," says
the speaker of "An Apologie . . ." (l.8) – an idea affirmed in *The
Flaming Heart* . . . in connection with the "advice to a painter"
topos (ll.13–74). Even so, the hymn attests spectacularly to
Crashaw's own wit in treating of sacred love, whether or not he
might have seen love as that wit's source. His fusion of the
hymn, the deliberative oration, and the *suasoria* is, to begin
with, a stroke of wit: *concordia discors*. But the truly remarkable wit in his poem lies in his icons of Teresa. The incongrui-
ties of Teresa's infant heroism are pictured in emotive paradoxes that bring together sublimity and pathos, fiery passion
and delicacy – and in conceits whose daring befits depiction of
the daring child (ll.25–28, ll.35–42, and so on). The mystical
experiences of the adult Teresa (which Crashaw presents as the
quintessence of her adult life) are imaged in intensely sensuous,
cumulatively forceful conceits that unite the language of her
autobiography with parody of the paradoxes and sexual word-
play of Petrarchan love verse and that cunningly rise to a
parody of sexual climax. Her apotheosis is pictured incandes-
cently, in glittering images of the moon and the stars, of snow
and fire, of gems, bright scars, and the white steps of the Lamb,
and by paradoxes mingled with hyperbole. Crashaw's baroque
style, as seen in his hymn's icons of Teresa, has a brilliance
unusual even in *his* religious verse.

For a poem to rival the hymn's wit of love, one turns not to
Crashaw's other Teresan poems but to *The Weeper*, which also
rivals the hymn as a study of sacred love's power. Focused on
the weeping eyes of the repentant Magdalen, the poem begins:

I.
Hail, sister springs!
Parents of syluer-footed rills!
  Euer bubling things!
  Thawing crystall! snowy hills,
Still spending, neuer spent! I mean
Thy fair eyes, sweet MAGDALENE!

II.
  Heauens thy fair eyes be;
Heauens of euer-falling starres.
'Tis seed-time still with thee

And starres thou sow'st, whose haruest dares
Promise the earth to counter shine
Whateuer makes heaun's forhead fine.

III.
     But we'are deceiued all.
Starres indeed they are too true;
For they but seem to fall,
     As Heaun's other spangles doe.
It is not for our earth & vs
To shine in Things so pretious.

IV.
     Vpwards thou dost weep.
Heaun's bosome drinks the gentle stream.
Where th'milky riuers creep,
     Thine floates aboue; & is the cream.
Waters aboue th' Heauns, what they be
We' are taught best by thy TEARES & thee.

V.
     Euery morn from hence
A brisk Cherub somthing sippes
Whose sacred influence
     Addes sweetnes to his sweetest Lippes.
Then to his musick. And his song
Tasts of this Breakfast all day long.

Meditating on the eyes and tears of the love-transformed
Magdalen (see the poem's epigraph and eighteenth stanza), the
speaker evolves his meditation as a colloquy with her eyes,
with her directly, and with her tears (sts 28–31); within the
fictional frame of his colloquy, he presents a series of lesser
fictions to interpret the spiritual significances of her weeping
(he interprets that, of course, for the reader, but insofar as they
are addressed to the saint – or to aspects of her – his lesser
fictions form homage to her, the poem thus being a meditation
akin to the ode).[35] An especially revealing feature of the
speaker's meditation is that he quite deliberately lays bare its
lesser fictions (1,6; 3,1; 7,6 and so on), making plain to the saint
whom he (notionally) addresses, and thus to the reader, that he

is not in the process of representing her eyes and tears "realisti-
cally" but as insight rather than sight might perceive them. In
fact, the speaker's perceptions of her, as is evidenced by the
stanzas quoted above, indicate that she in her penitence is more
rich, more wonderful, than her humility – much less the
physical dimensions or properties of her weeping – would
apparently suggest. The speaker's laying bare of his meditation's lesser fictions, then, implies that in transforming Mary
Magdalen sacred love necessarily and radically transformed
perception of her. He defamiliarizes the Magdalen's penitence
– and thereby Crashaw compels the reader to consider it anew.

To make what has just been proposed more specific, one has
to discuss in some detail the lesser fictions that open the poem.
There are primarily two fictions at the poem's beginning. The
first occurs in stanza one, the second in stanzas two to five. In
the first, the speaker fashions an image of higher nature, of
nature as pure, uncontaminated and, in marvellous transcendence of fallen nature's laws, giving of itself without depletion
(see especially 1,4–5). Only after he has fashioned that image
does the speaker draw attention to it as a fiction describing
Mary Magdalen's weeping eyes: "I mean / Thy fair eyes, sweet
MAGDALENE!" (1,5–6). Revealing the image to be not just a
fiction, but one that Mary Magdalen herself, and so the reader,
might not make sense of, the speaker identifies its subject and
thus implies its function to be other than that of merely
physical description. The speaker goes on to present the
second fiction similarly, if more elaborately. There he again
fashions an image and draws attention to its fictionality; again
he carefully identifies its subject and, in so doing, implies that
he is not attempting physically true description (2,1–2; 3,1–3).
The image is, moreover, again one of higher nature, in which
the laws of fallen nature are seen to be transcended. However,
now the speaker compares Mary Magdalen's eyes and tears not
to earthly things, but to the heavens and the stars (2,1–2ff.) –
stars which fall upwards – her tears then being pictured by him
as the cream of the milky way, sipped by an angel. The image is
perhaps better said to be of *natura redempta* than of higher
nature.

If the two fictions scarcely suggest the physical appearances
of Mary Magdalen's eyes and tears, what they evoke instead is,

of course, their spiritual significances: they clearly function to offer spiritually true images of Mary Magdalen's weeping. Those images seem to represent the repentant Magdalen as "a new creation," and to complement each other in portraying her in accord with that Pauline topos. St Paul's words are: "Therefore, if any one is in Christ, he is a new creation; the old has passed away, behold, the new has come" (2 *Corinthians* 5,17 – cf. 5,16). The first image of Mary Magdalen emphasizes the purity of her contrition ("syluer-footed rills"; "Thawing crystall! snowy hills"), implying her repudiation of her past and her renovation. It also indicates her unfailing, always-renewing, spiritual energy ("Euer bubling things!"; "Still spending, neuer spent!"). That is to say, it suggests the uncontaminated richness, the marvels, born of her penitential self-abasement. The second image both complements and amplifies the first. There the speaker in effect depicts the apotheosis of Mary Magdalen's eyes and tears. The preceding image pictures them in earthly terms; now, they are presented respectively as new heavens and extraordinary stars: "Heauens thy fair eyes be; / Heauens of euer-falling starres" (2,1–2). Furthermore, Mary Magdalen's tears are pictured not merely as transcending natural law, by falling upwards, but as transcending the physical heavens and heightening worship in heaven (sts 4 and 5, *passim*). The apotheosis of her eyes and tears implies her contrition to have been, in fact, a sequence of increasingly wonderful marvels, and to have had a purity, a richness, finally beyond earthly comparisons: to be compared, indeed, not even with the purity and richness of stars in the physical heavens, but rather to be seen as able to delight an angel and to enhance his celebration of God (5,4–6).[36] In the opening of *The Weeper*, the speaker images Mary Magdalen's eyes and tears as a new cosmology in order to celebrate her contrition as having made her a totally "new creation," a virtually perfect one, and so to identify anew why she is an archetype of true repentance.[37]

The speaker then seeks to confirm his Pauline study of Mary Magdalen's contrition and her gift of tears by surveying the natural world and asserting the inferiority of its "tears" to hers. He puts forward a series of fictions (sts 6–14) that imply the lesser beauty and value of fallen nature's "tears" to those of her pure contrition – of nature perfected, as it were, by grace. For example, he says in stanza thirteen:

> Golden though he be,
> Golden Tagus murmures tho;
> Were his way by thee,
> Content & quiet he would goe.
> So much more rich would he esteem
> Thy syluer, then his golden stream.

Thereupon he dramatically and climactically restates his perception of her as having become a totally new creation through her exemplary repentance (sts 15–18). Parodying the paradoxes of Petrarchan love verse, he indicates that as a new cosmos she is, like the other cosmos, a *discordia concors*; at the same time, however, he also indicates that her harmonious discord transcends it insofar as sacred love alone informs and orders her, resolving opposites into smooth amity:

> XV.
> O cheeks! Bedds of chast loues
> By your own showres seasonably dash't
> Eyes! nests of milky doues
> In your own wells decently washt,
> O wit of loue! that thus could place
> Fountain & Garden in one face.

> XVI.
> O sweet Contest; of woes
> With loues, of teares with smiles disputing!
> O fair, & Freindly Foes,
> Each other kissing & confuting!
> While rain & sunshine, Cheekes & Eyes
> Close in kind contrarietyes.

> XVII.
> But can these fair Flouds be
> Freinds with the bosom fires that fill thee
> Can so great flames agree
> Æternall Teares should thus distill thee!
> O flouds, o fires! o suns ô showres!
> Mixt & made freinds by loue's sweet powres.

He emphasizes sacred love as the cause of those marvels and ends triumphantly with an allusion to that love's goal:

> XVIII.
>   Twas his well-pointed dart
> That digg'd these wells, & drest this Vine;
> And taught the wounded HEART
>   The way into these weeping Eyn.
> Vain loues auant! bold hands forbear!
> The lamb hath dipp't his white foot here.

The speaker's image of the Lamb's "white foot" cunningly takes one back to the images of purity with which he began.

Having considered what Mary Magdalen's contrition made her, the speaker now meditates upon what, as "a new creation," she did. He images her as impelled by the sacred love which inspired her contrition to put the spiritual riches born of it in Christ's service: he implies that having become a richly "new creation," *multum in parvo*, she subsequently expressed her devotion to Christ (cf. st. 18) by expending herself, her precious new existence, in self-sacrificial – or, at the very least, self-denying – adherence to him (sts 19–27). The speaker says, for instance:

> XIX.
>   And now where're he strayes,
> Among the Galilean mountaines,
> Or more vnwellcome wayes,
>   He's follow'd by two faithfull fountaines;
> Two walking baths; two weeping motions;
> Portable, & compendious oceans.

> XX.
>   O Thou, thy lord's fair store!
> In thy so rich & rare expenses,
> Euen when he show'd most poor,
>   He might prouoke the wealth of Princes.
> What Prince's wanton'st pride e're could
> Wash with Syluer, wipe with Gold.

> XXI.
>   Who is that King, but he

Who calls't his Crown to be call'd thine,
That thus can boast to be
Waited on by a wandring mine,
A voluntary mint, that strowes
Warm syluer shoures where're he goes!

XXII.
    O pretious Prodigall!
Fair spend-thrift of thy self! thy measure
(Mercilesse loue!) is all.
Euen to the last Pearle in thy treasure.
All places, Times, & obiects be
Thy teare's sweet opportunity.[38]

It is apt that he suggests her tears to have been the true measure of her life (26,5–6).

The speaker ends his imaging of Mary Magdalen's contrite service to Christ, and thus the poem, with a fiction in which her tears themselves tell of that service (sts 28–31). In response to the speaker's question, "Say, ye bright brothers, / ... What make you here? what hopes can tice / You to be born?" (28,1,4–5), her tears reply:

XXXI.
    Much lesse mean we to trace
The Fortune of inferior gemmes,
Preferr'd to some proud face
Or pertch't vpon fear'd Diadems.
Crown'd Heads are toyes. We goe to meet
A worthy object, our lord's FEET.

Through those words, Crashaw's speaker has the Magdalen's tears confirm that her contrite service to Christ was indeed the self-sacrificial love of "a new creation" for her creator (see l.2, ll.5–6), and indicate that her apparent self-abasement in restating her complete repentance was in fact her apotheosis (ll.5–6). The speaker's meditation ends, that is to say, with his having Mary Magdalen's very tears attest to his interpretation of her as an archetype of penitence.

Although Crashaw's study of St Mary Magdalen differs

from his study of St Teresa in many ways, it is nonetheless, as was implied above, like that poem in the sophistication of its baroque style. The virtuosity with which Crashaw uses baroque strategies in the hymn to St Teresa has already been discussed; to examine, even briefly, how he does so in *The Weeper* will suggest why the stylistic achievements of the two poems can be equated. If, in the former, Crashaw cunningly mingles formal praise and formal argument, no less shrewd in the latter is his bringing together of the meditation and the epigram. Crashaw's meditative structures in his religious verse cannot often be identified precisely with the patterns of conventional meditative modes – as *The Weeper* illustrates. Perhaps, since the poem's compositions of place/analyses, and also its temper, recall what St Francis de Sales observes of devout wit and of the temper of meditation in his *Introduction to the Devout Life*, one could identify its meditative structure as having affinities with the Salesian meditative mode.[39] Be that as it may, fused with the meditative design of *The Weeper* is the epigram: each of the poem's stanzas is an epigram; the speaker's meditation evolves in sequences of epigrams.[40] There lies the basis of Crashaw's wit of love in the poem. Through the compacting of conceits in the epigrams, and the sudden juxtaposition of very diverse conceits as the epigrams succeed each other, he has his speaker, in meditating on Mary Magdalen's contrition and her gift of tears, confront the reader with changing visions of her. What makes those changing visions stylistically remarkable is that they emphasize Crashaw's protean use of the conceit. Almost all the conceits in the poem are sensuously affective, many being sensuously luxuriant. Many are flamboyantly paradoxical (as in sts 3 and 4); some are emblematic (as in sts 17–19); some are sacred parodies (see, for example, sts 15–16); many are scripturally allusive whilst others draw on classical myth (compare sts 21–22 and st. 25); some are conceptually intricate whereas some are fantastically playful (compare sts 19 and 5). One is reminded of Gracián's remark that producing wit is "an exaltation of man's mind that carries us to the summit of a strange, fanciful hierarchy."[41]

If, by drawing on devotional literary modes of the Counter-

Reformation, Southwell in effect introduced the devout aspect of the baroque into the verse of the English Renaissance, Crashaw in his religious verse made its presence there more brilliant than did any of his Catholic predecessors or contemporaries. The startling sensuousness and intellectual intricacy, the prolific creation of the marvellous, in so many of his religious poems indicate the uniqueness of his baroque style at its finest. The sophistication of that style, one could fairly add, surpasses the sophistication achieved by any of the other Catholic religious poets in any style. But Crashaw can be claimed the greatest Catholic religious poet of the English Renaissance for a further reason: his poems study nearly all the spiritual concerns in the verse of his fellow Catholics with a subtlety that they did not often equal. That becomes clear when, for a start, one considers Crashaw's poems in relation to Southwell's. Crashaw's poems suggest that whilst he shared Southwell's interest in illumination and in unitive experience, he studied them with a frequency and an acuteness with which Southwell did not.[42] His attention to the Eucharist, moreover, was closer than Southwell's. (Their works seem equally Christocentric, for all that, and seemingly place similar emphases on the divine *agape*.) Crashaw focuses on the spiritual nuances of penitence and of grief perhaps no more perceptively than does Southwell, but his spiritual admonitions are often more complex than those of his Jesuit predecessor.[43] His astute studies of female sanctity and religious experience do not have any real counterparts in Southwell's verse. Such contrasts become rather more obvious when one sets Crashaw's religious poems side by side with those of poets who were certainly not Southwell's equals. Crashaw apparently shared Constable's strong interest in female spirituality and in sacred *eros*, yet his examining of them is far more elaborate than Constable's.[44] Just so, he went beyond Alabaster in considering illumination, unitive experience, martyrdom, and almost everything else.[45] One hardly need go on to make similar points by contrasting Crashaw's religious poems with those of Beaumont and of Habington. It all but goes without saying that none of the other Catholic religious poets could rival him in the study of sacred love's intensity and power to transform human life and art. Crashaw's religious verse virtually sums up and perfects the works of his Catholic fellows from Southwell onwards (among them, only he could be mentioned in the same breath with Herbert); it is with him that one necessarily ends a critical history of Catholic religious poetry's major phase in the English Renaissance.

Appendix: Ralegh's Ocean to Scinthia

What we have of Ralegh's *Ocean to Scinthia* suggests that the poem is a turning point in his art.[1] The basis of the poem is the personal emblem by which Ralegh represents his relationship to the Queen: in it she becomes Cynthia, he the Ocean. Ralegh implies that, like the moon and the sea, Elizabeth and he are bound harmoniously together by natural law. Cunningly the emblem anticipates change as an element of the relationship and indicates an essential constancy behind it. But Ralegh's long poem, written during his disfavour at court, argues that whilst love may be seen as ordering life (as the poem's central emblem implies) that order is very precarious indeed, for when love fails then order ends and life becomes lonely, fragmentary, violent. With that argument comes Ralegh's rejection of the styles of elegance (the High Renaissance version of the middle style) and of magnificence (the High Renaissance version of the high style).

Ralegh's lament of his treatment by the Queen has the setting of a pastoral elegy. From being the Ocean at the poem's outset he becomes more specifically individualized as the Shepherd of the Ocean now confined to the land ("No feedinge flockes, no sheapherds cumpunye / That might renew my dollorus consayte ...," ll. 29–30): Ralegh's fusion of personal emblem and pastoral elegy lends unusual power to his complaint by making it at once intimate yet, given the images of moon and sea, of more than localized significance. As he and the Queen are sung in a pastoral setting they are involved in a pattern of natural correspondences. Those suggest the richness of life under royal favour (sometimes figured by the shining sun) or the frustration, disorder and sterility caused by royal displeasure (sometimes imaged as sunset). Yet the most telling and powerful images in the complaint remain those of moon and sea. Instead of to harmony, they now point to a terrible disjunction at once personal and – for the Ralegh persona – universal.

Ralegh's emblem defines Cynthia/Elizabeth as a mistress uniting a divine virtue with power and so as one who can truly ennoble her servant. Ralegh, in the iconic/pastoral role through which he conducts his lament, declares that in her service he could act with an epic spirit ("To seeke new worlds, for golde, for prayse, for glory, / To try desire, to try love severed farr," ll. 61–62) and hints that in doing so he would be restoring the heroism of times past (see ll. 63–64). Not merely obedience to a queen is indicated to create that heroic possibility. It is suggested that to serve Cynthia/Elizabeth is (of course) to serve the divine order and its values for she is

> ... natures wonder, Vertues choyse,
> The only parragonn of tymes begettinge
> Devin in wordes, angellicall in voyse;
> That springe of joyes, that floure of loves own settinge,
> Th' Idea remayninge of thos golden ages,
> That bewtye bravinge heavens, and yearth imbalminge,
> Which after worthless worlds but play onn stages. (ll. 344–350)

For all the celebration of her as a transcendent being, however, Cynthia/Elizabeth is presented as a paradox because within her enduring perfections lie caprice and instability:

> So hath perfection, which begatt her minde,
> Added therto a change of fantasye
> And left her the affections of her kynde
> Yet free from evry yevill but crueltye. (ll. 209–212)

Her arbitrary disfavour, the Ralegh persona suggests, brings ruin to the individual and discord to his world – she denies a beneficent and life-giving energy to both:

> Therfore all liueless, and all healpless bounde
> My fayntinge spirritts sunck, and hart apalde,
> My ioyes and hopes lay bleedinge on the grovnd
> That not longe since the highest heaven scalde. (ll. 161–164)

> When shee that from the soonn reves poure and light
> Did but decline her beames as discontented
> Convertinge sweetest dayes to saddest night;
> All droopes, all dyes, all troden under dust. (ll. 250–253)

Moreover, the Ralegh persona implies that when divorced from her he ceases to fulfil his role as her heroic agent; she can negate all heroic aspiration (see ll. 163–164 and ll. 65–68). The poem's opening stanzas stress, of course, that when the Ralegh persona can no longer serve his capricious mistress he loses his personal integrity as well as an heroic identity: in contrast to Cynthia/Elizabeth as the Astraean "Idea remayninge of thos golden ages" (l. 348) is his "Idea but restinge, of a wasted minde" (l. 12). That dwelling upon disjunction (within the speaker's personality, between him and his mistress, between him and the ordinary world, between his world and Cynthia/Elizabeth as the principle of creative order) culminates in the poem's most compelling image of discord:

> Bellphebes course is now observde no more,
> That faire resemblance weareth out of date.
> Our Ocean seas are but tempestius waves
> And all things base that blessed wear of late. (ll. 271–274)

The Ralegh persona depicts himself ultimately as a microcosm of his world's confusion. In reflecting a spiritual as well as a more encompassing incoherence, Ralegh's personal emblem itself breaks apart – the "faire resemblance" no longer seems true to experience. Silence is perhaps the poem's necessary end.

It can reasonably be suggested that the High Renaissance styles of elegance and magnificence which crown the Tudor aesthetic are based upon the concept of a love-ordered universe. In his long complaint Ralegh fables that love of Cynthia/Elizabeth and her love for those below her form the origin of all perfecting grace, of order, even of life itself. But when she denies love, when she – the "Idea" from whom life supposedly emanates – withholds herself, then love's failure generates a style of discord and disjunction. The High Renaissance styles cannot contain the violent fragmentation that Ralegh seeks to describe:

> Yet as the eayre in deip caves under ground
> Is strongly drawne when violent heat hath rent
> Great clefts therein, till moysture do abound,
> And then the same imprisoned, and uppent,
> Breakes out in yearthquakes teringe all asunder,
> So in the Center of my cloven hart,
> My hart, to whom her bewties wear such wounder,
> Lyes the sharpe poysoned heade of that loves dart. (ll. 450–457)

As its design and texture make apparent the poem is not just an amplified Petrarchan lament. It images disorder in whole and in part

– decorously so since it considers a disorder perceived as at once specific and encompassing. The poem has a beginning, yet no centre or end. Having begun, it oscillates uneasily between its speaker's minute studying of his own brokenness and his concentration upon different aspects of his paradoxical mistress, imperfectly perfect. Rather than conclude the poem, Ralegh interrupts its movement, within which one sees the styles of elegance and magnificence being distorted because they prove unequal to the violence of the Ralegh persona's situation. There are sudden moments of impotent heroic assertiveness:

> Shee is gonn, Shee is lost! Shee is found, shee is ever faire!
> Sorrow drawes weakly, wher love drawes not too.
> Woes cries, sound nothinge, butt only in loves eare.
> Do then by Diinge, what life cannot doo. (ll. 493–496)

The epic similes ironically scrutinize the speaker's experience in terms of the detail of natural law (natural law has of course all but been abrogated in his world); the forced calm of their scientific detachment and clarity only heightens one's sense of the obsessiveness in the speaker's self-examination. There are the "boddy violently slayne" and the "wheele" in the "fallinge streame" used as likenesses to the "withered mind." Elegant conceits mingle strangely or are compressed into obscurity (see for example ll. 143–149).

Here is something alien to the High Renaissance styles, obliquely challenging both their underlying assumptions and those of the Tudor aesthetic they crown: Ralegh's poem idiosyncratically traces a contradictory view of experience. It explores uncertainties, for with anguish the Ralegh persona confronts a private world perceived as divorced from its paradoxical principle of order. The oscillating movement of the poem reflects the lack of direction within and without the Ralegh persona and it also suggests the movement of his mind, his vacillating between "appearances and judgments" as he scrutinizes his own broken identity or the ambiguity of his mistress's, surveying everywhere a diversity he cannot unify. After *Ocean to Scinthia* all but one of Ralegh's significant poems deny that love orders and graces life – in fact they virtually deny that life has any order. The commendatory sonnet on *The Faerie Queene* is perhaps Ralegh's last attempt to describe life in terms of a style at once elegant and magnificent.

Notes

As the notes throughout this book tend to be fairly detailed, I have not provided a bibliography.

PREFACE

1. In this study I do not seek to put forward a new theory of the baroque; rather, I make use of topoi that have evolved throughout the long and protean discussion of that term and of the phenomena that it is used to describe. A broad range of views on the nature and historiography of the baroque can be seen in the following: Heinrich Wölfflin, *Renaissance and Baroque* (1888), trans. Kathrin Simon (London, 1971); *idem, Principles of Art History: The Problem of the Development of Style in Later Art* (1915), trans. M. D. Hottinger (1932; rpt. New York, 1950); Anthony Blunt, *Artistic Theory in Italy 1450–1600* (1940; rpt. Oxford, 1973), pp. 103–136; René Wellek, "The Concept of the Baroque in Literary Scholarship," *Journal of Aesthetics and Art Criticism*, 5 (1946), 77–109; Ellis Waterhouse, *Painting in Britain 1530 to 1790* (London, 1953), pp. 87–119; Odette de Mourgues, *Metaphysical, Baroque, and Précieux Poetry* (Oxford, 1953); Rudolf Wittkower, *Art and Architecture in Italy: 1600–1750* (Harmondsworth, 1958); René Wellek, *Concepts of Criticism* (New Haven, 1963), pp. 69–127; Frank J. Warnke, *Versions of Baroque: European Literature in the Seventeenth Century* (New Haven and London, 1972); Rudolf Wittkower and Irma B. Jaffe, eds, *Baroque Art: The Jesuit Contribution* (New York, 1972); John Rupert Martin, *Baroque* (London, 1977); M. J. Woods, *The Poet and the Natural World in the Age of Góngora* (Oxford, 1978), esp. pp. 176–204; José Antonio Maravall, *Culture of the Baroque: Analysis of a Historical Structure*, trans. Terry Cochran (Manchester, 1986); J. W. Van Hook, "'Concupiscence of Witt': The Metaphysical Conceit in Baroque Poe-

tics," *Modern Philology*, 84 (1986), 24–38. See also: Christopher Norris, "Paul de Man and the Critique of Aesthetic Ideology," *AUMLA*, 69 (1988), 3–47.

2. Crashaw has received, however, a good deal of perceptive, responsive, and scholarly attention.

3. Habington's connection (which I take to be slight indeed) to the baroque is through the courtly culture centred on Henrietta Maria; his poetry seems rather to have affinities with mannerism.

4. As is indicated by the table of contents, I have included in this study only those poets who are definitely known to have been Catholics (some definitely Catholic, but also very minor, poets have been excluded). Thus Davies of Hereford and Davenant, for example, are not discussed or mentioned as Catholic poets. Davies of Hereford may have been a Catholic in and after 1611 – one cannot be certain; even less clear is whether he may have been a Catholic prior to that year. Davenant's religious allegiance remains equally unproven.

5. Barbara Kiefer Lewalski, *Protestant Poetics and the Seventeenth-Century Religious Lyric* (Princeton, 1979). John N. King, *English Reformation Literature: The Tudor Origins of the Protestant Tradition* (Princeton, 1982).

6. Herford and Simpson suggested years ago that some of the religious poems belong to the latter part of his life, when he was again a Protestant. Jonson's authorship of the poem "Here, are five letters in this blessed Name," remains uncertain.

7. On the history of the English Catholics in Tudor and Stuart times, see: David Mathew, *Catholicism in England 1535–1935* (London, 1936); Martin J. Havran, *The Catholics in Caroline England* (California, 1962); Pierre Janelle, *The Catholic Reformation* (1963; rpt. Middlesex, 1980), pp. 250–274.

8. They were literary dissidents, that is, insofar as they introduced elements of the Counter-Reformation baroque into English Renaissance poetry.

9. See Pierre Janelle, *Robert Southwell the Writer: A Study in Religious Inspiration* (London, 1935), pp. 154–156. See also Christopher Devlin, *The Life of Robert Southwell Poet and Martyr* (1956; rpt. London, 1967), pp. 105–324.

10. See William Habington, *The Poems*, ed. Kenneth Allott (Liverpool, 1969), pp. xi–xliv, and Martin Butler, *Theatre and Crisis 1632–1642* (Cambridge, 1984), pp. 62–83. My remarks about Habington's life refer to what we actually know of it, and apply especially to the years prior to 1650.

CHAPTER ONE: *English and Counter-Reformation Traditions*

1. That is by no means to deny or to underestimate the value of a reader's knowing biographical and socio-political information; rather, the point is to suggest that primacy must be given to knowledge of devotional literary tradition.

2. See: D. W. Robertson, Jr, trans., *On Christian Doctrine* (1958; rpt. Indianapolis, 1979), "Translator's Introduction," xii; James J. Murphy, *Rhetoric in the Middle Ages* (Berkeley, Los Angeles, London, 1974), pp. 326–330.

3. Augustine's work is already a standard authority; that of Erasmus, at once popular and fashionable, significantly pre-dates both Calvin's commentary on Seneca and his *Institutes*. In what follows, I should not be taken as implying that there was a distinctively *Catholic* theory or practice of the religious plain style.

4. St Augustine's enthusiasm for Cicero is evinced in *Confessions*, 3,4 (reference here, as below, is to Watts's translation of 1631, reprinted in the *Loeb Classical Library*, 1912). In *De Doctrina Christiana* he alludes often to Cicero, see for example 4,12,27 (reference here, and subsequently, is to Robertson's translation cited above). See also Murphy, *Rhetoric in the Middle Ages*, pp. 286–287.

5. Cf. *De Trinitate*, 1,1,2.

6. Cf. *De Catechizandis Rudibus*, 9,13.

7. Cicero delivers his argument about the high style and its function through Crassus in *De Oratore*. For St Paul, see 1 *Cor.* 1,17–2,5. Augustine's exegetical methods in *De Doctrina Christiana* are of course heavily indebted to the writings of St Paul. Reference to and quotation from Scripture throughout this book rely upon the *RSV*.

8. D. W. Robertson cites an interesting Erasmian allusion to *De Doctrina Christiana* in the introduction to his translation, xii. All reference to *Sileni Alcibiadis* is from M. M. Phillips, trans., *The Adages of Erasmus* (Cambridge, 1964).

9. Erasmus, *The Colloquies*, trans. Craig H. Thompson (Chicago and London, 1965), p. 68. On Socrates, see *De Oratore*, 2,67,270 and *De Officiis*, 1,30,108 (cf. 1,1,3).

10. Erasmus, *The Praise of Folly*, trans. Betty Radice (Harmondsworth, 1971), esp. pp. 198–199.

11. Erasmus, *Ciceronianus*, trans. Izora Scott (Albany, 1908), p. 66.

12. See for instance the allusion to Cicero in *De Doctrina Christiana*, 4,10,24.

13. This is made especially clear in *The Praise of Folly*.

14. On the dates and order of the paraphrases see the editions by F. M. Padelford (rev. edn 1928; rpt. New York, 1966), pp. 228–231, and Emrys Jones (1964; rpt. Oxford, 1970), p. 153. On those matters I am indebted also to W. McGaw, who is preparing an edition for Oxford University Press. The last of the paraphrases, that of psalm 55, need not be last in sequence of composition; however, as reproduced in manuscript order it nonetheless appears last before the reader. Further reference to Surrey's verse is from Jones's edition. For another view of Surrey's paraphrases, see Rivkah Zim, *English Metrical Psalms: Poetry as Praise and Prayer 1535–1601* (Cambridge, 1987), pp. 88–98.

15. On Surrey's indebtedness to Campensis see Jones's edition, pp. 153–154, p. 158. (See also his references to H. A. Mason on this topic.)

16. Reference to Vaux's poem is from Alexander B. Grosart, ed., *Miscellanies of the Fuller Worthies' Library*, 4 vols (Blackburn, Lancashire, 1872–1876), 4, 367–369.

17. Reference here is to the most accessible text of Huggarde's verse, that of I. L. Guiney in her *English Recusant Poets* (London, 1938), no. 45.

18. The problem of distinguishing between role playing and ineptitude arises as well with Tregian and some other very minor poets.

19. As regards chronology, it should be noted that Pontanus's work first appeared in 1594; Tasso's appeared – in final form – in 1594, and Gracián's, also in finished form, in 1648.

20. See for example, Pierre Janelle, *The Catholic Reformation* (1963; rpt. Middlesex, 1980), pp. 64–91, 137–158.

21. That is clear from the texts themselves but was first noted in Pierre Janelle's pioneering account of the topic, wherein he first drew readers' attention to Pontanus. See his *Robert Southwell the Writer* (London, 1935), p. 119. I am indebted to Janelle's early discussion; even so, my differences from his views will be apparent.

22. Jacobus Pontanus, *Poeticarum Institutionum Libri Tres*, 2nd edn (1595; rpt. Lugduni, 1607), 1,2,6. Reference is by book, chapter, page number; all following references are to this edition.

23. I translate *"compositissima"* as "euphonious" not only because of its lexical probability but also because *compositio* is the rhetorical term familiarly used for "euphony" in writing or speech.

24. Torquato Tasso, *Discourses on the Heroic Poem*, trans. Mariella Cavalchini and Irene Samuel (Oxford, 1973), p. 10. Further reference to Tasso, unless otherwise noted, is to this edition.

25. Torquato Tasso, *Prose*, ed. Ettore Mazzali (Milan and Naples, 1959), p. 505.

26. Baltasar Gracián, *The Mind's Wit and Art*, trans. L. H. Chambers, 2 vols (Ph.D. dissertation, University of Michigan, 1962), 2,92. Further reference is to this translation, by discourse and page.

27. As S. L. Bethell first noted. See his "The Nature of Metaphysical Poetry," *Northern Miscellany* (1953), reprinted in Gerald Hammond, ed., *The Metaphysical Poets* (London, 1974), p. 135.

28. Emanuele Tesauro, *Il Cannocchiale Aristotelico*, 2nd edn (Venezia, 1663), p. 54. Further reference is to this edition.

29. Tesauro, pp. 68–69.

30. Cf. 3,103 on wit and action of the soul.

31. Something similar can be seen in this remark by Tesauro on metaphor: "*Onde maggiore è il tuo diletto: nella maniera, che più curiosa & piaceuol cosa è mirar molti obietti per vn' istraforo di perspettiua, che se gli originali medesimi successiuamente ti venisser passando dinanzi agli occhi*" (p. 276).

32. Plotinus, *The Six Enneads*, trans. Stephen MacKenna and B. S. Page (Chicago and London, 1952), 5,9,11. Further reference is to this edition.

33. Tesauro, p. 645.

34. George Puttenham, *The Arte of English Poesie*, eds Gladys Doidge Willcock and Alice Walker (Cambridge, 1936), p. 108. Later reference is to this edition.

35. Henri Estienne, *The Art of Making Devises*, trans. Thomas Blount (London, 1646). Further reference is to this edition.

36. The relationship between poetic imagery and universals in the Renaissance was first discussed at length by Rosemond Tuve in her *Elizabethan and Metaphysical Imagery: Renaissance Poetic and Twentieth-Century Critics* (Chicago and London, 1947).

37. According to Tesauro, too, emblems are designed for "instruction of the people" (p. 646) – but not, he adds, of "*la ignara Plebe*" (*ibid.*).

38. Cf. Pontanus, 1,5,18.

39. Otho Vaenius, *Amoris Divini Emblemata* (Antverpiae, 1615). Further reference is to this edition.

40. As far as I have been able to see, the *navis animae* image descends from Plotinus, St Augustine and, most popularly, Petrarch.

41. Hermann Hugo, *Pia Desideria Emblematis Elegiis & affectibus S.S. Patrum illustrata* (Antwerpiae, 1624). Further reference is to this edition.

42. That argument pervades the first two books.

43. St Augustine, *On the Holy Trinity, Doctrinal Treatises, Moral Treatises*, eds and trans. Philip Schaff, *et al.* (1887; rpt. Michigan, 1978), 12,15,25 and 13,1,2. Further reference is to this edition.

44. Augustine's *Soliloquies* and *"Meditations"* show his own bringing together of those things.

45. On the popularity of Walter Hilton in England see Janelle, *The Catholic Reformation*, p. 186.

46. St Ignatius Loyola, *The Spiritual Exercizes* (1533), trans. Anthony Mottola (New York, 1964), pp. 38,54,82–83. Further reference is to this edition.

47. There can be three preludes, if desired, the additional one being a "history of the event." See pp. 92–93.

48. *The Arte of English Poesie*, p. 238. Puttenham's account of *demonstratio* is representative, as *Ad Herennium* (4,68) indicates.

49. Louis L. Martz, in *The Poetry of Meditation* (New Haven and London, 1954), notes the Augustinian analogy between the soul and God but does not elaborate on the point and does not consider the issue of *sapientia* (see pp. 34–36).

50. Anon., *Certayne deuout Meditations very necessary for Christian men dououtly to meditate vpon Morninge and Eueninge, euery day in the weeke: Concerning Christ his lyfe and Passion, and the fruites thereof* (1576), eds D. M. Rogers and A. F. Allison (Yorkshire, 1969). See "Saterday," Dv1^r–Dv8^v. According to Ignatius, *compositio loci* can be variously placed in a meditation.

51. Fulvio Androzzi, *Meditations vppon the Passion of Ovr Lord Iesvs Christ* (1606), ed. D. M. Rogers (Yorkshire, 1970), p. 96. Subsequent reference is to this edition.

52. Nicolas Berzetti, *The Practice of Meditating with Profit the Misteries of Ovr Lord, the Blessed Vergin and Saints* (1613), ed. D. M. Rogers (Yorkshire, 1970), p. 13, and quoted at length from pp. 25–26.

53. Luis de la Puente, *Meditations vpon the Mysteries of Ovr Faith* (abridged edn, 1624), ed. D. M. Rogers (Yorkshire and London, 1976). Reference is to this edition.

54. St Francis de Sales, *Introduction to the Devout Life*, ed. and trans. John K. Ryan (1950; rpt. New York, 1966), p. 28. "Inability" of course here means inability to depart from established truth. Further reference is to this edition.

55. Similarity can also be seen in St Francis' adoption from St Ignatius of the "two standards" motif (see p. 58).

CHAPTER TWO: *St Robert Southwell*

1. See Robert Southwell, S.J., *The Poems*, eds James H. McDonald and Nancy Pollard Brown (Oxford, 1967), lxxx, lxxxix, xcii–cii. All further reference to Southwell's poems is from this edition.
2. Southwell, *The Poems*, xciii–xcix.
3. I am not suggesting, however, that Southwell draws directly on St Augustine in planning *The Sequence*.
4. For other views of *The Sequence* see: Pierre Janelle, *Robert Southwell the Writer: A Study in Religious Inspiration* (London, 1935), pp. 162–166. (Later in his study Janelle traces the "open throats and silent mouthes" image cited above to Tansillo. See *Robert Southwell*, p. 214.); Louis L. Martz, *The Poetry of Meditation: A Study in English Religious Literature of the Seventeenth Century* (New Haven and London, 1954), pp. 102–107. Martz considers *The Sequence* in connection with the rosary. As the reader will recognize, my thinking on *agape* is indebted to Nygren and Outka.
5. Emanuele Tesauro, *Il Cannocchiale Aristotelico*, 2nd edn (Venezia, 1663), p. 458. Subsequent reference to Tesauro is from this edition.
6. Tesauro, p. 458.
7. Walter Hilton, *The Ladder of Perfection*, trans. Leo Sherley-Price (Harmondsworth, 1957), pp. 33–34. Here Hilton refers to love *for* God.
8. Robert Southwell, *S. Mary Magdalens Fvnerall Teares* (1616), ed. D. M. Rogers (Menston, Yorks., 1971), pp. 70–71.
9. Moreover, the language of the profane "I" anticipates that of the vision.
10. The redeemed self who narrates is not, of course, an identity in opposition to Christ.
11. A point clearly implied in "The Author to his loving Cosen," ll.12–16.
12. In ll.9–12, the rhetoric of the profane "I," like his language, anticipates that of the vision. See n.9.
13. St Thomas Aquinas, *Summa Theologica*, trans. Fathers of the English Dominican Province, 3 vols (New York, 1947), Pt 1, Q.88, Art.3. Cf. *De Veritate*, Q.22, Art.2, Ad.1.
14. St Thomas Aquinas, *Summa Contra Gentiles*, in *Basic Writings of Saint Thomas Aquinas*, ed. Anton C. Pegis, 2 vols (New York, 1944), 3,37.
15. St Thomas Aquinas, *Summa Theologica*, trans. Fathers of the English Dominican Province, Pt 1–2,Q.3, Art.8.

16. Cf. Robert Southwell, *Spiritual Exercizes and Devotions*, ed. J.–M. de Buck, S.J., trans. P. E. Hallett (London, 1931), p. 39, p. 45. Southwell is fond of such dicta, as "The burning Babe" attests.

17. The speaker's reflections may in fact approximate to the form of Ignatian meditation, for they can be seen as points followed by a composition of place and then a colloquy.

18. There is a profane counterpart to this manifestation of the topos in Donne's "The Sun Rising" – the topos in fact recurs throughout his secular love poems.

19. Here Southwell's modern editors quote in apparent comparison from the last words of his *A Short Rule of Good Life* (see p. 124 of their edition), but a broader look at its close shows the contrast between the endings of the two works to be as striking as the likeness.

20. For a discussion of typology in Southwell's verse, see Ira Clark, *Christ Revealed: The History of the Neotypological Lyric in the English Renaissance* (Gainesville, 1982), pp. 29–51. For a discussion of the poem as connected with the Eucharist, see Carolyn A. Schten, "Southwell's 'Christs Bloody Sweat': A Meditation on the Mass," *English Miscellany*, 20 (1969), 75–80.

21. More's poems, although derived from that tradition, reflect Attic notions of the plain style and are clearly born of the Humanist milieu of his youth.

22. Cf. Vaenius' emblem "*Odit Moras*." Another context for the poem is Scupoli's *The Spiritual Combat*.

23. For another view of Southwell's neoplatonism in the poem, see Pierre Janelle, *Robert Southwell the Writer*, pp. 270–271 (see also pp. 267–269).

24. *S. Mary Magdalens Fvnerall Teares*, ed. D. M. Rogers, p. 154.

25. Here I follow McDonald and Brown in assuming that the shorter poem is the earlier (*The Poems*, lxxxix). How significantly "unrevised" the longer poem may be, if it is so, would seem to be unknowable.

26. For the text of the medieval poem, see Douglas Gray, ed. *A Selection of Religious Lyrics* (Oxford, 1975), p. 41.

27. The seminal discussion of the poem was by Pierre Janelle, *Robert Southwell the Writer*, pp. 205–227. His account of Southwell's indebtedness to Tansillo in the poem remains standard. For another view of the poem (in fact, of its dramatic centre), see Louis L. Martz, *The Poetry of Meditation*, p. 186. Cf. Helen C. White, "Southwell: Metaphysical and Baroque," *Modern Philology*, 61 (1964), 159–168.

28. The *navis animae* topos recurs many times in Southwell's poems, sometimes being combined with the *naufragium* topos.

29. Robert Southwell, *An Epistle of a Religious Priest vnto His Father*, [1596–1597], ed. D. M. Rogers (Menston, Yorks., 1971), pp. 33–34.

30. Cf. ll.166–168. Contrast ll.235–236, ll.385–390. For comparisons and contrasts between the poem and the prose works, see: *A Short Rule of Good Life* [1596–1597], ed. D. M. Rogers (Menston, Yorks., 1971), p. 24; *An Epistle of a Religious Priest*, pp. 19–20, p. 29, p. 34; *S. Mary Magdalens Fvnerall Teares*, p. 144, p. 154, p. 156; *An Epistle of Comfort, to the Reverend Priestes* [1587–1588], ed. D. M. Rogers (Ilkley, Yorks., 1974), pp. 167–168, pp. 176–177. Those comparisons and contrasts are equally relevant to the earlier poem.

31. For another view of the poem's structure, see Nancy Pollard Brown, "The Structure of Southwell's 'Saint Peter's Complaint,'" *Modern Language Review*, 61 (1966), 3–11.

32. They may even have been composed at the same time; in any case, the poems would seem to be very close chronologically.

33. For a more detailed account of Ralegh's poem see below, "Appendix: Ralegh's *Ocean to Scinthia*."

34. In blaspheming against Christ, they pit human words against the Word and hence against God.

35. The meditation can be seen as approximating to the Ignatian form, a brief history of the event being followed by an analysis interwoven with a colloquy (see especially ll.373–378).

36. For an opinion of St Ignatius on the gift of tears see his letter to Father Nicholas Gaudano, in *Letters of St Ignatius of Loyola*, sel. and trans. William J. Young, S.J. (Chicago, 1959), pp. 311–312.

37. Throughout the poem Peter is conscious of the divine love but here, where he is particularly so, his sense of wretchedness intensifies – see ll.367–372, wherein Peter considers himself as a deformed *imago dei*. (At this point in the poem, Peter is no longer "in hell" because he has been saved through the gift of tears; even so, he still has not escaped from a Christless existence.)

38. There is also a very indirect allusion here to *eros* not aroused because of worldliness (ll.415–416).

39. Here those strategies set in perspective Southwell's other uses of them, in particular where he has Peter unname himself (e.g. ll.121–126, ll.169–174, l.613) and where he has Peter examine his own displacement in the world (e.g. ll.25–30, ll.139–150).

40. There are too many instances for them all to be cited, however

see: *Saint Peters Complaint*, ll.727–732; "Loves servile lot," ll.57–60; "Lewd Love is Losse," ll.19–24; "From Fortunes reach," l.3.

41. George Eliot uses the phrase "sacred parody" when discussing Savonarola. Louis L. Martz applies it to Southwell in *The Poetry of Meditation*, pp. 184–193. Certainly the idea is interesting and describes some of Southwell's poems well; nonetheless, to define the boundaries of sacred parody in Southwell's verse seems very hard, because the idea is far from precise, and much that might be claimed for sacred parodies could equally be claimed for poems that aren't sacred parodies at all. Cf. Rosemond Tuve, "Sacred 'Parody' of Love Poetry, and Herbert," *Studies in the Renaissance*, 8 (1961), 249–290.

42. The idea was first generally raised by Pierre Janelle, *Robert Southwell the Writer*, pp. 34–60.

43. This is true even of "S. Peters afflicted minde," and of "Mary Magdalens blush."

CHAPTER THREE: *Henry Constable and William Alabaster*

1. See: Henry Constable, *The Poems*, ed. Joan Grundy (Liverpool, 1960); William Alabaster, *The Sonnets*, eds G. M. Story and Helen Gardner (Oxford, 1959). Further reference to Constable and to Alabaster is from those editions. On the dating of Constable's *Spirituall Sonnettes* see Grundy, p. 59; on that of Alabaster's *Divine Meditations*, see Story and Gardner, pp. xxxvi–xxxviii. Constable may have written either before or after Alabaster. Here he is discussed first because he is the elder poet.

2. Baldesar Castiglione, *The Book of the Courtier*, trans. Charles S. Singleton (Garden City, New York, 1959), 4,64.

3. Although Constable is here offering a sacred parody of Castiglione or, perhaps, of some other courtly writer, and although the idea of spiritual union in love is fashionable at court, the idea has of course many theological counterparts and is not solely a courtly one.

4. In the writings of Castiglione and of other neoplatonic authors (such as Ficino), secular love is not considered necessarily to be profane.

5. See St Bonaventure's *The Soul's Journey into God*, Prologue, 2–3, and *The Life of St Francis*, 9,1–3, in *Bonaventure: The Soul's Journey into God. The Tree of Life. The Life of St Francis*, trans.

Ewert Cousins (London, 1978). Bonaventuran analogues to passages in Constable's poems were first noticed by Grundy, who cites in her notes on this poem a different analogue from either of those just suggested.

6. Criticism is implied perhaps especially of the notion of the mistress as godlike. In his secular verse, Constable simultaneously puts forward the notion and undercuts it (through a rhetoric whose elaborate symmetries at once celebrate, confine, and diminish the mistress' supposed power). Here, the phrase "True God of Love" by implication dismisses the notion completely.

7. If the manuscript order of the *Spirituall Sonnettes* followed by Grundy is Constable's, then the poems have a numerological coherence; if not, then they merely have strong numerological elements – as in the play on six, the Augustinian perfect number, in "To St Peter *and* St Paul."

8. Cf. Jean de la Ceppède, "*Soit que je vo' reçoive*," in Frank J. Warnke, ed., *European Metaphysical Poetry* (1961; rpt. New Haven and London, 1974), pp. 102–103.

9. In the manuscript ordering of the sonnets, single poems to the Virgin and to Mary Magdalen are soon followed by triads to each. Hence the grouped poems are the second, third, and fourth sonnets to either figure. Whether or not Constable intended such an ordering of the sonnets, those grouped are very closely related.

10. More than a third of Constable's poems are acts of courtiership. On Constable's non-literary activities as a courtier, see Grundy, pp. 21–50. Grundy's introduction to her edition offers the best account of Constable's life as it does the best criticism of his poems.

11. For example, see Grundy, pp. 46–48.

12. In fact almost all Constable's political verse is pervaded by secular *eros*.

13. The elaborate harmonies of the poem image a moral order that the persona wants, not has.

14. In her notes, Grundy cites an interesting account from *The Soul's Journey into God*; however, equally relevant ones can be seen in: *The Tree of Life*, 11,44, and 12,48; *The Life of St Francis*, 9,1–4. There are of course analogues to be seen also in St Augustine and St Bernard of Clairvaux.

15. In the sonnets, the purgative and illuminative ways tend to merge, as do the illuminative way and imagined experience of the unitive way.

16. That is certainly true as regards its experience of sacred *eros* (ll.9–16), but also as regards its experience of profane *eros*, for the soul – as a "female" entity – knows sexual desire (ll.5–6) and seems in close sympathy with the Magdalen's past experience of passion's "feaver" (cf. l.3).

17. On the medieval inheritance, including that of typology, in Alabaster's *Divine Meditations*, see Story and Gardner, pp. xxiii–xxxiii. For another discussion of typology – and an account of Petrarchan elements – in the poems, see Ira Clark, *Christ Revealed: The History of the Neotypological Lyric in the English Renaissance* (Gainesville, Florida, 1982), pp. 51–63. Clark's criticism of Alabaster seems to be the best yet written.

18. The general title *Divine Meditations* of course refers to all seventy-seven of Alabaster's religious sonnets. Reference to the numbers of the sonnets, and to their individual titles, comes from those used by Story and Gardner.

19. As Story and Gardner also note in their commentary.

20. Nothing in sonnets 1–11 seems to suggest that Alabaster had yet read *The Spiritual Exercises*. Story and Gardner point out (on p. xxvii, see p. xvi) that "The Jesuit, John Gerard, gave Alabaster the *Exercises* in 1598," but it is not known what poems he wrote before, or after, receiving Loyola's work. As will be argued below, however, some of the sonnets strongly indicate Ignatian influence.

21. Most of that praise has been oblique, implied by the poem's inclusion in anthologies.

22. On the title of the poems, see Story and Gardner, p. 51.

23. Evelyn Underhill, *Mysticism: A Study in the Nature and Development of Man's Spiritual Consciousness* (1911; rpt. New York, 1961), p. 227. The "oneness" referred to above does not, of course, imply spiritual union with Christ but rather gaining a sense of his presence.

24. The experience of purification here does not include mortification.

25. The opening couplet implies how Christ has acted for and upon the speaker.

26. Again, though one cannot know whether Alabaster had read *The Spiritual Exercises* by the time of the sonnets' composition, an Ignatian influence seems present in the poems. Moreover, although one cannot know to what degree Alabaster was acquainted with Counter-Reformation poetic theory and/or practice, emblem theory and/or practice, he certainly writes here and elsewhere as if he were indeed acquainted with them.

27. To be fair, some of Alabaster's worst poems also appear among the penitential poems (see 16).
28. See the notes by Story and Gardner on this poem for discussion of the allusion to *The Song of Solomon*.
29. For another view of the sonnet see Clark, pp. 54–55.
30. Juan Luis Vives, *A Fable about Man*, trans. Nancy Lenkeith, in Ernst Cassirer, Paul Oskar Kristeller, and John Herman Randall, Jr., eds, *The Renaissance Philosophy of Man* (1948; rpt. Chicago and London, 1967), pp. 389–390.
31. Should Constable not be, chronologically, a Tudor poet then he is still one in his favouring the sonnet form and in many aspects of his style.

CHAPTER FOUR: *Sir John Beaumont, William Habington, and Some Others*

1. Reference is to: Sir John Beaumont, *The Poems*, ed. A. B. Grosart (n.p., 1869); British Museum Additional Manuscript 33,392 (for Beaumont's *The Crowne of Thornes*); William Habington, *The Poems*, ed. Kenneth Allott (Liverpool, 1969).
2. What influence Counter-Reformation poetic practice and/or theory may have had on Beaumont is not known; nor is how emblem theory and/or practice may have influenced him. His writing in *The Crowne of Thornes* often accords with the poetics of Pontanus. The best critical account of Beaumont's epic, that by Ruth Wallerstein, speculates interestingly on those matters. See her "Sir John Beaumont's *Crowne of Thornes*, A Report," *Journal of English and Germanic Philology*, 53 (1954), 410–434. There is a brief and useful account of Beaumont's verse as a whole by Douglas Bush in his *English Literature in the Earlier Seventeenth Century 1600–1660*, 2nd edn (1945; rpt. Oxford 1962), p. 89.
3. The "Augustan" aspect of Beaumont's verse is frequently noted (see, for instance, Bush, cited above). His use of the couplet indicates, of course, his indebtedness to Jonson.
4. Beaumont recurrently considers the limitations of human knowledge; here he seems to anticipate Rochester.
5. St Augustine, *The Confessions*, trans. Watts, 1, 1. Cf. "In Spirituall Comfort," *passim*. In his edition, Grosart suggests the poem's last line to be possibly indebted to that passage in *The Confessions*.

6. The "crowne" is literally, as the poem makes clear, a "garland" or "wreath".

7. There are still, perhaps, some traces of unevenness in the poem (see ll. 39–40).

8. For a more detailed account of the epic's organization, see Wallerstein's article (cited above), pp. 414–422. Cf. John Abbot's *Iesvs Praefigured* (1623), Book 1, *passim*, on the theme of England's being restored to Catholicism.

9. Naturally, the inference could not reasonably be drawn from the poem's opening that the crown of thorns would form the epic's dominant emblem, nor could that emblem's main functions be likewise inferred.

10. The chronology indicated by ll. 15–16 is ambiguous.

11. That is to say, those are the main concerns, or emphases, within the poem's celebration and interpretation of Christ as the centre of the universe.

12. I am not saying that those rhetorical figures are found only in the high style, but that here they combine with others to make the passage high-styled.

13. Wallerstein notes the affinities between Beaumont's verse in the epic and Jesuit emblem verse as well as the verse in Jesuit books of elegies – which implies the association of his epic with other aspects of Jesuit meditation than the formally Ignatian (see her article, p. 415).

14. See, for example, 2,73–120 and 3,1–90 (among many instances).

15. That there is, furthermore, a consciously Dantesque element in Beaumont's epic seems evident from the likeness of its introduction to the opening of Dante's *Inferno*.

16. The idea is introduced in ll. 1–3 by a play on the *exegi monumentum* topos.

17. See also: "*Solum mihi superest sepulchrum. IOB*"; "*Deus Deus Meus.* DAVID"; "*Quoniam ego in flagella paratus sum.* DAVID"; "*Vias tuas Domine demonstra mihi*"; "*Cogitabo pro peccato meo*"; "*Recogitabo tibi omnes annos meos. ISAY.*"

18. It is not suggested that the biblical titles to Habington's religious poems make all their personae Davidic, Jobean, or other scripturally based figures.

19. The second poem clarifies, too, the references in its predecessor to writing of love. Virtually all the rest of Habington's religious poems to some degree treat of *contemptus mundi* and/or *contemptus hominis*.

20. Cf. Fanshawe's "A Rose," Herbert's "The Flower," "Vertue," "Life," and Herrick's "To the Virgins, to make much of Time."

21. That is to say, the poem in fact opens with a meditation on a scriptural text concerned with *contemptus hominis*.

22. Nicolas Caussin, *The Holy Covrt in Three Tomes* (1634), trans. Thomas Hawkins, ed. D. M. Rogers (London, 1977). Subsequent reference to the work is from this edition.

23. *The Holy Covrt*, 2, p. 254. Not only courtly ladies, of course, are said to aspire to, or to realize, that state – but the point is that the true courtly lady must do both.

24. Sir William Davenant, *The Shorter Poems and Songs from the Plays and Masques*, ed. A. M. Gibbs (Oxford, 1972), p. 241. On the courtly milieu to which Habington belonged, see Martin Butler, *Theatre and Crisis 1632–1642* (Cambridge, 1984), pp. 25–83, and Kenneth Allott's edition of the poems, pp. xxiii–xl. Allott's is still the best critical account of the poems, secular as well as religious (see the introduction to his edition, pp. liii–lx).

25. See l. 8 of the former poem and ll. 1–5 of the latter. Reference is to John Donne, *The Complete English Poems*, ed. C. A. Patrides (London, 1985).

26. The theme of retirement and the figure of the (Horatian) stoic wise man feature also in Habington's secular verse. Cf. Maren-Sofie Røstvig, *The Happy Man. Studies in the Metamorphoses of a Classical Ideal*, vol. 1, 2nd edn, rev. (Oslo and Oxford, 1962), pp. 160–176.

27. Reference is to H. E. Rollins, ed., *The Paradise of Dainty Devices (1576–1606)* (Cambridge, Mass., 1927). See Louis L. Martz, *The Poetry of Meditation*, pp. 182–183, and R. C. Bald, *John Donne: A Life* (Oxford, 1970), pp. 39–42, 44–45, 52, 64.

28. Reference is to the edition of D. M. Rogers (Menston, Yorks., 1970). See Rivkah Zim, *English Metrical Psalms*, pp. 4, 129–132, 133, and 85.

29. Reference is to the edition of D. M. Rogers (Menston, Yorks., 1969).

30. Reference to each is from the editions by D. M. Rogers (Menston, Yorks., 1971 and London, 1975 respectively). See: Rosemary Freeman, *English Emblem Books* (London, 1948), pp. 173–198, 243–248; Wolfgang Lottes, "Henry Hawkins and *Partheneia Sacra*," *Review of English Studies*, N.S. 26 (1975), 271–286.

31. Reference is to Patrick Cary, *The Poems*, ed. Sister Veronica Delany (Oxford, 1978). Even though Cary wrote a little after Crashaw's death, he could hardly be omitted. On the dating of his religious poems, see Delany's edition, p. lxx.

CHAPTER FIVE: *Richard Crashaw*

1. Reference to Crashaw's verse is from Richard Crashaw, *The Poems English Latin and Greek*, ed. L. C. Martin, 2nd edn (1957; rpt. Oxford, 1968). When a poem exists in more than one version, quotation is always from the final version.

2. The phrase comes from the title of his pathfinding volume, *Richard Crashaw: A Study in Baroque Sensibility* (London, 1939). For other accounts of Crashaw, see: Mario Praz, *The Flaming Heart: Essays on Crashaw, Machiavelli, and Other Studies in the Relations between Italian and English Literature from Chaucer to T. S. Eliot* (1958; rpt. New York, 1973), pp. 204–263; Ruth C. Wallerstein, *Richard Crashaw: A Study in Style and Poetic Development* (Madison, 1935); A. F. Allison, "Crashaw and St François de Sales," *Review of English Studies*, 24 (1948), 295–302; Louis L. Martz, *The Poetry of Meditation* (New Haven and London, 1954), pp. 61–67, pp. 115–117; Margaret Claydon, A. M., *Richard Crashaw's Paraphrases of the Vexilla Regis, Stabat Mater, Adoro Te, Lauda Sion, Dies Irae, O Gloriosa Domina* (Washington, 1960); Mary Ellen Rickey, *Rhyme and Meaning in Richard Crashaw* (Kentucky, 1961); Lowry Nelson, Jr, *Baroque Lyric Poetry* (New Haven and London, 1961), pp. 26–27, pp. 53–55; George W. Williams, *Image and Symbol in the Sacred Poetry of Richard Crashaw* (Columbia, 1963); Anthony Raspa, "Crashaw and the Jesuit Poetic," *University of Texas Quarterly*, 36 (1966), 37–54; Louis L. Martz, *The Wit of Love: Donne, Carew, Crashaw, Marvell* (Notre Dame and London, 1969), pp. 113–147; Earl Miner, *The Metaphysical Mode from Donne to Cowley* (Princeton, N.J., 1969), esp. pp. 186–188; Marc F. Bertonasco, *Crashaw and the Baroque* (Alabama, 1971); Frank J. Warnke, *Versions of Baroque: European Literature in the Seventeenth Century* (New Haven and London, 1972), pp. 32–40, pp. 52–54; Anthony Low, *Love's Architecture: Devotional Modes in Seventeenth-Century English Poetry* (New York, 1978), pp. 116–159; R. V. Young, *Richard Crashaw and the Spanish Golden Age* (New Haven and London, 1982); Walter R. Davis, "The Meditative Hymnody of Richard Crashaw," *ELH*, 50 (1983), 107–129; Laurence Lerner, "Poetry as the Play of Signifiers," *Essays in Criticism*, 35 (1985), 238–259.

3. For another view of the poem, see especially Steven Blakemore, "The Name Made Flesh: Crashaw's Celebration of 'The Name Above Every Name,'" *Concerning Poetry*, 17 (1984), 63–77.

4. There is an interesting analogue to Crashaw's image of the bees in *Paradiso* 31,7–12.

5. The notion of light's spiritual aspect is familiar from Dante and Ficino. Cf. Crashaw's *In the Gloriovs Epiphanie* ...

6. On the dating of the poem, see Martin's edition p. xcii.

7. See George Walton Williams, ed., *The Complete Poetry of Richard Crashaw* (New York, 1970), p. 186. Reference to "*Dies Irae*" is from his edition. To disagree with Williams about "The Hymn of the Chvrch ..." is not to imply, of course, criticism of his valuable edition.

8. That inverts the allusion to the "interiour RAY" in l. 2 of the hymn to the Holy Name.

9. The "individual soul" being the persona's and thence the reader's, for the reader shares in the poem as a hymn.

10. Cf. *John* 3,16 and 1 *John* 4,10. Christ is, of course, sacred love's origin insofar as he expresses God's redemptive love for the world in the world.

11. The hymns appear in 1648. There is no evidence to suggest that they are early works; however, they cannot be dated with certainty.

12. Illumination connected with Christ's spiritual presence – the poem has nothing to do with the idea of transubstantiation.

13. St Teresa, *The Life of Teresa of Jesus: The Autobiography of St Teresa of Avila*, trans. and ed. E. Allison Peers (Garden City, New York, 1960), ch. 15, p. 154. Cf. St Francis de Sales, *Treatise on the Love of God*, trans. John K. Ryan, 2 vols (1963; rpt. Rockford, Illinois, 1975), 1, pp. 289–299.

14. Crashaw knew her autobiography, but one could hardly say that images of illuminative calm in his verse should be thought of as essentially Teresan.

15. Nor, likewise, should images of fervent illumination in his verse be thought of as essentially Salesian.

16. St Francis de Sales, *Introduction to the Devout Life*, trans. John K. Ryan, pp. 82–83. Crashaw certainly knew this work; however, some affinities between it and his works may be accidental.

17. Dated 1 January 1608. Crashaw may have been acquainted with the saint's letters. See: St Francis de Sales, *Selected Letters*, trans. Elisabeth Stopp (London, 1960), no. 34, p. 144. Cf. St Francis de Sales, *Treatise on the Love of God*, 1, pp. 304–306.

18. *The Life of Teresa of Avila*, ch. 18, p. 174, ch. 19, pp. 180–181.

19. There appears to be a difference in time here, however. Crashaw seems to image heroic resolve as present in, as enacted during, spiritual union; St Teresa writes of "heroic resolutions" as

formed after the experience of mystical union has passed. Nonetheless, see *The Life*, ch. 18, p. 175. The main point would seem to be their mutual connection of union with violent self-sacrifice for God.

20. I am conscious of no major exceptions in his verse.
21. See, for example, the account of Huggarde in Chapter One.
22. See the twenty-eighth and twenty-ninth *Articles of Religion*.
23. One assumes that Crashaw himself gave the poem its title – there is as yet no reason to believe otherwise.
24. He ends in faith, a degree of hope and, arguably, also in a state of love (for Christ).
25. *Luke* 2,49.
26. *Luke* 9,22 is only in part fulfilled by the Crucifixion. It is worth noting here that the persona speaks in the dramatic present tense of meditation. Moreover here, as elsewhere in his religious verse, Crashaw seems influenced by Salesian ideas of meditation, see *Treatise on the Love of God*, trans. John K. Ryan, 1, pp. 312–313.
27. Instances of the idea can be seen in Ficino, Castiglione, Spenser, Shakespeare, and Donne.
28. Cf. his Latin epigrams of 1634.
29. Cf. "On Mr. G. Herberts booke ... the Temple... ." One assumes that the title *Steps to the Temple* was Crashaw's own; if it were not, it nonetheless captures his early indebtedness to Herbert.
30. For another view, see H. Swanston, "The Second 'Temple,'" *Durham University Journal*, 56 (1963), 14–22.
31. And by Tesauro, moreover.
32. See ll. 49–56. For other views of the poem than that given here, see especially: Frank J. Warnke, *Versions of Baroque: European Literature in the Seventeenth Century*, p. 63; Walter R. Davis, "The Meditative Hymnody of Richard Crashaw," *ELH*, 50 (1983), 107–129; Frank Fabry, "Richard Crashaw and the Art of Allusion: Pastoral in 'A Hymn to ... Sainte Teresa,'" *English Literary Renaissance*, 16 (1986), 373–382.
33. In the transverberation episode of her autobiography, St Teresa talks not of Christ but of "the Lord" or "God," nor does she refer to the Spiritual Marriage, as Crashaw does in ll. 79–87 – a distinct shift in emphasis occurring in the hymn.
34. Crashaw identifies sacred love in heaven chiefly in terms of the Spiritual Marriage, but he also represents it as expressed in familial affection and in pure, neoplatonic desire of the Good and the Beautiful.

35. He is in colloquy, momentarily, also with her cheeks (15,1–2). For other views of the poem, see especially: George W. Williams, *Image and Symbol in the Sacred Poetry of Richard Crashaw*, p. 103; R. V. Young, *Richard Crashaw and the Spanish Golden Age*, pp. 38–39; Carroll Viera, "Crashaw's 'Saint Mary Magdalen; or, The Weeper,'" *Explicator*, 43 (1984), 21–22.

36. The angel is, moreover, possibly one of the Cherubim, the second highest angelic order.

37. Implicit in his doing that is his illustrating why she almost uniquely manifests the preciousness of the gift of tears (St Peter being her counterpart).

38. Here, in stanzas 21–22, there seem to be allusions to giving God the things due him, to serving God rather than Mammon, to laying up treasures in heaven, to the parable of the pearl, to the parable of the Widow's mite. Cf. St Francis de Sales, *Treatise on the Love of God*, 1, pp. 300–302.

39. Marc F. Bertonasco, in his *Crashaw and the Baroque*, quite firmly identifies *The Weeper* with Salesian meditation (see pp. 104–116; cf. pp. 44–90). It seems fair to suggest that Crashaw's religious verse often has closer similarities to the Salesian form of meditation than to other meditative forms.

40. Mario Praz first connected *The Weeper* with the (Counter-Reformation) epigram in his essay on Crashaw reprinted in *The Flaming Heart*. See pp. 218–219 of that work.

41. *The Mind's Wit and Art*, disc. 2, p. 92.

42. The early paraphrase of psalm 23, the hymn on the Holy Name, the Teresan poems, the poems to the Virgin, the hortatory poems to the Countess of Denbigh and to "a young gentlewoman," and *The Weeper* help to confirm such an assertion.

43. See, for merely two examples, the poems to the Countess of Denbigh and to "a young gentlewoman."

44. As the poems to the Virgin, the Teresan poems, and *The Weeper* indicate. He did not, however, consider the male self's "female" spirituality as did Constable.

45. Alabaster arguably considered purgative experience, contrition, and individual psychology in connection with martyrdom more variously and more closely than did Crashaw.

APPENDIX: *Ralegh's* Ocean to Scinthia

1. Reference to the poem is from *The Poems of Sir Walter Ralegh*, ed. Agnes M. C. Latham (London, 1951). Dating of the poem remains

uncertain. Stylistically – and for other reasons – it would seem to come after 1591 at least (1592 being an obvious date to suggest for the poem), but there is no evidence which definitely alters the conventional dating of 1589. Cf. Latham's Introduction, pp. xxxv–xlv. If the poem was written after 1591 then of course Ralegh's sonnet on *The Faerie Queene* precedes it (see the last paragraph of this discussion).

Index of Names